MYSTICISM AND
PHILOSOPHICAL ANALYSIS

MYSTICISM AND PHILOSOPHICAL ANALYSIS

EDITED BY
STEVEN T. KATZ

L A Cunningham

New York
Oxford University Press
1978

First Published in Great Britain in 1978
by Sheldon Press, Marylebone Road, London NWI 4DU

First published in the United States in 1978
by Oxford University Press, New York

Library of Congress Cataloging in Publication Data
Main entry under title:

Mysticism and philosophical analysis.

Includes index.
1. Mysticism—Addresses, essays, lectures.
I. Katz, Steven T., 1944-
BL625.M89 1978   291.4′2   78-5958
ISBN 0-19-520027-6

Printed in the United States of America

Contents

Acknowledgements

Thanks are due for permission to quote from the following copyright sources:

The Cult of the Seer in the Ancient Near East by Violet Macdermot: Copyright © 1971 by The Wellcome Institute of the History of Medicine reprinted by permission of the University of California Press and The Wellcome Institute of the History of Medicine.

'East Coker' and 'Burnt Norton' in *Four Quartets* by T. S. Eliot: Faber and Faber Ltd, London, and Harcourt Brace Jovanovich Inc., New York.

The Life of St Teresa of Jesus translated by E. Allison Peers: Image Books, Doubleday & Co. Inc., New York.

Mysticism and Philosophy by W. T. Stace: Copyrighted © 1960 by W. T. Stace; Macmillan, London and Basingstoke, and J. B. Lippincott Company, New York.

Editor's Introduction

Mysticism is a subject with a special fascination. It derives this fascination from its subject matter as well as from its forms of expression which seem to promise something for everybody if not everything to everybody. In the last hundred years or so, these alluring characteristics have generated a broad scholarly interest in the subject which has given rise to a large body of secondary literature, dealing with the variegated and polychromatic aspects of the subject with varying degrees of competence. The majority of this literature was generated as a consequence of two primary intentions. The first was an ecumenical desire, for good and bad reasons, to find something common in the spiritual life of all the world's people despite the clear differences between, and the wide variety of organized, orthodox, religious traditions around the globe. This motive was given special impetus by the shrinking nature of our world and the rise of a new awareness of our global interdependency. Benares is now only a day's journey from New York, only half a day from London or Paris. The second causal factor was the hope of finding some universal spiritual resource that could restore meaning to contemporary life in the face of the cultural crisis of modern society, marked out perhaps most clearly in the decline of the power of organized, positive religion, especially in intellectual and academic circles. Mysticism, in various guises, was now sought out to replace traditional piety as the authenticating dimension of human life. The existential crises of twentieth-century living were now resolved by an appeal to an intuitively available transcendental realm which was not susceptible to more pedestrian theological or philosophical criticism. The cure for the *anomie* created by our revolutionary contemporary awareness of man's finitude, mortality, and freedom was now sought in a renewed, immediate, non-critical, largely non-cognitive, contact with the mystical depths of Being itself (whatever that is!). And this appeal to a re-established contact with the transcendental has not been devoid either of large-scale cultural seductiveness or of ardent intellectual support in many quarters.

These two motivations in all their different forms, and the intellectual phenomena which attend them, are however, whatever their appeal or merit, not conducive to the rigorous analytic investigation of the subject matter, or even to a coherent understanding of the kinds of intellectual challenges which the study of mysticism raises. Rather, they create a body of literature which is primarily enthusiastic, committed, and personal rather than sober, careful, and reasonable. Thus, generally, the studies produced under these inspirations have the dubious distinction of preaching to the converted while dismissing the 'unenlightened' as poor souls who must still await their entrance into this enchanted mystical paradise. At the same time such approaches usually limit, *a priori*, all serious conversation about the subject and certainly preclude it altogether between mystic and non-mystic, or between mystics who have different accounts of what mysticism is – a common phenomenon despite the widespread myth to the contrary. There have, of course, been a number of important at least partial exceptions to this rule, to which all students of mysticism are indebted. In this connection one thinks, for example, of William James's *Varieties of Religious Experience*, Evelyn Underhill's *Mysticism*, as well as her other works, and the explorations of Dean Inge, Baron von Hügel, Rufus Jones, Aldous Huxley, Charles Bennett, J. Maréchal, James Pratt, and Rudolf Otto, to name only the most important pioneers in the academic study of mysticism. Yet, as noted, even these valuable early works only *partially* avoid the criticisms made above, for all of them manifest strong biases and problematic presuppositions about what mysticism is and how it should be studied – biases which colour their investigations from the outset and which significantly diminish the value of their results.

More recently, three scholars in particular have undertaken fresh researches which command both respect and attention and which have raised the debate as to the nature, content, and philosophical relevance of mysticism to a new level of sophistication. The three are, of course, W. T. Stace, R. C. Zaehner, and Ninian Smart. Though differing amongst themselves and manifesting biases of their own, each in his own way has made a fundamental contribution to our understanding of mysticism and what is involved in its serious study. Yet even their work is still preliminary in two senses: first, there is a great deal more 'technical' work to be done on the mystical material itself, i.e. in the understanding of texts, linguistic researches, editions of material, 'form-criticism' of sources, etc.; and secondly, there are philosophical issues which are essential to an accurate and complete understanding of mysticism which need either to be further refined or to be rethought *in toto*. Nonetheless, the work of these three scholars, as well as the work of the earlier researchers, has provided the impetus and encouragement for a fresh interest in the subject which the present volume hopes to continue and improve upon.

II

The original letter of invitation to possible contributors explaining the intent of the present symposium stated:

> The aim of the collection is to investigate various aspects of the subject [of mysticism] from a sensitive yet rigorous philosophical perspective. The object is to try to advance the discussion and analysis of the subject beyond James and Otto, Stace and Zaehner. We would like to have essays which investigate and clarify basic aspects of the subject so that we can move beyond the position which is philosophically unsophisticated and fails to distinguish between various types of mystical experience on the one hand and the logic and language of different types of mystical claims on the other. Alternatively, we want to avoid the extremes of positivist-like rejections of such experience as 'nonsense' as well as the position which rejects logic, criteria, and analysis on the dubious grounds that they are out of place in the discussion of mysticism.

In response to this editorial challenge the contributors to the present volume have produced, both individually and as a group, essays which it is hoped will be seen to be of fundamental importance for all future students of the subject. Professor Ninian Smart has contributed an essay on 'Understanding Religious Experience' which has been placed first in the collection because it raises certain essential epistemological and methodological issues for any and all inquiry in this area. It is to Professor Smart's credit that he stresses the complexity of the issues involved and opts for a subtle mediating methodological position between the 'all or nothing' views of the majority of earlier, more naive, students of the *corpus mysticum*, i.e. that either one is a mystic and sees the issues with total clarity, or one is not a mystic and thus must remain silent as one's remarks are always going to be wide of the mark. The single area which Professor Smart's essay especially focuses on and clarifies is the meaning of 'experience' as used in the context of the discussion of religious experience, a topic which certainly calls for considerable clarification, further phenomenological inquiry, and additional precision. The point that emerges clearly from this opening paper is the need for all investigators to be more intellectually open as well as hermeneutically sophisticated in the topics they treat as well as in the manner in which they treat them.

The second essay, 'Language, Epistemology, and Mysticism', is by the editor. As to its content, only two descriptive remarks need be made by way of introduction. The first is that the essay concentrates on the pre-experiential conditions of the mystic's circumstance and how this pre-experiential pattern informs the resultant experience. The second and related concern that should be noted is that the essay argues against the thesis that there is a 'common core' (*à la* Stace, for example) to all mystical experiences. It is hoped that the essay will at least force those interested in the subject to reconsider their views on these two issues and also to take a very much closer and tougher look at the original sources in their social, religious, historical, and philosophical context.

Professor Carl Keller's informative and significant paper on 'Mystical Literature' is our third contribution. The merit of this essay derives from Professor Keller's expertise in handling a wide range of cross-cultural mystical sources. This breadth allows him to make intelligent judgements as to the differing *forms* that mystical literature takes and the way in which these forms impose order and even content on the mystical experience itself as well as on the way it is reported in the many-sided mystical literature of the world's religions. Almost always we hear of 'mysticism' or 'mystical literature' without significant, if any, recognition of the diverse nature of this material in structure and conceptual content. Professor Keller's reflections should put an end to this sort of superficial discussion, for what they begin to do is to chart the way for a 'form-critical' study of mystical documents, an essential prolegomenon to any conclusive study of the topic. In order to alert readers to this basic methodological concern we have placed the essay near the beginning of our symposium.

The issues of intellectual openness, epistemological rigour, linguistic precision, and the need for a close study of the texts are all reinforced, elaborated upon and clarified by Dr Peter Moore's wide-ranging paper, 'Mystical Experience, Mystical Doctrine, Mystical Technique'. As he describes it, his contribution aims at two interrelated goals: 'on the one hand the identification and classification of the phenomenological characteristics of mystical experience, and on the other the investigation of the epistemological and ontological status of this experience'. Dr Moore's work gains its strength from his careful delineation of the philosophical issues concerned and his useful attempt to construct a more precise phenomenological account through which to approach the 'raw data'. He is sensitive to the absence of conceptual exactness which has plagued previous attempts to build a phenomenological framework through which to study mysticism and without which all claims to a 'common mystical core' are unsubstantiable. Dr Moore's essay, taken together with the three papers which precede it, begins to provide the basis for a sound hermeneutical and epistemological approach to the corpus of mystical reports.

Our fourth contribution is by Professor Donald MacKinnon. Professor MacKinnon, well known for his interest in the philosophy of religion and Kant, reflects on some of the epistemological problems which arise as a consequence of mystical reports which claim that through the vehicle of mystical apprehension the mystic gains a 'knowledge of the wholeness of reality'. It is clear that the mystical claim to grasp in one powerful intuitive insight the unity of all reality presents fundamental puzzles for any epistemology and is all the more problematic for a Kantian-like one. These difficulties force a basic reconsideration of the Kantian schema on the one hand, as well as a re-examination of the mystical claims on the other. Professor MacKinnon's paper indicates some of the ways in which this mutual interrogation can be seen to be fruitful for both more ordinary epistemological investigations, as well as the more unusual areas which force themselves into consideration by the novel claims of the world's mystics.

All too often studies of mysticism are written by westerners who are expert only in the western, or even more narrowly Christian, mystical traditions but who nonetheless feel competent (or incompetent!) to extrapolate their findings to cover *all* mystical traditions, east and west alike. However, in fact, this ignorance of Asian experience and tradition negates from the outset any and all possibilities of constructing sound cross-cultural phenomenological descriptions of mystical experience, if such descriptions be possible at all. In the light of this real danger of western provincialism and its attendant distortions, we are especially glad to have the contributions of

Professor Fred Streng and Dr Robert Gimello, two scholars who possess the rare combination of philosophical agility and mastery of Asian religious traditions.

Professor Streng's 'Language and Mystical Awareness' brings together his expertise in matters Indian and phenomenological and focuses on the central issue of the relation of language to mystical experience. Professor Streng subtly develops the essential thesis, long recognized by analytic philosophers but not employed fruitfully in the study of mysticism, that language functions in a variety of different ways and the assumptions that one makes about language will affect the way in which one considers the soteriological significance of alternative sorts of mystical awareness. In this connection, the significant philosophical dichotomy between the 'descriptive' and the 'transformative' functions of language, to use Streng's terms, is developed with clarity and insight. What Professor Streng's paper does especially well is to demonstrate further the need for a far more differentiated, pluralistic account of mysticism than has been given heretofore and to insist on a more profound recognition of the way in which the different orthodox religions shape the mystical experience of their respective mystics.

Dr Gimello, our seventh symposiast, also primarily reflecting on the lessons to be learnt from Buddhist materials, concentrates on the relation of, and the meaning of the relation of 'Mysticism and Meditation'. Dr Gimello sets out three basic philosophical areas in which he believes clarification will be gained by properly attending to the details of this relationship. These areas are no less than the central ones dealing with: (*a*) the relation of experience to its interpretation; (*b*) the relation of a given experience to truth claims purportedly based on that experience; and (*c*) the relation of mysticism to other areas of human concern. On the basis of detailed study of the exact meaning of meditation as it manifests itself in Buddhist practice and ideology, Dr Gimello offers three important conclusions relative to the three issues mentioned and goes so far as to suggest that: 'Buddhist mystical experiences [are] deliberately contrived exemplifications of Buddhist doctrine'.

The second half of this volume deals with 'Verificationist Issues' and contains essays by Mr Renford Bambrough, Professor Nelson Pike, and Professor George Mavrodes respectively. Mr Bambrough's paper provides the ideal transitional link between the epistemological and linguistic issues dealt with in the first part of this volume and the issues of criteria, truth-claims, and verification raised in the contributions classed together in the second part. In 'Intuition and the Inexpressible' Mr Bambrough, through concentration on the issues raised by Rudolf Otto's classic account of the 'numinous', raises the very propriety of asking for confirmatory evidence in certain areas of human life. Using a Wittgensteinian-like approach, the whole question of what a 'proof' is and when 'proof' is properly asked for and properly provided is considered. In addition, his essay intelligently raises questions about our very understanding of both mystical as well as more ordinary experiences and the nature of any account of either taken separately or together. In his conclusions Mr Bambrough might be classed as an anti-verificationist but of a very complex and sophisticated kind. His main emphasis is centred on the important point that we must not too narrowly construct our vision of the 'possible' nor 'try to settle bounds and limits to what can be understood and to what can be expressed'.

In another and quite different move in the 'verificationist' debate, Professor Nelson Pike, working primarily from the evidence supplied by Catholic mystics, argues that though, on the one hand, critics like A. McIntyre are correct to stress certain circularities in the reasoning of mystics and those who would employ mystical evidence in support of more general theological or philosophical positions, on the other hand, these critics themselves ask the wrong sorts of questions and try to use the mystical data in ways that are also insensitive to the legitimate intentions of their original mystical authors. To evaluate properly the meaning and significance of mystical texts one must refrain from first making a caricature of them, and then dismissing them on this criterion. Professor Pike's discussion of these issues is finely argued, representing the kind of nuanced reasoning that scholars will appreciate, and all readers will learn from.

Finally, our tenth and last contribution, by Professor George Mavrodes on 'Real *v.* Deceptive Mystical Experiences', is a decided counterpoint to the anti-verificationist theses of Bambrough and Pike. Professor Mavrodes takes up and scrutinizes St Teresa's doubts about whether her mystical experiences are caused by the Devil. He persuasively suggests, on the basis of a tightly constructed four-step argument, that Teresa cannot frame a criterion which will allow her decisively to determine whether or not her experiences are authentic or whether it is the Devil who is deceiving her. However, the point of this logical debate is not only that Teresa cannot be sure about the Devil but also, and more importantly, that we can never be *certain* that any of our experiences have their source in a transcendental reality, rather than in human error or some other point of non-Divine origin. All who would use mystical experience as a foundation on which to construct a more elaborate theological edifice will do well to ponder Professor Mavrodes's rigorous argument on this issue.

What emerges from our brief review, which we hope will have whetted the appetite of the reader, is the strong impression that the contributors have made essential contributions to the study of the subject under discussion. The editor is especially struck by the variety of insights and accounts which have been advanced both intentionally and indirectly against the 'common core' thesis, either in whole or in part. This near-consensus in such diversity is all the more striking in that each of the essays was written independently and without elaborate, if any, communication between the authors. As a consequence, this collection represents in itself, and argues for more generally, a strongly pluralistic position in the study of mysticism, and this on several levels: with regard to the methodological tools used to study the data; with regard to the variety of traditions to be considered; with regard to the variegated features or aspects of the subject to be concentrated upon; with regard to the richness of the philosophical perspectives and arguments to be employed; and finally, with regard to a pluralistic account of the very nature of mystical experience itself. Anyone who hereafter wishes to work seriously in the garden of mystical delight will have to consider fully the position advanced in this volume and respond accordingly.

III

A few final odds and ends. Though no separate bibliography of mystical works has been appended it should be noted that the sources and titles referred to in the substantial notes which follow each of the essays make up collectively quite a complete 'bibliography for further study'.

Before concluding I should like to thank Professor Peter Baelz, the general editor of this series, for his initial enthusiasm for the present symposium and for his encouragement as it went along. Thanks also are due to the two splendid and long-suffering editors at Sheldon Press, Darley Anderson and Celia Kent, who dealt with this project throughout its long gestation period.

STEVEN KATZ

Understanding Religious Experience

NINIAN SMART

The three terms in the phrase 'understanding religious experience' contain ambiguities. Let us look first at the concept of understanding.

In this context, it sometimes seems as if understanding is 'all-or-nothing'. This is perhaps because sometimes philosophers concentrate upon possible unintelligibility, and see intelligibility as the straight alternative. But in fact understanding is a matter of degree. Unintelligibility is the limiting case. (If you like, it is a special form of intelligibility as rest is of motion.) So when we explore how it is that we may understand someone else's religious experience, it will be a matter of what degree of understanding can be obtained and in what circumstances. This simple observation may already suggest that the thesis that you need to belong to religious tradition T in order to understand it has an air of unreality. It is rare that a binary theory applies properly to a continuum.

There is a set of distinctions which is also important for understanding understanding. There are two different forms of intelligibility we need to contemplate here. Thus first there is what may be called existential understanding, namely understanding what a given experience is like. Thus a person who has been tortured with electric shocks can be said to know what that experience is like. I have never undergone this experience, so my understanding of what it is like is not very good, though of course I can imagine. Second, there is understanding the explanation of something. Thus we might be uncertain as to how we should understand Paul's conversion. Was it due to an inner psychological crisis of some kind? Was it really Jesus speaking to him? This kind of understanding may be called *theoretical* understanding. Since there are different sorts of theories which may or may not be overlapping or compatible, there are in effect different species of theoretical understanding. As for compatibility and overlap, it could be that the psychological and theological accounts of Paul's conversion can be held together. One of the vital questions concerning religious experience is whether it is possible to have any adequate theoretical understanding without existential understanding. To such matters I shall return.

Next we may briefly contemplate the question of what counts as a religious experience. It is, I think, useful to distinguish between religion and religions, or to put it another way between religion and a religion. This is similar to the distinction between sport and sports. A religion is a given tradition of a religious kind, and so religious experience is often picked out by considering crucial experiences in the lives of those who belong to such traditions. But it ought to be noted that there is quite a lot of evidence about experiences which hit people out of the blue, even though they do not belong to a given tradition. In the case of conversions, often the experiences occur at the frontier between non-belonging and belonging to a given tradition. So the first conclusion we can draw is that, though we should start with traditions in pinning down religious experience, we should not confine religious experience to this area. Another observation to be made is that, though we can pick out certain traditions as being religious, there are other traditions or movements which may not normally be called religious but which nevertheless have formal characteristics making them analogous at least to religions, and which represent similar human feelings, impulses, and thoughts. Thus I have argued in my book *Mao*[1] that Maoism has an analogy to the traditional religions of China, however much it may also differ in content.

Briefly, the argument is as follows. If a religion typically contains various aspects or dimensions as I have elsewhere named them,[2] viz. doctrine, myth, ethical teaching, ritual, experience, and social institutionalization, then Maoism is analogous to a religion. It has doctrines, namely Marxism as mediated by Mao; myth, such as the story of the Long March and the dialectic of history; ethics, namely its Red puritanism and evaluation of different elements in human society; the rituals of rallies and little red book-waving; experiences of conversion and exaltation; and the institutions of party and cadres. Further, the anarchist elements in Mao's thought echo Taoist themes, and Mao's anti-Confucianism replaced the Confucian ethic with a new mode of education. Marxist eschatology draws on sentiments earlier expressed in Buddhist devotionalism. Hence it is unwise to draw a sharp boundary between religion and ideological system, and consequently religion should not be narrowly defined.

Third, it may be noted that there are dramatic events in human life which have religious significance. Thus facing death is sometimes a profound and awe-inspiring experience, which naturally raises questions about human destiny and the meaning of life, and which therefore marches upon religious concerns. We may call these dramatic experiences. Religious experiences of the tradition-oriented kind may also indeed be dramatic, but conventionally let us simply refer to these as religious experiences.

Fourth, there are experiences which may have religious significance, but which are not *necessarily* religious in character. Thus if I am a pious Christian I may think of my daily work as done to the glory of God, but that work does not need to be seen in this way. I ·have elsewhere referred to this phenomenon as a matter of superimposition. Thus I have elsewhere [3] sketched the following picture of the relationship between morality and religion. While injunctions such as 'It is wrong to steal' can exist and be justified independently of religious belief, they are frequently interpreted as both ethical and religious. Thus Brother Lawrence in *The Practice of the Presence of God* depicts everyday duties as modes of worshipping God. (Naturally there are some specifically religious duties which would not occur in a 'secular' morality, such as the injunction to keep the Sabbath holy.) To use different language, daily activities seen in the light of religious commitment involve *interpreted* experiences. This is, of course, a pregnant sense of 'interpreted'. To sum up so far: there can be existential and/or theoretical understanding (of different degrees) of religious, dramatic, and/or interpreted experiences, which crop up inside or outside religious and analogous traditions.

To some issues arising from these distinctions I shall come back, but meanwhile let us contemplate 'experience'. It seems to be rather specially used in the context of religion. We can see this by indulging in a little experiment. Consider some typical uses of the term 'experience' and then see what happens if we slip in 'religious' before it. Contemplate the following locutions:

1. 'He is a person of wide experience.' Compare: 'He is a person of wide religious experience.' Still, we probably are not interested in this sense of the term anyway, viz. the sense in which it has to do with having lived with a problem, various circumstances, etc.

2. 'Parachute-jumping is an interesting experience': what sort of event would need to be the subject of the sentence if we were to slip in 'religious'? In fact, the term 'experience' here often seems just to be a way of bringing out the existential aspect of an outer event or circumstance.

3. 'My experience of Henry is that he is unpredictable.' This at first might seem to be like 'my experience of God'. But slipping in 'religious' is somewhat incongruous, even if we substituted God for Henry.

It seems that when writers speak of religious experience they use it in a special sense, meaning something like a vision or an intuition. Mystical unions, prophetic visions, psychic ascents to heaven, ecstasies, auditions, intoxications – it is such things that typically get bracketed as religious experiences, and a subclass of these is mystical. And here we come to another tricky term.

I consider that it is clearest if we use the term 'mysticism' and its relatives to refer to those inner visions and practices which are contemplative. Briefly, yoga is a typical kind of mysticism, for it is a certain method or group of methods concerned with contemplation, yielding what is taken to be a fundamental insight into the nature of reality. Again, such persons as Teresa of Avila, Eckhart, Buddhaghosa, Shankara, and Rumi are mystics, for the centre of their religious life was inner contemplation. This does not exclude outer visions, for a mystic may have more than mystical experiences, and he may interpret his own quest in terms of non-contemplative religion also. For example, he may interpret his quest as part of worship which would then constitute another layer of superimposition. For though there are forms of contemplation, for instance those found in Theravāda Buddhism, which are not seen in relation to the worship of God, it is possible to interpret the yogic quest this way, just as we can also see washing dishes as a form of service to God. Also, I think it is a fair observation to make that the numinous experience so brilliantly described in Otto's *The Idea of the Holy* has an outer and thunderous quality not characteristic of the cloud of unknowing within. For this reason, it is best to draw a rough distinction between numinous and mystical experience.

But it has sometimes been fashionable among writers to count the 'panenhenic' Wordsworthian experiences of a mysterious harmony with nature as being mystical. I would rather place them near the numinous type. In any case, we are still in the early stages of any kind of refined classification of the varieties of religious experience, and unfortunately some writers, notably Zaehner, have mixed up classification problems with theological judgements. My own strictures[4] on this muddle, which are now admirably reinforced by the critique of Zaehner and others found in Fritz Staal's recent *Exploring Mysticism*,[5] can be summed up briefly as follows.

Zaehner is keen to show that there is a vital distinction between theistic and monistic mysticism (such a distinction has, of course, certain possible apologetic uses). But under the latter head he includes Sānkhya-Yoga, Advaita Vedānta, Buddhist mysticism – in short systems respectively involving many souls but no union with God; one Soul or Self identical with the Divine; and no souls at all. Mind you, Zaehner strives to get souls back into Buddhism, and this in my view involves a distortion of the relevant texts as well as contradicting the overwhelming bulk of Buddhist testimony. But if so many varieties of doctrinal milieu and interpretation of the mystical fall under the monistic bracket is it not artificial? What if I put first what I have bought into two baskets: in the one I put grapes, and in the other persimmons, pineapples, and peas, on the ground that the second group are not used to make wine. I have one basis for sorting, but not a basis which points to serious resemblances in other respects. The distinction between Advaita and theism may be less than the distinction between Advaita and Theravāda Buddhism (roughly, I believe it *is* less). So Zaehner should not have two but many baskets – or alternatively one, ascribing differences of description to doctrinal interpretation.

It may perchance be replied that such criticism relies upon this distinction between actual experience and doctrinal interpretation – and such a clear distinction cannot be drawn, for experiences are always in some degree interpreted: they as it were contain interpretation within them. No perception can be quite neutral. To this I would reply that there are differing degrees of interpretation, and the distinction being made is heuristically useful in providing a directive to be as phenomenological as possible about the experiences being reported. A way of illustrating the point is as follows. If I see a man in a white cassock driving past in a black chauffeur-assisted car, I should not jump to the conclusion that it is the Pope. It may well be the Pope (and to understand this description I have to know quite a bit about Christian institutions): but what I can report is first of all the 'lesser' description. Similarly, one needs to be on one's guard in evaluating mystics' reports, since the existential impact and sacred context of the inner visions can naturally lead to wider claims for them than the phenomenology might warrant. Now it still might be argued that such a deflationary method may prove misleading. For if I describe a goal being scored at football simply as a round piece of leather whizzing into a net slung from wooden posts, I am both literally correct and misleading. However, what is reasonably well established is that there are similarities in differing cultures between mystical reports, while at the same time there are rather divergent doctrinal claims made in the relevant traditions. It is on this basis, partly empirical, that one has reason to keep the heuristic model. If Siberians think of wolves as grey spirits of the dead and if Italians think of them as dangerous animals, reports from both quarters would reasonably raise the question of whether it is the same sort of being that is being spoken of. It is when this is established that we can go on to consider how far further attitudes to wolves are to be justified.

There is of course an important corollary of these remarks, and I mention it only because, though obvious, it is frequently ignored in philosophical practice. It is this: that philosophizing must rest here upon a reasonable knowledge of the empirical facts concerning religion and religions. The number of varieties of religious experience is largely an empirical question, though as in other inquiries there are conceptual issues too. There are thus severe limitations upon the philosophical discussion of mysticism in the abstract. The comparative study of religion thus becomes an indispensable basis of the philosophy of religion. (Naturally there are some problems where this is less directly true: as with the classical discussion of the problem of evil.)

I now turn, in view of the distinctions I have rather simply made, to certain problems which appear to arise in the exploration of mystical and more broadly religious experience. First, let us consider what limitations may exist in regard to existential understanding. Is it necessary to have a given type of religious experience in order to understand what it is like? Well, such a question has to be re-framed in view of our first point, about the degree-character of understanding. The question perhaps can be reshaped: Could one have an adequate understanding of a type of religious experience if one had never had it? Otto seemed to go far in his negative answer to this question. But it obviously spawns another: adequate for what? In the context of philosophy, the answer to this question relates to theoretical understanding. We want to know enough about religious experience to discuss intelligently theories of their genesis and validity – theories which are necessarily entangled with each other.

One criterion of adequacy here is: Do we have enough understanding of what the experiences are like to be reasonably persuaded that experiences E, F, G, and so on from different contexts are pretty similar? For if they are, then some conclusions may follow about genesis and validity. Thus if one culture has quite different family arrangements from another, but similar numinosities, then psychoanalytic accounts of genesis which relate to early childhood experience may need to be revised. And again if E and F are rather similar and E occurs in the context of a possibly true religion, then the religion in which F occurs is possibly not wholly false.

Given these reflections, we may now ask whether the diagnosis of such similarities relies in part upon existential understanding. It is perhaps theoretically possible that one might get by without an inkling of what the experiences are like, for I suppose the reports of different Martians, if available to us, concerning some type of experience which we simply do not have because we are built so very differently, might constitute some evidence of similarity. But it would surely be easy in such circumstances to be thoroughly misled – as an ignorant man might think that a person shouting 'Love' at tennis had amorous thoughts. In any case, mystics, prophets, and shamans are not Martians, and it would be surprising if we had no inkling of their sensations. For it often happens that there are analogies in experience.

This is perhaps brought out, ironically, by Otto's *The Idea of the Holy*. For Otto, the numinous experience is *sui generis*: but in fact by skilful use of analogies he brings out the flavour of the *mysterium tremendum et fascinans*. Nor was Oppenheim wrong to call his book on the nuclear bomb *The Light of a Thousand Suns*, for the theophany of Krishna/Vishnu in the Gita is like a spiritual atomic explosion.

In so far as we use our imagination negatively also to understand certain experiences, there is a method, as it were, of visualizing contemplative experiences. Thus the emptying of the mind of mental images and discursive thoughts can be imagined, and I use this technique in trying to explicate the stages of *jhāna* in Theravāda Buddhism, in my *Reasons and Faiths* (1958). The meditative exercises are, fortunately, described in quite a lot of detail, and this makes the process of visualization easier. Thus the various levels of consciousness can be imagined much as one might be able to imagine what it is like to be weightless even though one has not experienced the state. I use the term 'imagined' here, despite its paradoxical air – the imagination produces, so to speak, a blank picture.

Still, there is no reason in principle why it should not be possible for the philosophical evaluator of mystical experience to go in for spiritual practices himself. This point is made with some force by Fritz Staal, in his afore-mentioned *Exploring Mysticism*. It might be objected that the foretaste of the beatific vision or whatever is a gift from God and not to be induced by human effort. But we climb mountains which we do not make ourselves. And the fact that something is a divine gift should not lead to human paralysis. The account in terms of grace may simply be superimposed upon an account in terms of human effort (the effort itself is a gift of God!).

A somewhat different objection might be this – that it is impossible to imagine what most mystical experiences are like since so frequently, perhaps universally, mystics refer to their experiences as ineffable, or at any rate to the 'object' of their experiences as ineffable. There is indeed a whole battery of expressions liable to occur in this context – such as 'indescribable', 'inexpressible', 'unspeakable', 'indefinable', 'unutterable', 'incomprehensible', and so on. Relatedly it is not surprising that the author of a famous account should refer to a cloud of *unknowing*. However, one should not assume that such expressions are to be taken as quite excluding describability. This is so for several reasons.

First, there is about them in any event an ambiguity. To say that God is incomprehensible may be to say not that he is utterly incomprehensible but that he is not *totally* comprehensible. There would seem to be a contradiction in saying he is utterly incomprehensible – thus nothing could be known about him including anything that might form a basis for referring to him as God.[6] Perhaps the Mādhyamika account of the Void (and so of nirvāṇa) is that nothing can be said about it whatsoever, but there have been severe difficulties about sticking to the corollary of this 'account', namely that the Mādhyamika does not have a position but only dialectically knocks down all theories, thus eliminating all apparent alternatives to a golden silence. I have argued against the consistency of this in *The Yogi and the Devotee*,[7] with the further point that a similar western view, that of Dean Mansel, also suffers from self-contradiction. T. R. Miles's 'silence qualified by parables' also may fall into the same sort of trouble.[8] The argument regarding Nāgārjuna, Mansel, and Miles is basically as follows: If we say that the religious ultimate, whether this be *śūnya* (Void) or God, is indescribable (and/or incomprehensible, etc.) and mean this literally and rigorously, then how can either the Buddha or Christ be specially connected with it? For if it is just an X then everything and nothing bears its imprint equally. Thus as a position it is empty, and cannot hope to explicate the tradition which it is used to illuminate. And if it could it could exclude no other tradition, and all religions would become equally valid including those whose positions are attacked, e.g. in the Mādhyamika, dialectically. In brief it is one thing to say X is incomprehensible, indescribable, etc., in that there is something about it which transcends description, comprehension, etc., and another thing to say that it totally eludes any sort of human grasp.

Second, we should notice the performative aspect of the string of expressions in question. Consider the following locutions: 'This news is indescribably wonderful'; 'These are the unspeakable gifts of God'; 'I simply cannot tell you how grateful I am'. In the last of these, I am actually expressing my gratitude by saying how I cannot do it! The point is: I cannot sufficiently express it by mere words, but I can show through words how my gratitude transcends the usual courtesies and formulations. There is nothing mysterious here (beyond the whole mystery of feelings and their outer manifestations); and if it is frequent to advert in religion to the unutterable this is at least partly because powerful and existential feelings come into play, and joys thought greater than the more usual earthly ones. Hence the string of expressions in question are used in a context of what may be dubbed 'performative transcendence', namely performatively using words to sketch expression beyond their conventional limits. Performative transcendence is, as I have indicated, by no means at all confined to religious contexts.

All this may be reinforced by reflecting that religion (like swearing, humour, and courtesy) fights a running battle against debasement of the currency. Repetition of words in sacred contexts may enhance their numinosity, as with the formulae of solemn liturgies; but repetition in sermons and hymns and radio broadcasts can make words lose their existential edge, their force. We need slang as a means of re-supplying vividness to our expressive language; and the indescribability of God is a reminder that likewise creativity is required in maintaining and reinforcing the means of expressing the wonder and depth of God and Brahman.

There are two further ways at least in which religious experience can be indescribable (and so on). One has to do with problems of adequacy, as above discussed; and is perhaps simply an extension of the idea of performative transcendence. It could be that for certain purposes no description is *adequate*. To this I return in a moment. The second way is just that in which *every* experience in some sense eludes description: as it were, the ocean of nuances in actual life is infinite or at least indefinitely explorable, and we can always find new things to say and subtleties to add. Even if a pre-Raphaelite can get all the details in, his 'King Cophetua and the Beggar Maid' would suffer a sea-change if Gauguin were to get at them, or Braque. But let us return to the extension of performative transcendence.

Regarding *adequacy* of descriptive utterance having a strong performative aspect, one may consider the various functions the relevant utterances may be expected to fulfil. Leaving aside attempts, for the moment, to further the scientific understanding of religion, consider the following functions – to praise God, to convert others, to arouse in others similar feelings and/or insights, to express joy. Such functions can, quite clearly, overlap. As for worship and praise – no words will do it adequately in that the meaning of God's infinity is that he is infinitely to be praised. As for conveying feelings and/or insights – the problem is that words alone cannot quite do it: something beyond them has to be there (the correct disposition of the hearer, the activity of the Holy Spirit, or whatever).

To sum up this part of the discussion: the notion of the inexpressibility of religious experience has various roots, and these centre upon forms of performative transcendence and criteria of adequacy. It is incorrect to conclude either that ineffability is a unique characteristic of religious experience or that it is absolute (for herein lies contradiction).

A further problem may be thought to arise in relation to what I have called performative transcendence. It may be said that the 'object' of religious experience is itself transcendent and so a discussion which assimilates it to 'worldly' objects of experience is misleading. Performative transcendence, or rather the need for it, really arises because of ontological transcendence. Now it would be tedious here to analyse the concept of transcendence, e.g. the transcendence of God, and in any case I have done this elsewhere in an article on 'Myth and Transcendence'.[9] Briefly I considered there divine transcendence to mean that God is non-spatial, that God and the cosmos are non-identical, and that the cosmos is pictured as a screen concealing and secretly also containing the holy God – a picture connected with religious practice and the sense of the numinous. First, not all objects of religious experience are transcendent in the sense of which a sole God is – the monotheos, so to say. For the sun-worshipper will perchance feel awe at the glorious deity, who is admittedly for him more than a red ball, a star. The monotheos's outer manifestation is the cosmos, by contrast. Second, one aspect of the idea of God's transcendence is in any case performative transcendence. Third, it does not follow that because God is conceived as distinct from the cosmos he cannot be assimilated in some degree to it and conversely; however we may regard the source of knowledge about God there will exist an *analogia*, whether *entis* or *gratiae* or *experientiae*, or all three, etc. If not, we relapse into speechlessness, and in the absolutely unutterable there is nothing worth discussing. Consequently, God lies, as it were, along the spectrum of our experiences, and his transcendence cannot absolutely hide him away. Since anything human can be investigated and scientifically explored, so to the extent that God and nirvāṇa may appear in human experience they too can be explored, and the goal of a greater understanding of religious experience need not elude us.

There is one final issue I would like to explore concerning this search for understanding religious experience. It might be that ultimately the only *real* understanding must depend upon a theory which would incorporate within it some judgement or otherwise on the *validity* of religious experience. Genesis may be vital for true understanding. Since supposedly scientific theories, e.g. projectionist ones such as those of Freud and Marx, are liable to be in conflict with theologies, and since the evaluation of theologies is partly a matter of faith, it could therefore be held that in some manner understanding religious experience depends upon commitment. We are not in an area of 'neutral' investigation. There may be truth in this; but I would be disinclined to proclaim such a truth too loudly. For what is often forgotten is that we have a long and delicate path to pick before we are really in a position to make an evaluation; and that path is phenomenological. It means that we must be able to disentangle varieties of religious experience, have a nose for degrees of interpretation in their descriptions, see what they mean existentially, place them in their living contexts and so on. We are still in a very early stage of scientific and human inquiry along these lines, and that inquiry is ill-served if we speed too hastily into questions of theology and evaluation.

NOTES

1 Ninian Smart, *Mao*. London, 1974.
2 Ninian Smart, *The Religious Experience of Mankind* (London, 1969), ch. 1.
3 Ninian Smart, 'Gods, Bliss and Morality' in I. T. Ramsey, ed., *Christian Ethics and Contemporary Philosophy*. London, 1966.

4   Ninian Smart, 'Interpretation and Mystical Experience' in *Religious Studies*, vol. I, No. 1 (1965).

5   Fritz Staal, *Exploring Mysticism*. London, 1975.

6   See further on this Steven Katz 'Logic and Language of Mystery' in S. Sykes and J. Clayton, eds., *Christ, Faith and History*. Cambridge, 1972.

7   Ninian Smart, *The Yogi and the Devotee*. London, 1968.

8   See T. R. Miles, *Religion and the Scientific Outlook*. London, 1959.

9   See Ninian Smart, 'Myth and Transcendence' in *The Monist*, vol. 50, No. 4 (October 1966).

NINIAN SMART, M.A., B.Phil. (Oxon), D.H.L. (Loyola). Professor Smart is the author of numerous publications, among which the most important are: *Reasons and Faiths* (1958); *Philosophers and Religious Truth* (1964); *Doctrine and Argument in Indian Philosophy* (1964); *The Religious Experience of Mankind* (1976[2]); *The Concept of Worship* (1972); *The Phenomenon of Religion* (1973). He has also published several dozen articles and reviews in such leading philosophical and religious journals as *Mind, Philosophical Quarterly, Religion, Religious Studies*, and *Philosophy*. He was Professor of Theology at the University of Birmingham from 1961 to 1967 and then became the first Professor and Chairman of the Department of Religious Studies at the University of Lancaster, England, a post he held from 1967 to 1975. He has also been a visiting Professor at Princeton, University of Wisconsin, and Benares Hindu University. At present he holds two chairs, one at the University of Lancaster and the other at the University of California at Santa Barbara, spending half a year at each.

Language, Epistemology, and Mysticism

STEVEN T. KATZ

I should like to start by raising several standard elements in the discussion of mysticism and mystical experience in order to dispose of them at the outset. This will leave us free to concentrate on our main epistemological concerns. The first such feature is actually not one issue but a set of related issues having to do with the nature and referent of claimed mystical states. The easiest way to introduce these concerns is by referring to the terms' 'interpretation' and 'verification' and all that these notions suggest to the philosophically perceptive reader. Let us first deal with the issue of verification. There are major, perhaps insuperable, problems involved in the issue of trying to verify mystical claims, if by verification we mean the strong thesis that independent grounds for the claimed event/experience can be publicly demonstrated. Indeed, it seems to me, though I will not try to justify this position here, that it is not possible to provide 'verification' of this sort. As a corollary of this view it also seems correct to argue that no veridical propositions can be generated on the basis of mystical experience. As a consequence it appears certain that mystical experience is not and logically cannot be the grounds for *any* final assertions about the nature or truth of any religious or philosophical position nor, more particularly, for any specific dogmatic or theological belief. Whatever validity mystical experience has, it does *not* translate itself into 'reasons' which can be taken as evidence for a given religious proposition. Thus, in the final analysis, mystical or more generally religious experience is irrelevant in establishing the truth or falsity of religion in general or any specific religion in particular.[1]

Despite the strict limitation being placed on the justificatory value of mystical experience, it is *not* being argued either that mystical experiences do not happen, or that what they claim may not be true, only that there can be no grounds for deciding this question, i.e. of showing that they are true *even* if they are, in fact, true. Moreover, even this disclaimer requires the further declaration that, though no philosophical argument is capable of proving the veracity of mystical experience, one would be both dogmatic and imprudent to decide *a priori* that mystical claims are mumbo-jumbo, especially given the wide variety of such claims by men of genius and/or intense religious sensitivity over the centuries as well as across all cultural divisions. Nor does it seem reasonable to reduce these multiple and variegated claims to mere projected 'psychological states' which are solely the product of interior states of consciousness.

The related topic of 'interpretation' also needs brief mention both because the ordinary sense in which this notion is taken in relation to our subject is *not* our direct concern, and also because the work done here seems to me, despite the beginnings of some valuable investigations in this area, to be still preliminary in terms of its methodology as well as its results. When I speak of 'interpretation' here I mean to refer to the standard accounts of the subject which attempt to investigate what the mystic had to say *about* his experience. This interpretative enterprise is, of course, carried on at several different removes and in several different ways. Among these are: (*a*) the first-person report of the mystic; (*b*) the mystic's 'interpretation' of his own experience at some later, more reflective, and mediated, stage; (*c*) the 'interpretation' of third persons within the same tradition (Christians on Christian mysticism); (*d*) the process of interpretation by third persons in other traditions (Buddhists on Christianity); and so on. In addition, all these forms of interpretation can be highly ramified or not as the case may be.[2] Though all these stages in the 'interpretation' of mystical experience are of importance, and in the later parts of this paper we shall have occasions to return to certain aspects of them they are, for the most part, only tangential to our essential, still more basic, 'preinterpretive' concern.

The issue of 'interpretation', however, raises another standard feature of the analysis of mystical states which does move us directly to were we want to concentrate our epistemological attentions. Here I have in mind the almost universally accepted schema of the relation which is *claimed* to exist between one mystic's experience (and his report of the experience) and the experience of other mystics. This schema takes three forms, one less sophisticated, the other two, in differing degrees, often highly sophisticated. The less sophisticated form can be presented as follows:

(*I*) All mystical experiences are the same; even their descriptions reflect an underlying similarity which transcends cultural or religious diversity.

The second, more sophisticated, form can be presented as arguing:

(*II*) All mystical experiences are the same but the mystics' *reports about* their experiences are culturally bound. Thus they use the available symbols of their cultural-religious milieu to describe their experience.

The third and most sophisticated form can be presented as arguing:

(*III*) All mystical experience can be divided into a small class of 'types' which cut across cultural boundaries. Though the language used by mystics to describe their experience is culturally bound, their experience is not.

A word has to be said about each of these. Thesis I is more commonly found in the early literature on the study of mysticism, much of it having been generated by missionary and related activity which sought to find some common denominator among people of widely diverse religious backgrounds. This ecumenical desire coloured much of the early investigation of the subject as well as being responsible for making it a popular subject of study. Again, a second less ecumenical feature, also at least in part tied to the early missionary enterprise, which often prompts this sort of argument is the dogmatic consideration, i.e. all religions, even if appearing different, really teach x – the definition of x being variously supplied on the basis of the particular dogmatic beliefs the given interpreter happens to hold, e.g. the Christian finds the x to be the Christian God.[3] Among the results of this paper one will be to show that Thesis I is mistaken. There is no *philosophia perennis*, Huxley[4] and many others notwithstanding.

Thesis II, though more sophisticated than I, can also be made for the same ecumenical and dogmatic reasons as I, as it also supports such enterprises. The ecumenicist or dogmatist is still able to argue on the basis of II that underneath or above all differences there is one common Truth, and this is what he is after in any case. That this sort of essentialist reductionism, i.e. reducing all reports of x to one claimed essence y, is usually not open to falsification, nor to any clear hermeneutical, methodological, or metaphysical procedure is of little account to well-meaning ecumenicists or dyed-in-the-wool dogmatists. If one differs with the essentialist over the meaning of a specific mystical report or mystical reports in general, for example, by pointing to variations between them, one is dismissed as not understanding them, and all disagreement is accounted as the result of such 'misunderstanding'. There is, however, something more to say about Thesis II for it has also come into prominence for at least one good reason, i.e. the more, if still not completely, dispassionate study of the relevant mystical data. To serious academic students of the subject who owed some allegiance to the academy as well as to a given tradition it became unavoidably obvious that not all mystical experience was *reported* in ways that easily suggest that they are all reports of the same experience. Despite this last virtue Thesis II is also to be rejected as inadequate for dealing with all the relevant evidence.[5]

Thesis III is more sophisticated still, recognizing a disparity both of content and of form in mystical reports. The best recent studies of mysticism belong under this rubric, as, for example, the work of R. C. Zaehner,[6] W. T. Stace,[7] and N. Smart.[8] It is to their credit to have recognized the deep problems involved in trying to classify various mystical experiences as the same. Yet even the positions of Zaehner,[9] Stace,[10] and Smart[11] are unsatisfactory because they try to provide various cross-cultural phenomenological accounts of mystical experience which are phenomenologically as well as philosophically suspect. The positive position argued later in the present paper will materially bear on this topic of cross-cultural phenomenological categorization for it will try to demonstrate that even these comparatively sophisticated accounts have remained too close to Thesis II which will be shown, as noted, to be unacceptable, even if a marked improvement over Thesis I. By way of anticipation and as an interim conclusion, it will suffice here to suggest that, for example, the phenomenological typologies of Stace and Zaehner are too reductive and inflexible, forcing multifarious and extremely variegated forms of mystical experience into improper interpretative categories which lose sight of the fundamentally important differences between the data studied. In this sense it might even be said that this entire paper is a 'plea for the recognition of differences'.

II

Our interest, however, is only incidentally concerned with the adequacy of framing a typology for the study of mystical experience for this, despite its occupying the centre stage of almost all the important research on mysticism from William James's classic *Varieties of Religious Experience*, through the work of Underhill, Inge, Jones, Otto, Zaehner, and Stace, is a second-order inductive procedural concern. It is a second-order concern to the more basic inquiry into why the various mystical experiences are the experiences they are.[12]

To get a clearer conception of what this paper is after when it speaks of the issue of 'Why mystical experiences are the experiences they are', let me state the single epistemological assumption that has exercised my thinking and which has forced me to undertake the present investigation: *There are* NO *pure (i.e. unmediated) experiences*. Nether mystical experience nor more ordinary forms of experience give any indication, or any grounds for believing, that they are unmediated. That is to say, *all* experience is processed through, organized by, and makes itself available to us in extremely complex epistemological ways. The notion of unmediated experience seems, if not self-contradictory, at best empty. This epistemological fact seems to me to be true, because of the sorts of beings we are, even with regard to the experiences of those ultimate objects of concern with which mystics have intercourse, e.g. God, Being, nirvāṇa, etc. This 'mediated' aspect of all our experience seems an inescapable feature of any epistemological inquiry, including the inquiry into mysticism, which has to be properly acknowledged if our investigation of experience, including mystical experience, is to get very far. Yet this feature of experience has somehow been overlooked or underplayed by every major investigator of mystical experience whose work is known to me.[13] A proper evaluation of this fact leads to the recognition that in order to understand mysticism it is *not* just a question of studying the reports of the mystic after the experiential event but of acknowledging that the experience itself as well as the form in which it is reported is shaped by concepts which the mystic brings to, and which shape, his experience. To flesh this out, straightforwardly, what is being argued is that, for example, the Hindu mystic does not have an experience of x which he then describes in the, to him, familiar language and symbols of Hinduism, but rather he has a Hindu experience, i.e. his experience is not an unmediated experience of x but is itself the, at least partially, pre-formed anticipated Hindu experience of Brahman. Again, the Christian mystic does not experience some unidentified reality, which he then conveniently labels God, but rather has the at least partially prefigured Christian experiences of God, or Jesus, or the like. Moreover, as one might have anticipated, it is my view based on what evidence there is, that the Hindu experience of Brahman and the Christian experience of God are (not) the same. We shall support this contention below. The significance of these considerations is that the forms of consciousness which the mystic brings to experience set structured and limiting parameters on what the experience will be, i.e. on what will be experienced, and rule out in advance what is 'inexperienceable' in the particular given, concrete, context. Thus, for example, the nature of the Christian mystic's pre-mystical consciousness informs the mystical consciousness such that he experiences the mystic reality in terms of Jesus, the Trinity, or a personal God, etc., rather than in terms of the non-personal, non-everything, to be precise, Buddhist doctrine of nirvāṇa.[14] Care must also be taken to note that even the plurality of experience found in Hindu, Christian, Muslim, Jewish, Buddhist mystical traditions, etc., have to be broken down into smaller units. Thus we find, for example, in Hinduism[15] monistic, pantheistic, and theistic trends, while Christianity knows both absorptive and non-absorptive forms of mysticism. And again close attention has to be paid to the organic changes in ideology and historical development which specific traditions undergo internally, and how these changes affect the mystical experiences of mystics respectively in each tradition. For example, absorptive mysticism is not found in the earliest strata of Christian mysticism, while again the Jewish mystical experience of Talmudic times known as *merkabah* mysticism based on the chariot vision of Ezekiel is different from the Zoharic (late thirteenth century) and Lurianic (sixteenth century on) mysticism of the later Middle Ages more thoroughly suffused as it is by gnostic elements. And, I repeat, the remainder of this paper will attempt to provide the full supporting evidence and argumentation that this process of differentiation of mystical experience into the patterns and symbols of established religious communities is experiential and does not only take place in the post-experiential process of reporting and interpreting the experience itself: it is at work before, during, and after the experience.

We can see the significance, as well as the failure to recognize the significance, of the issue being raised if we look at W. T. Stace's[16] extremely influential discussion of mysticism and philosophy. Stace begins with an opening chapter entitled 'Presuppositions of the Inquiry' as part of which he takes up the familiar distinction between experience and interpretation and argues that this is a distinction which must be respected, though he holds that it generally is not, even by the best investigators into the subject. In the course of this discussion he gives the following opening example which seems most promising.

It is probably impossible . . . to isolate 'pure' experience. Yet, although we may never be able to find sense experience completely free of any interpretation, it can hardly be doubted that a sensation is one thing and its conceptual interpretation is another thing. That is to say, they are distinguishable though not completely separable. There is a doubtless apocryphal but well-known anecdote about the American visitor in London who tried to shake hands with a waxwork policeman in the entrance of Madame Tussaud's. If such an incident ever occurred, it must have been because the visitor had a sense experience which he first wrongly interpreted as a live policeman and later interpreted correctly as a wax figure. If the sentence which I have just written is intelligible, it proves that an interpretation is distinguishable from an experience; for there could not otherwise be two interpretations of one experience.[17]

Stace goes on to add the further correct observation regarding the event at Madame Tussaud's.

There were two successive interpretations, although it may be true that at no time was the experience free of interpretation and even that such a pure experience is psychologically impossible. No doubt the original something seen at the entrance was immediately recognized as a material object, as having some sort of colour, and as having the general shape of a human being. And since this involved the application of classificatory concepts to the sensations, there was from the first some degree of interpretation. It seems a safe position to say that there is an intelligible distinction between experience and interpretation, even if it be true that we can never come upon a quite uninterpreted experience.[18]

Yet after this most auspicious beginning to his inquiry, indeed in the very argument which Stace generates from it, it is clear that Stace fails to grasp clearly the force of this concern about the impossibility of 'pure' experience and what this entails. For Stace turns this discussion into a discussion of the post-experience interpretation placed on the experience rather than pursuing *in any sense at all* the primary epistemological issues which the original recognition requires. He immediately turns to 'the difficulty of deciding what part of a mystic's descriptive account of his experience ought to be regarded as actually experienced and what part should be taken as his interpretation'. Then he again simple-mindedly turns to the issue of whether all mystical experiences are the same or not based on the discussion of their post-experiential reports.

Now the first question – how far the mystical experiences *reported* by Christians, Muslims, Jews, Hindus, and Buddhists,

and also by mystics who have not been adherents of any specific
religious creed, are similar or different – is one of extreme difficulty. We shall have to struggle with it, but we cannot hope to get
anywhere near a true answer unless we make the distinction between experience and interpretation and endeavour to apply it to
our material. The reason for this may be made clear by the
following example.

The Christian mystic *usually says* that what he experiences is
'union with God'. The Hindu mystic *says* that his experience is
one in which his individual self is identical with Brahman or the
Universal Self. The Christian *says* that his experience supports
theism and is not an experience of actual identity with God, and
he understands 'union' as not involving identity but some other
relation such as resemblance. The Hindu insists on identity, and
says that his experience establishes what writers on mysticism
usually call 'pantheism' – though Hindus usually do not use that
western word. The Buddhist mystic – at least according to some
versions of Buddhism – does not speak of God or Brahman or a
Universal Self, but interprets his experience in terms which do
not include the concept of a Supreme Being at all.

There are thus great differences of belief here, although the
beliefs are all equally said to be founded on mystical experiences.[19]

Stace's failure to appreciate the complexity of the nature of 'experience' with its linguistic, social, historical, and conceptual contextuality, and the severe limitations of his concentration on a naively
conceived distinction between experience and interpretation
become clear when he takes up what he considers to be Zaehner's
position as argued in *Mysticism Sacred and Profane*. Zaehner
argues that the original mystical reports reveal *different* experiences, not only different reports of the same experience; that is, it is
not just a case of recognizing the distinction of experience and
interpretation and then simply comparing alternative interpretations of the same given. Stace tries to reply to Zaehner's thesis by
suggesting that:

Professor Zaehner, who is a Roman Catholic, insists that their
experiences [of Christian and Hindu mystics] must have been
different because Eckhart and Ruysbroeck *built their accounts of
the experience into the orthodox Trinitarian theology which they
accepted from the Church, whereas the Hindus understood it pan-
theistically* – pantheism being, according to Catholic theologians,

a serious 'heresy' ... the point is that Professor Zaehner's conclusion simply does not follow from the mere fact that the *beliefs* which Christian mystics *based upon their experiences* are different from the *beliefs* which the Indians *based on theirs*. And the difference of beliefs is really the only evidence which he offers for his view. A genuine grasp of the distinction between experience and interpretation, and especially of the difficulties involved in applying it, might have resulted in a fuller, fairer, and more impartial examination and treatment of the two possible hypotheses.[20]

It is highly instructive to note that Stace tries to reject Zaehner's charge on the basis of the distinction between experience and interpretation without at all recognizing the need to ask the fundamental question: what does the Christian bring to his experience and how does it affect that experience, and what does the Hindu bring to his experience and how does it affect that experience? The focus of Stace's remarks is on the relation between the mystics' experience and 'the beliefs which the mystics based upon their experiences'. Here the symmetry is always one-directional: from 'experience' to 'beliefs'. There is no recognition that this relationship contains a two-directional symmetry: beliefs shape experience, just as experience shapes belief. To take, for the moment, a non-controversial example of this, consider Manet's paintings of Notre Dame. Manet 'knew' Notre Dame was a Gothic cathedral, and so 'saw' it as a Gothic cathedral as testified to by his paintings which present Notre Dame with Gothic archways. Yet close examination will reveal that certain of the archways of Notre Dame which Manet painted as Gothic are in fact Romanesque.[21] As Coleridge reminded us: 'the mind half-sees and half-creates'. Reflection now also reminds us that Stace failed in a similar fashion to appreciate the need to investigate the deep issues involved in what the American visitor at Madame Tussaud's brought to his experience. In order to treat adequately the rich evidence presented by mystics, concentration solely on post-experiential reports and the use of a naive distinction – almost universally held by scholars – between claimed 'raw experience' and interpretation, will not do.

As Stace has mentioned Zaehner, the other leading modern investigator of the subject, let us briefly look at his account. Zaehner, in contradistinction to Stace, is aware both by virtue of training, being a most eminent Orientalist and holder of the Spalding Chair in Eastern Religions at Oxford University from 1953 to 1967, as well as in respect of personal experience,[22] that it is not so easy to

55555555555555

draw all mystical experience together in one basically undifferentiated category.[23] Indeed, in his Gifford lectures he writes with especial regard to Hinduism, but in order to make a more general point, that Hinduism 'gives the lie ... to the facile assumption that "mysticism is essentially one and the same whatever may be the religion professed by the individual mystic"'.[24] Zaehner, in addition, goes on to note correctly that the view that mysticism is 'a constant and unwavering phenomenon of the universal longing of the human spirit for personal communion with God'[25] while true of western mysticism and thus pardonable as a description of western mysticism, is inappropriate, nay even inaccurate when applied to 'the kind of mysticism with which we became acquainted in the Upanishads, let alone with the experience of nirvāṇa as described in early Buddhist texts'.[26] Yet, despite Zaehner's insight into the need to acknowledge the diversity of the mystical evidences, there are severe weaknesses in his position which prevent it from making the contribution to the subject it promised. These weaknesses are of three kinds: first, there is the correct objection that Zaehner's evidence is made up exclusively of post-experiential testimony which, on the one hand, neither respects the experience-interpretation distinction in a fashion which is sufficiently rigorous to satisfy Stace, nor on the other – and this is the crucial point for our concern of which Stace is oblivious – makes the necessary inquiry into the logical and social-contextual conditions of mystical experience which would justify rejecting Stace's simplistic distinction. Secondly, Zaehner's own strong Catholic biases colour his entire investigation and make much of his work appear to be special pleading for Catholic Christianity, or at least for western monotheism over against eastern monism. For example, in his *Hindu and Muslim Mysticism* Zaehner injudiciously, not to say dogmatically, writes: 'Both Najm al-Dīn Rāzī, defending Islamic orthodoxy, and Ibn Tufayl, defending sanity, expose the monist's pretension to be God as the "misgrounded conceit" it so manifestly is.'[27] While again in his *Mysticism Sacred and Profane* he attempts to relate the different types of mysticism, especially that between what he calls monistic and theistic mysticism to his own christological understanding of Adam's fall.[28]

Lastly, Zaehner's phenomenology is not adequate. It *is more* sophisticated than Stace's and that of almost all earlier investigators, and its real achievements should be acknowledged. Yet Zaehner's views will not do as a final statement of the problem, or indeed even of an interim one, because it stops too short in its search for the full and diverse meaning(s), leading to a recognition of the relevant diversity, of the nature of mystical experience, especially in terms of its contexts, conditions, and relation to language, beliefs, and cultural configurations. As a consequence his threefold typological distinction for handling cross-cultural mystical experiences – the theistic, the monistic, and the naturalistic ('panenhenic' in Zaehner's vocabulary) – turns out to be an advance over most alternative accounts, as we have said, though overly simplistic and reductionistic. For example, both Jewish and Christian mystics are for the most part theistic in the broad sense, yet the experience of Jewish mystics is radically different from that met in Christian circles. And again the 'theism' of the Bhagavad Gita or of Ramanuja is markedly different from the theism of Teresa of Avila, Isaac Luria, or Al Hallaj. Alternatively, the monism of Shankara is not the monism of Spinoza or Eckhart. And again Buddhism, for example, though classified according to Zaehner's phenomenology as monistic, is really not to be so pigeon-holed.[29] Zaehner achieves this 'monistic' identification of Buddhism only by misusing the texts, and attributing to Buddhism doctrines it does not hold, especially surprising in this respect being his attribution of the doctrine of Ātman, the doctrine of a substantial self, to the Buddha. Zaehner notwithstanding, the Buddha seems to have made the denial of the ātman doctrine which was central to Hinduism, a central, if not *the* central basis for his own revolutionary position. Thus, the supposed 'monism' of the Buddhists who deny the existence of a substantial self or soul can hardly be equated, except by manipulation of evidence and ignoring of facts, with, say the Advaitan monistic experience which claims that there is one universal Self, Brahman, which is the ground of all being and in which each particular individual participates and finds his ultimate salvation. Zaehner's well-known investigations flounder because his methodological, hermeneutical, and especially epistemological resources are weak. Indeed, his researches reinforce the felt pressing need to pursue such inquiries in more sophisticated conceptual terms.

This failure to investigate or to consider in one's investigation of mystical experience the *conditions of experience* in general and the specific conditions of religious/mystical experience in particular is a deficiency which skews the entire discussion in ways which distort any and all conclusions or suggestions made. Let us return, therefore, to this topic. We recall, at the outset, the wisdom of the remark, 'the child is father to the man'. This holds for epistemic inquiry also, in regard both to the logical-conceptual aspect of the inquiry and to the cultural-social aspect, though, of course, the logical-conceptual aspect involves ideas and conditions which are, on another level, to be strictly divorced from this sort of approach, as we shall see. Let us investigate the methodological significance of this phrase as it applies in the case of a Jewish mystic, as an opening gambit.

In the cultural-social sphere the Jewish mystic will have learnt and been conditioned in all kinds of ways from childhood up that: (1) there is more to reality than this physical world; (2) that this 'more' than physical reality is an ultimate Reality which is a personal God; (3) that this God created the world and men; (4) that men have spiritual souls that commune with God; (5) that God enters into covenants with men; (6) that even in covenants He remains distinct; (7) that God's Being and man's being are ontologically distinct; (8) that God entered into special covenants with Abraham and his heirs, Israel; (9) that these covenants are expressed in the acts of circumcision and the giving of the Torah; (10) that the Torah and its commandments (*mitzvot*) are the most perfect expression of God's Will as well as the most perfect means of relation between man and God, and so on. Moreover, the Jewish mystic will have learnt to fit all these items into a special 'mystical theology' known by the broad term of Kabbalah, in which the visible and perceivable is the unreal and the unperceived and non-sensual is the real. One could extend this comparatively small list at great length. All these cultural-social beliefs and their attendant practices, especially in the myriad practice of the *mitzvot*, clearly affect the way in which the Jewish mystic views the world, the God who created it, the way to approach this God, and what to expect when one does finally come to approach this God. That is to say, the entire life of the Jewish mystic is permeated from childhood up by images, concepts, symbols, ideological values, and ritual behaviour which there is no reason to believe he leaves behind in his experience. Rather, these images, beliefs, symbols, and rituals define, *in advance*, what the experience *he wants to have*, and which he then does have, will be like. Without making the discussion too complex in its detail of Jewish mystical theory and practice (traditionally called theoretical Kabbalah and practical Kabbalah, though there is much overlap and the latter is predicated on the theology of the former), let us consider the most essential feature of Jewish mystical thinking and its related behaviour, unique to Jewish mystics, namely, the centrality of the performance of the *mitzvot* (commandments) for reaching the mystic goal and how this interpenetration of ritual and ethical actions (*mitzvot*) with the goal of relation to God affects the kind of experience one *anticipates* having and then, *in fact*, does have.[30]

The Jewish mystic performs the *mitzvot* as a necessity on the mystic's way because he conceives of himself, the world (or cosmos), and God in a very special light. Foremost, perhaps, among the elements of his self-consciousness is his conception of God as the sort of Being who is in some sense personal and, even more, who is ethically and evaluatively personal, i.e. a God who is affected by good deeds and acts of obedience, and the relation to Whom is affected by the proper performance of prescribed actions. Thus, the Jewish mystic's experience is a preconditioned experience of a (moral-personal) God. We see this pre-experiential configurative element, for example, in the details of the central Kabbalistic doctrine of the relation of human action and the *Sefiroth* (Divine Emanations which comprise the highest levels of the upper worlds) in which every *Sefirah* is related to a human ethical counterpart, so that the perfect performance of ethical behaviour becomes, above all, the way towards relation with these Divine Emanations. More generally the level of one's experience with the different rungs of the *Sefiroth* (of which there are ten) is dependent on one's ethical and ritual behaviour (*mitzvot*), and especially on prayer done with the right commitment and concentration (known as *kavvanah*). The Jewish mystics believe that such mystical prayer leads the soul on its upward ascent because mystical prayer leads to a recognition of, and contact with, the true meaning of God's 'Names' which are the real ontological structure of the upper worlds.[31]

That this complex pre-experiential pattern affects the actual experience of the Jewish mystic is an unavoidable conclusion. It can be ascertained clearly in the Jewish mystic's experience or perhaps a better way to describe it might be to refer to the Jewish mystic's 'non-experience'. That is to say, the Jewish conditioning pattern so strongly impresses that tradition's mystics (as all Jews) with the fact that one does *not* have mystical experiences of God in which one loses one's identity in ecstatic moments of unity, that the Jewish mystic rarely, if ever, has such experiences. What the Jewish mystic experiences is, perhaps, the Divine Throne, or the angel Metatron, or aspects of the *Sefiroth*, or the heavenly court and palaces, or the Hidden Torah, or God's secret Names, but not loss of self in unity with God. The absence of the kinds of experience of unity one often, but mistakenly, associates with mysticism, even as the 'essence of mysticism', in the Jewish mystical context, is *very* strong evidence that pre-experiential conditioning affects the nature of the experience one actually has. Because the Jew is taught that such experiences of unity do not happen for reasons flowing out of the Jewish theological tradition, he does not, in fact, have such experiences.[31A] This is a formative pre-experiential element rather than only a post-experiential fact necessitated by Jewish orthodox requirements, as Stace might suggest, being of the essential character of the experience itself. The logic of experience requires the adoption of this account and the evidence supports it.[32]

There is no evidence but *a priori* theorizing in the face of the actual evidence to the contrary, that this non-unitive characterization of the experience of the Jewish mystic is *merely* the product of the post-experiential report, whose form is necessitated by social or religious orthodoxies and imposed on what, in fact, was basically an experience of an altogether different (unitive) sort. Rather, these orthodox concerns, which are indeed very real, are much more deeply rooted and much more powerful, shaping the imaginative and experiential capacities of the Jewish mystic from childhood up and pre-forming his organizing perceptual schema. However, Stace, for example, only sees this constructive aspect of the external factors as they work on one's internal consciousness in terms of the post-experiential report rather than in terms of both their before and after character – a curious blindness in support of a passionately held theory.

Let us stay with this example a little longer and develop its deepest implication. In the Jewish mystical tradition the ultimate state of mystical experience is called *devekuth*, which literally means 'adhesion to' or 'clinging to' God. That is to say, in the Jewish tradition the strong monotheistic emphasis on God's uniqueness is understood to entail not only his numerical unity and perfection but also his qualitative, ontological, distinction from his creations. And even though this distinction is blurred somewhat in the Zoharic and later Lurianic Kabbalah, with their theories of emanation rather than creation, even there God's transcendental majesty and distinctiveness is essential and is retained by the reference to God in himself as *Eyn Sof*, literally 'without end', but used more broadly to refer to God's ultimate and radical Otherness and unknowability, both epistemologically and ontologically. As a consequence, Jewish mystics envisioned the ultimate goal of mystical relation, *devekuth*, not as absorption into God, or as unity with the divine but rather as a loving intimacy, a 'clinging to' God, a relation which all the time is aware of the duality of God and mystic, i.e. which *experiences* God as Other rather than Self. All Jewish mystical literature reflects this teaching of *devekuth* as the goal to be sought and, even more importantly, all Jewish mystical testimonies conform to this pattern. Now one could say: 'but this is because of social pressure' – but what evidence is there for saying this? Moreover, is it not more reasonable to relate the formative milieu to the experience itself and then read the available evidences as confirmation of the milieu-affecting character of the totality of the experience, rather than accounting for the material in more artificial ways?

To bring our point into still sharper focus let us shift our concern and compare the Jewish experience of *devekuth* to a radically different mystical experience found in a mystical tradition near the other end of the mystical spectrum, that of the Buddhist. The preconditioning of the Buddhist consciousness is very different from that of the Jewish and this difference generates the radically different mystical experience which the Buddhist aims at and reaches. Consider, for example, the following concrete elements which the Buddhist *learns* from his tradition starting with the 'four noble truths' which are the foundation of his tradition. These Truths are:

(*a*) 'Birth is suffering, old age is suffering, disease is suffering, death is suffering, association is suffering, separation from what is pleasant is suffering, not obtaining what one desires is suffering . . .';

(*b*) The cause of suffering is 'craving' or 'desire', 'craving for sensual desires, and craving for becoming, and craving for nonexistence';

(*c*) Suffering can be overcome by the proper discipline and understanding;

(*d*) There is an eightfold path which leads to the cessation of suffering (i.e. *nirvāna*).

These eight ways are: (1) Right understanding, i.e. understanding the four noble truths; (2) Right thought, i.e. thought free from desire and craving and cruelty. It is referred to as *saṃkalpa*, the proper 'shaping together' of one's consciousness; (3) Right speech, i.e. refraining from lying, slander, malicious gossip, frivolous speech; (4) Right action, i.e. the avoidance especially of killing, stealing, and general misconduct; (5) Right livelihood, i.e. not earning a living by inappropriate means, for example, as an astrologer; (6) Right effort, i.e. striving to purify oneself of evil thoughts;

(7) Right mindfulness, i.e. being properly mindful of the nature of one's body and mind; (8) Right concentration, i.e. practising the proper meditation patterns especially the four *dhyānas* or trance states. Thus we see that the Buddhist is conditioned to reach *nirvāna* by *sīla* or moral behaviour, *samādhi* or concentration and *prajña* or wisdom.[33]

These elements of the four noble truths were then further elaborated upon in the Buddha's second great sermon, the 'Discourse on the Marks of Not-Self' in which he taught the essential doctrines of 'no-self', i.e. that there is no simple, pure substance which is permanent and which has its own independent substantial existence analogous to the doctrine of the soul in the western traditions or to *ātman* in Hinduism. Indeed, the no-self *anātman* doctrine is a reaction to the Hindu emphasis. Related to this no-self doctrine is also the important doctrine of *pratītyasamutpāda*, 'dependent origination'. We are also taught the doctrine of the impermanence of all things. The only 'something' – or is it a nothing? – which avoids *anītya* (impermanence) and which we have as our goal is *nirvāna* wherein we avoid the wheel of suffering which is the condition of all existing realities. The stages of sanctification that carry a man upwards towards *nirvāna* have been summarized as follows:

In passing from existence as a common person (*prthagjana* to experiencing nirvāna, several stages can be delineated. The first task is to become a member of the family of spiritually elect noble personages (*ārya pudgalas*). To do this one must first make himself fit to commence the practices that will make him an *ārya pudgala*. Even to begin this quest is significant, resulting in the stage of *gotrabhū* or member of the family (of *āryas*). From here, depending on temperament and capability, one of two courses is open: either the follower in faith (*skaddhān-usārin*) for those with mild faculties, or the follower of Dharma (*Dharmānusārin*), for those of keen intellect. By progressively gaining insight into each of the four noble truths, one becomes, at the culmination of the process, a *srotāpanna* or 'streamwinner', the first class of the *ārya pudgalas*. Having abandoned totally belief in the self, doubts about the Three Jewels (i.e. Buddha, Dharma, Samgha), and belief in the efficacy of rituals, the streamwinner is assured of enlightenment within one more lifetime. Progressing further still, the adept becomes an *anāgāmin* or 'non-returner', assured of enlightenment during his current lifetime. When all negative qualities have been eradicated and the adept is pure in all respects, he is able experientially to realize nirvāṇa, thus becoming an *arhant*, and establishing himself as a true saint in Buddhism.[34]

This brings us directly to *nirvāṇa*, the goal of the entire Buddhist enterprise in all its elaborate detail. While it is a subject of fiercely debated divergent opinion among Buddhologists, for our purposes it seems fair to say that *nirvāṇa*: (1) is the recognition that belief in the phenomenal 'self' of mundane existence is an illusion; (2) is most especially characterized by the extinction of 'suffering' which is the predominant feature of ordinary reality; (3) is not a conditional or conditioned reality; (4) is in some positive way the attainment of unique wisdom or insight into the impermanence (*anītya*) of all existing things; (5) is not a Being; (6) is a state or condition, i.e. in the sense of being 'Nirvanaized'; (7) is not a relational state of being.[35]

From this complex structure let us concentrate especially on two cardinal features of the Buddhist account. First, the basis of the entire system is the awareness of suffering in the world and the goal of the system is the extinction of suffering; secondly, the goal, *nirvāṇa*, is not a relational state in which the finite self encounters a saving or loving transcendental Being – God – but rather is a new ontological (if this term is not inappropriate) state of being (if these terms are not inappropriate). That there is no encounter of any sort results from the fact that there is no real self and no transcendental other self. Again, it should also be noted that in the Buddhist doctrine there is no divine will which plays any role as there is no divinity. Rather one has in place of the divine will the strict law of ethical causality, *Karma*, which is at the root of the causal chain of existence, re-existence or reincarnation, and release.[36]

Just setting this Buddhist understanding of the nature of things over against the Jewish should, in itself, already be strong evidence for the thesis that what the Buddhist experiences as *nirvāṇa* is different from what the Jew experiences as *devekuth*. However, let us draw this out more clearly. To begin, when the Jewish mystic performs his special mystical devotions and meditations, *kavvanot*, he does so in order to *purify his soul*, i.e. to remove the soul from its entrapment in the material world in order to liberate it for its upward spiritual ascent culminating in *devekuth*, adhesion to God's emanations, the *Sefiroth*. The Buddhist mystic, on the other hand, performs his meditative practices as an integral part of the Buddhist mystical quest, not in order to free the soul from the body and purify it, but rather in order to annihilate suffering by over-coming any notion of 'self', holding that the very notion of a sub-stantial 'self' or 'soul' is the essential illusion which generates the entire process of suffering. Buddhist literature specifically represents the Buddha as criticizing the belief in a permanent or substantial self (the Hindu doctrine of *ātman*) as a false, even per-nicious, doctrine which, paradoxically, in so far as it encourages egoism in one's pursuit of one's own eternal happiness, makes the fulfilment of one's happiness an impossibility.

In addition to its insistence on the extinction of suffering through the elimination of the 'self' *nirvāna* is also not a relational state, i.e. it is *not* the meeting of two distinct selves or realities who come together in loving embrace. *Nirvāna* is the absence of all relation, all personality, all love, all feeling, all individuality, all identity. *Nir-vāna* is the achievement (if we can use this term, but we have no better one) of calm, of peace, of tranquillity. While it is the banish-ment of care or anxiety, of concern or striving, it is not the creation of a new condition of meeting. *Nirvāna* is no 'something', nor does it contain or permit the continued existence of either individual beings or one grand Being. Its ontology can not even be easily classed as theistic, monistic, or naturalistic. In the world of religious ideas it comes the closest to reminding one of Wittgenstein's remark made in another connection about 'not being a something nor a nothing either'.[37] Moreover, and this cannot be emphasized too strongly, it is this theoretical structure of the impermanence of all existence, the resultant suffering of all beings, and the doctrines of no-self, meditation, etc., upon which the whole of Buddhist life and its goal, *nirvāna* is built. The Buddhist understanding of reality generates the entire elaborate regimen of Buddhist practice, and it is this understanding of reality which defines in advance what the Buddhist mystic is seeking and what we can tell, from the evi-dence, he finds. To think that his pre-conditioned consciousness of how things are and how to find release from suffering in *nirvāna* is extraneous to the actual Buddhist mystical experience is bizarre.

Whatever *nirvāna* is, and indeed whatever *devekuth* is, in so far as words mean anything and philosophical inquiry has any signifi-cance, there is no way one can describe, let alone equate, the experi-ence of *nirvāna* and *devekuth* on the basis of the evidence. There is no intelligible way that anyone can legitimately argue that a 'no-self' experience of 'empty' calm is the same experience as the experi-ence of intense, loving, intimate relationship between two substantial selves, one of whom is conceived of as the personal God of western religion and all that this entails. The losing of self is not equivalent to the finding of another, especially when this other is conceived of as the God of Jewish tradition. To emphasize one key issue: one is especially struck in Jewish mysticism by the imagery of love, even including very pronounced sexual imagery, which is used to express all sorts of 'relations' relevant to the kabbalistic mind. This aspect is totally absent from early Indian Buddhism which equates sexuality with desire and sees desire as the basic element which causes suffering and which is to be overcome in *nirvāṇa*. Now, this is not to *evaluate* either the truth-claims of the sought and reported experiences in Judaism and Buddhism, etc, or to presume to rank them in terms of better or worse as Otto and Zaehner, for example, quite arbitrarily do, or again, as D. T. Suzuki does, but now reversing the dogmatism and opting for the superiority of Zen Buddhism. What I wish to show is only that there is a clear causal connection between the religious and social structure one brings to experience and the nature of one's actual religious experience.

A further logical point needs to be made. This deals with my opening remark in the previous paragraph that if words mean anything my position seems to be the only reasonable one to adopt. Many students of mysticism might see this remark as their 'escape hatch' for avoiding my conclusion. After all, they might argue, all mystics are wary about using language to describe their experience, and many are absolutely opposed to its employment, arguing a form of 'I don't mean what I say and I don't say what I mean'. Also, we are sure to be reminded of the well-known mystical penchant for paradox and ineffability as relevant at this point. However, this 'escape' is no escape at all. It fails to provide the desired way out because it fails to realize that, if the mystic does not mean what he says and his words have *no* literal meaning whatsoever, then not only is it impossible to establish my pluralistic view, but it is also logically impossible to establish any view whatsoever. If none of the mystics' utterances carry any literal meaning then they cannot serve as the *data* for any position, not mine, and certainly not the view that all mystical experiences are the same, or reducible to a small class of phenomenological categories.

We can shed further light on this issue by moving only a short sideways step in the study of mysticism and introducing one further tradition, Christianity, that seems close to the Jewish but which, in fact, introduces new elements which are clearly reflective of a larger theoretical pattern moulding the mystical consciousness of the Christian mystic. Space prevents us from spelling out the forces at work in Christian traditions in the same detail as we have for Judaism and Buddhism, but let us consider this one essential element. In Christian mysticism we have two types of mystical experience, the non-absorptive type which is reminiscent of Jewish mysticism and its doctrine of *devekuth*, though still with a difference, and the absorptive (or unitive) type in which the goal sought and experience reached is a transcendence of the distinction between self and God and the absorption of the self into God in an all-embracing unity. This absorptive type is certainly a common type of Christian mystical experience and is what students of mysticism often, though perhaps mistakenly, consider the paradigm of Christian mysticism. The great Flemish mystic, John Ruysbroeck (1293–1381), is thus able to express his experience in the fascinating expression 'To eat and to be eaten! This is union! . . . Since his desire is without measure, to be devoured of him does not greatly amaze me.'[38] That is to say, in more extreme form, what others have referred to as the loss of self in the 'ocean pacific' of God, or what Eckhart refers to when he writes: 'If I am to know God directly, I must become completely he and he I: so that this he and this I become and are one I.'[39] What permits, perhaps even encourages, this unitive, absorptive mysticism of the divine he and the finite I found in Christian mysticism, though absent from its Jewish counterpart, is, I believe, the formative influence of the essential incarnational theology of Christianity which is predicated upon an admixing of human and divine elements in the person of Jesus which is outside the limits of the Judaic consciousness. Thus, an essential element of the model of Christian spirituality is one of divine-human interpenetration on the ontological level which allows for a unity of divine and human which Judaism rules out. Essential here too is the Neoplatonic influence on Christian thought, especially for Christian mysticism as represented by the greatest of all Neoplatonic mystics, Plotinus.[40] Moreover, to classify this *unio mystica* of the Christian mystic, or rather of some Christian mystics, is not as easy a task as it has appeared to most investigators. The difficulty emerges because union with the divine, when the divinity is understood in christological and incarnational terms is not equatable with either (*a*) the dualistic experience of *devekuth*; (*b*) the no-self, no-God, no-relation experience of *nirvāna*; (*c*) the naturalistic mysticism of those like Richard Jefferies; (*d*) the non-absorptive mysticism of non-Jewish mystics whose experiences differ from that of *devekuth*; or even (*e*) the absorptive mystics who superficially seem closest, such as the Advaitans.

It should also be noted that even the absorptive, non-absorptive dichotomy at work in Christian mysticism which might appear to contradict the contextual rootedness of mystical experience in fact supports it. The unitive Christian mystics are invariably those such as Eckhart, Tauler, and Suso, who have been schooled on Plotinus, Dionysius the Areopagite, and Augustine, i.e. the strong Neoplatonic current in Christian intellectual history. Book VI of Plotinus's *Enneads* provides the inspiration for this conceptualization of the final ascension of the soul into unity ($\xi\nu\omega\sigma\iota\varsigma$) with the Good. Plotinus describes it as a final ineffable absorption of the self back into the perfect absolute One which transcends $\psi\nu\chi\eta$ or $\nu\hat{o}\hat{\nu}\varsigma$; back into the One which alone exists: $M\epsilon\tau\alpha\xi\hat{\upsilon}\ \gamma\grave{\alpha}\rho\ o\hat{\upsilon}\delta\acute{\epsilon}\nu,\ o\hat{\upsilon}\delta'\ \check{\epsilon}\tau\iota$ $\delta\acute{\upsilon}o,\ \grave{\alpha}\lambda\lambda\grave{\alpha}\ \check{\epsilon}\nu\ \check{\alpha}\mu\phi\omega.$[41] The study of Plotinus and the Neoplatonic mystical tradition shaped the mystic's 'mind's eye' so that his experience conformed to it. To think that the 'unitive' mystic merely describes his experience in this way is to distort the situation which gave rise to the experience, the experience itself, and the report of the experience. Thus, for example, seriously to credit that Augustine did not have the unitive experience described in his *Confessions* (Bk. 9) but only used this language is unwarranted for two strong reasons at least: (1) surely an Augustine would not consciously *mis*describe his experience; (2) the theory of misdescription due to orthodox pressures is untenable in Augustine's case because, in fact, the unitive account he gives is more in conflict, though little did he seem to know it, with Christian orthodoxy than a relational description would have been. The evidence for this second contention is the sad fate which some of Augustine's 'absorptive' heirs met at the hands of the Church. Dogmatic reasons aside, be they philosophical dogmas or theological ones, there is no good evidence for denying that Augustine's experience was of the *unitive* character he describes it as possessing. On the contrary, his entire life was a long preparation for just such an experience: 'Thou hast made us for thyself and our hearts are restless until they rest in thee.'

If we stay with the theme of theological and social contextualism a little longer, we shall also notice one further feature of importance deserving of note, as well as of further study. In almost all mystical traditions, we find the importance of a teacher or *guru* who leads the novice along 'the way'. In the Jewish tradition, there is a strong aversion to auto-didacticism both in traditional rabbinic and even more in mystical matters. Indeed, in the Jewish tradition, until the historic calamity of the expulsion from Spain in 1492 called for a radical new approach to mysticism, mystical wisdom was always held very close by its devotees and was only taught in small circles to a select few. The constant fear was expressed that this knowledge, if obtained by the unlettered without the guidance of a teacher, could lead to antinomianism and heresy, as indeed happened in the seventeenth-century pseudo-messianic movement known as Sabbatianism[42] and the eighteenth-century pseudo-messianic movement known as Frankism.[43] As a consequence, Jewish mystics show a close conformity of ideological background, shared experience, and theological reflection. This feature is pronounced in Jewish mysticism, moreover, because of the believed ability of Jewish mystics to escape from a mystical solipsism through the 'public' language of the Torah which served as a mystical lexicon in Jewish mystical circles and which also accounts for its eventual, highly structured, systemic nature, paradigmatically represented in the Zoharic[44] and Lurianic[45] schools. Mention of the Lurianic 'school' is especially noteworthy because it demonstrably reinforces the shared, taught, communal nature of this mystical theory which emerged in the town of Safed[46] in northern Israel in the sixteenth century. The development of Lurianic mysticism into the mass mystical movement surrounding the pseudo-messiah Sabbatai Zevi in the seventeenth century is also further weighty evidence to be considered.

In the Buddhist tradition, one also finds the same emphasis on being guided along the path towards *nirvāṇa* by a qualified teacher. Only *a* Buddha reaches self-enlightenment, all others must be helped towards this end. No less an authority than the late Richard Robinson has argued: 'Every form of Buddhism has held that guides are necessary.'[47] Here too, one sees not only the importance of a qualified teacher or *bhiksu*, but also how this insistence on proper instruction grew into the widespread institution of Buddhist monasticism,[48] with all its strict discipline and ideological commitments. And these emphases, of course, are not unique to Buddhism, the institution of the *guru*-like master being found in all eastern traditions, as for example, Hinduism especially in its Trantric variety, and Zen. The Zen tradition is highly instructive here, for though it made spontaneity the great virtue in achieving *satori*, this spontaneity was achieved through the mediating role which the Zen master played in the 'enlightenment' of his disciples. Not only were the Zen masters considered the paradigms of Zen practice to be emulated by their disciples, but they even became the objects of Zen meditation for their disciples. Even more importantly, it is the Zen master, through the seemingly meaningless *koans* which he sets his students to meditate upon as well as in the purposeful physical and mental abuse he subjects his students to, who destroys the illusions in which the disciple is imprisoned and which prevent him from reaching *satori*. The master induces in the disciple the condition of 'Zen sickness' which allows the disciple to break the bonds of conditional experience and to encounter reality as it really is, in its 'suchness'.[49]

Again, this aspect of the mystical situation is highly focused in the history of Sufism which developed a widespread, highly refined, tradition of Sufi-schools which aided the believer *salak aṭ-ṭariq* ('travelling the Path'). The essence of these mystical Orders, often centred in special Sufi monasteries known as *khānaqāhs*, was the formal relation of master and disciple, of *murshid* and *murid*, based upon the ideology that, though each man, potentially, latently, possessed the ability to merge with Allah in ecstatic union (*fana*), this potency could be actualized only with the assistance of a qualified master (except in the case of a small spiritual élite or elect known as *khawāṣṣ* or *Ṣūfiyya* on whom Allah has bestowed special favour). The disciple followed the *tariqa* ('the way') which was a *practical* method for moving upward through a succession of stages (*maqāmāt*) culminating in the experience of *fana* – unity in Allah. The *tariqa* consisted of set prayers, supererogatory exercises, other varied liturgical and penitential acts, fasts, retreats, vigils and the like. This highly structured procedure prepared the disciple for his experience, i.e. it 'prepared' him in the sense of putting him in the specifically Sufi frame of consciousness both ideologically and existentially, for his ecstatic experience, the form of which was also anticipated in advance.[50] Likewise, the overwhelming preponderance of Christian mystics are found in monasteries and holy orders with their lives centred around chastity, 'good works', and an extremely rigorous regimen of prayer. Fritz Staal has also recently reminded us that the Mexican Indian teacher, Don Juan, is essential for Castaneda's remarkable experiences, whatever one thinks of Castaneda's experiences.[51]

In all these instances, one must ask 'what does the *guru* teach?' The answer is that he teaches a *specific* way and a *specific* goal; his students follow him along the former because they want to reach the latter. Thus, to take one example, the Buddhist 'seeker' comes to his master (and the *Sangha*) and follows his prescribed meditations

and yoga practices to reach that state in which suffering is an-
nihilated and the erroneous notion of self, known as the doctrine of
anātmavada, is completely overcome. Alternatively the Hindu 'seeker'
loyally adheres to his *guru*'s instructions because he desires to
affirm the ultimacy of his self and its relation to the universal self,
known as *atmavada*. Again, the *Murid* is loyal to the rigorous discipline of his *Murshid* because he seeks to merge his soul with the
personal God of Islam; while the Jewish Kabbalist practises his
regimen of prayer and asceticism to find *devekuth* with God's exten-
ded-emanated being manifest in the *Sefiroth*. The Buddhist *guru*
does *not* teach what the Hindu *guru* teaches, though superficial
association of the term confuses the unwary. The *Murshid* does not
teach what the Kabbalist teaches, nor again does Teresa of Avila
teach St John of the Cross the same 'way' as Don Juan [52] or the
Taoist Master. Decisive proof of this is found not only in a close
examination of the respective 'teachings' of the various teachers but
also in the polemical spirit manifest by many, if not most, mystical
masters. Shankara does not shrink from entering into heated
polemics with his Buddhist opponents about the meaning of the
ultimate experience, understood by him in a non-personal monistic
way, or again with his more theistically-minded Hindu colleagues –
and of saying that they are wrong! They do not understand! They
do not have the ultimate experience! – only he and *his* students find
the ultimate experience because only they are properly equipped
to find it. Alternatively, in the Christian tradition we find, for
example, Ruysbroeck prepared to criticize those mystics for whom
mystic experience does not involve moral imperatives as inferior,
while Zen Buddhists have tests and rules for investigating whether a
person really has achieved *satori* or *nirvāna*.[53] For example, the
great Zen master Hakuin records in his autobiography, the *Itsu-
made-gusa*, that after an early experience he was convined that he
had reached the condition of enlightenment and set off to report this
good news to Etan, the aged hermit of Shojuan. Upon interrogation by the Master, Hakuin was found to be still wanting and was rebuked with the epithet, 'You poor child of the devil in a dark dungeon'.
After further study Hakuin reports that 'the enlightenment flashed
upon my mind', and when he was tested anew by Etan 'the master
now stroked my back with his fan' (i.e. a sign of approval).[54] It
should also be noted that classical mystics do not talk about the abstraction 'mysticism'; they talk only about their tradition, their 'way',
their 'goal': they do not recognize the legitimacy of any other. The
ecumenical overtones associated with mysticism have come pri-

marily from non-mystics of recent vintage for their own purposes.

Though we have just begun the description and study of the enormous, even bewildering, variety of specific detail which the technical study of specific mystical traditions reveals, I believe that it has been sufficiently demonstrated that it will not do either to argue that the empirical evidence indicates that all mystical experiences are the same or that such experiences are contextually undetermined or under-determined. The evidence we have considered to this point, in fact, points in the opposite direction: namely, mystical experience is 'over-determined' by its socio-religious milieu: as a result of his process of intellectual acculturation in its broadest sense, the mystic brings to his experience a world of concepts, images, symbols, and values which shape as well as colour the experience he eventually and actually has.

III

Let us now turn to some of the further curious logical-philosophical problems inherent in the study of mysticism which reinforce the contextual thesis here being argued.

The initial factor that needs to be considered is the meaning or meanings of the terms used by mystics to describe or interpret their experiences, for it is this factor that misleads those like Underhill, Otto, Stace, Bucke, Arberry, and Zaehner, among others, into thinking that all mystics are referring to the same experience or to a small number of similar experiences. For example, Stace,[55] in his argumentation for the existence of a 'universal core' common to all mystical experiences compares, among others, Eckhart's Christian experience, the Jewish Kabbalist's experience of *devekuth*, and the Buddhist doctrine of *sunyata* or the Void. In each case, Stace believes that the use of apparently similar language reflects an underlying 'core' experience. For example, he holds that the 'fact' that in each of these mystical reports it is claimed that there is no empirical content in the experience,[56] and that all such mystics seem to describe their experience as being non-spatial, non-temporal, beyond language and ineffable, paradoxical, sublime, and joyful among other traits, is clear evidence for his views regarding the existence of a 'common core'. Stace, however, and the others who follow a similar procedure and arrive at similar results are here being misled by the surface grammar of the mystical reports they study. That is to say, what appear to be similar-sounding descriptions are not similar descriptions and do *not* indicate the same experience. They do not because language is itself contextual and words 'mean' only in contexts. The same words – beautiful, sublime, ultimate reality, ineffable, paradoxical, joyful, transcending all empirical content, etc. – can apply and have been applied to more than one object. Their mere presence alone does not guarantee anything; neither the nature of the experience nor the nature of the referent nor the comparability of various claims is assured by this seemingly common verbal presence alone. Consider the following exercise. A Jew could use all these terms to refer to his experience of *devekuth* with the moral, personal Absolute Being he calls God. At the same time, the Buddhist could use all these phrases to refer to the absence of all being in *nirvāṇa*, while the Hindu could use them to refer to his experience of absorption into the Impersonal Absolute Brahman. Again, the Taoist could use these terms, as well as Plotinus or the nature mystic in referring to Nature. We can express this clearly through the following example. Consider the ambiguity of the proposition:

> *x* transcends all empirical content, is beyond space and time, is ultimate reality, gives a sense of joy, is holy, can only be expressed in paradoxes and is actually ineffable.

Where *x* can be replaced by several, radically different, and mutually exclusive candidates, e.g. God, Brahman, *nirvāṇa*, Nature.

What emerges clearly from this argument is the awareness that choosing descriptions of mystic experience *out of their total context* does *not* provide grounds for their comparability but rather severs all grounds of their intelligibility for it empties the chosen phrases, terms, and descriptions of definite meaning. This logical-semantic problem plagues all the attempts which various scholars, from William James on, have made to provide a common phenomenological description of mystical experience. The fact is that these lists of supposedly common elements not only always *reduce* the actual variety of disparate experiences to fit a specific theory (in each case the context for the terms used being the specific investigator's own system which varies the lists accordingly and which demonstrates, if nothing else, that the material can be arranged in different ways according to alternative ulterior purposes), but they also turn out to be of little help in understanding mystical experience because they are so broad as to fit any one of several mutually exclusive experiences. Consider, for example, James's list in his famous *Varieties of Religious Experience.*[57] James suggests four common characteristics of mystical experience: (1) ineffability; (2) noetic quality; (3) transiency; and (4) passivity. Without too detailed a review let us consider as models the terms 'ineffability' and 'noesis' which James himself considered the most important. 'Ineffability' James rightly defines as an experience or subject that 'defies expression, that no adequate report of its content can be given in words', and goes on to conclude as a consequence that 'it follows that its quality must be directly experienced; it cannot be imparted or transferred to others'.[58] While an accurate description of 'ineffability' James's definition is not the basis on which one can compare experiences, nor the basis on which one can conclude that different experiences have something in common in the sense that they are both instances of the same or similar situations or reflective of experience with a common 'object' or reality. Though two or more experiences are said to be 'ineffable', the term 'ineffable' can logically fit many disjunctive and incomparable experiences. That is to say, an atheist can feel a sense of dread at the absurdity of the cosmos which he labels ineffable, while the theist can experience God in a way that he also insists is ineffable. Thus in *I and Thou*, Buber describes the dialogical encounter with God, the *Absolute Thou*, as ineffable, whose 'meaning itself cannot be transferred or expressed',[59] while Kafka, whose brilliant and haunting tales also suggest the ineffability of existence intends no such encounter,[60] nor reflects any faith in the existence of an *Absolute Thou*. To argue that because both Buber and Kafka see their respective experiences as ineffable, the dialogical experience of Buber's relational *I* with the *Absolute Thou* is the same as or similar to the experience of the lost souls in Kafka's *The Castle* is absurd. Where one finds 'meaning confirmed',[61] the other finds 'emptiness'. Again, 'ineffable' *nirvāna* is not the ineffable *Allah* of the Sufi, nor the 'ineffable' *Allah* of the Sufi the 'ineffable' *Tao* of Taoism. The ontology or reality of Brahman/Atman that lies 'beyond all expression' in the *Mandukya Upanishads* is not the 'ineffability' encountered in Eckhart's Christian experience. 'They were dumb because the hidden truth they saw in God, the mystery they found there, was ineffable.' Even less comparable is Eckhart's 'ineffable' God, like the reality being pointed to, yet held 'ineffable' in the following Zen tale: A Zen master was asked 'What is the Buddha?' to which he replied (in quite typical Zen fashion), 'A dried shit stick.'[62]

Let us also briefly consider James's emphasis on the universality of 'noesis' as a distinguishing and comparable element in mystical experience. James defines this characteristic in the following way: 'Although so similar to states of feeling, mystical states seem to those who experience them, to be also states of knowledge.'[63] That is, he continues, 'states of insight into depths of truth unplumbed by the discursive intellect'. James has caught something important in calling attention to the noetic element in mystical experience, but it is nonetheless not an element that provides the desired commonality. Consider, to begin with, the variety of different knowledge claims which could fit James's definition and which his own examples acknowledge, i.e. this characteristic has been claimed for such differing experiences as those which might be classed as aesthetic, ethical, natural, religious, and mystical. To argue, as James does, that because each such experience claims to give 'insight into depths of truth unplumbed by the discursive intellect' all the experiences are the same, fails to recognize both the variety of 'insights' one could have into the 'depths of truth' and the variety of 'truths' which can lurk in these depths waiting to be 'plumbed'. The varying claims made for such knowledge of the 'truth' is staggering, running from Pythagorean speculations to voodoo, animism, and totemism, to Madame Blavatsky's theosophy and Huxley's and Ramakrishna's *philosophia perennis*, to say nothing of the variety of more traditional religions.

Compare the two contemporary examples of Castaneda and Suzuki. The 'truth' Don Juan discloses to Castaneda through the use of the hallucinogenic peyote plant bears little or no resemblance to the 'truth' of *satori* extolled by the Zen master. The 'noetic' quality of these two experiences is obviously *not* ground for their comparability or equation.

To make the significance of this point in more breadth, consider also W. T. Stace's attempt to construct a list of common mystical characteristics which cut across the cultural or temporal limits of mystical experience. Stace first lists as follows the characteristics of what he considers the two basic types of mystical experience:[64]

COMMON CHARACTERISTICS OF EXTROVERTIVE MYSTICAL EXPERIENCES

1. The Unifying Vision – all things are one
2. The more concrete apprehension of the One as an inner subjectivity, or life, in all things
3. Sense of objectivity or reality
4. Blessedness, peace, etc.

COMMON CHARACTERISTICS OF INTROVERTIVE MYSTICAL EXPERIENCES

1. The Unitary Consciousness; the One, the Void; pure consciousness
2. Nonspatial, nontemporal
3. Sense of objectivity or reality
4. Blessedness, peace, etc.
5. Feeling of the holy, sacred, or divine

COMMON CHARACTERISTICS
OF EXTROVERTIVE MYSTICAL
EXPERIENCES – *contd.*

COMMON CHARACTERISTICS
OF INTROVERTIVE MYSTICAL
EXPERIENCES – *contd.*

5. Feeling of the holy, sacred, or divine
6. Paradoxicality
7. Alleged by mystics to be ineffable

6. Paradoxicality
7. Alleged by mystics to be ineffable.

He then concludes that, 'characteristics 3, 4, 5, 6, 7 are identical in the two lists and are, therefore, *universal common characteristics of mysticism in all cultures, ages, religions, and civilizations of the world*'.[65] Even more, Stace adds one final word on the matter: 'extrovertive experience, although we recognize it as a distinct type, is actually on a lower level than the introvertive type'.[66] Though this final position is clearly reflective of Stace's own monistic, introvertive bias, it gives us a straightforward claim to deal with regarding the supposed common mystical characteristics of: 'the sense of objectivity or reality'; 'Blessedness, peace, etc.'; 'feeling of the holy sacred, or divine'; 'paradoxicality' and 'ineffability'. Let us take no. 3, 'the sense of objectivity or reality' as our model for examination. While it is the case that all mystics claim that theirs is an experience of reality – actually reality with a capital R – this seemingly common claim provides no basis for Stace's extreme conclusion about the 'universal common characteristics of mysticism'. It does not because the terms 'objectivity' and 'reality' are as notoriously elusive as they are seductive. Every system and every mystic had made claims to ultimate objectivity and to discovered Reality, but the claims are more often than not mutually incompatible. For example, while objectivity or reality (Reality) in Plato and Neoplatonism is found in the 'world of Ideas', these characteristics are found in God in Jewish mysticism and again in the *Tao, nirvāṇa,* and Nature, in Taoism, Buddhism, and Richard Jefferies[67] respectively. It seems clear that these respective mystics do not experience the same Reality or objectivity, and therefore, it is not reasonable to posit that their respective experiences of Reality or objectivity are similar. As presumably few of my readers have had a mystical experience, perhaps this point can be reinforced by comparing the terms 'Reality' in, say, Marxism, where Reality is equated with the economic and material, as against Freudianism where Reality is defined in terms of the psychological or alternatively in empiricism where Reality is equivalent to the sensible or that which is derived from the sensible as compared to the Idealist 'Reality' which is ideational and non-sensible. The presence of the term 'Reality' is no guarantee of either a common experience or again of a common language and metaphysics.

Careful inspection thus shows that while lists of supposed phenomenological characteristics seem to help in delineating what mystical experience is, and also in establishing what ties seemingly different experiences together as a class of like experience, such lists, in fact, are so general that even though they serve to *exclude* certain types of experience as, for a bizarre example, contemplating one's navel, as a mystical experience, they remain so general as not to suffice to delineate what mystical experience actually is, nor again are they sophisticated in their recognition of the contextual basis of language and thus are incapable of sorting out the actual meaning of mystical reports. Henry Suso's 'intoxication with the immeasurable abundance of the Divine House ... entirely lost in God [of Christianity]',[68] the *Upanishads* 'sat [what is] ... is expressed in the word *satyam*, the Real. It comprises this whole universe: Thou art this whole universe',[69] as well as the Buddhist's 'dimension of nothingness' (*ākincaññāyatana*)[70] all can be included under these broad phenomenological descriptions of 'Reality', yet for the reasons already advanced it is clear that Suso's Christian God is not equivalent to the Buddhist's 'nothingness', and that the experience of entering into the Divine House is not equivalent to losing oneself in Buddhist 'nothingness'. It becomes apparent on reflection that *different* metaphysical entities can be 'described' by the same phrases if these phrases are *indefinite* enough, as are the very general descriptive phrases used in our phenomenological lists. While appearing to delineate quite concrete phenomena these lists do not have the power to provide definite descriptions of any specific discrete phenomena: neither the claimed universal, common mystical experience nor anything else.[71]

The mention of different ontological realities being covered by the same term is an issue that raises severe difficulties of a logical, semantical, and metaphysical sort. Consider, for example, the use of the term 'nothingness' which has just been mentioned in the context of the Buddhist 'experience of nothingness'. When comparisons are made, based on the presence of this term without careful inquiry, insuperable problems emerge. For one has to ask at the outset about the precise use of the term. Is it being used as a subjective description of an experience or a putative objective description of an object or objective ontological state of being? This is the difference between using the term in a way analogous to the

subjective use of 'happiness', i.e. 'I experience happiness' as compared to the objective (and object) claim 'I experience God'. The problem of reification of course enters the picture too. This distinction
already indicates that the utterance of the term 'nothingness' does
not suffice to assure the univocal use of the term. Again, this usage
encourages one to reflect on the ontological claims that lie beneath
and are necessary correlates of language. Even agreeing that in two
or more cases the term 'nothingness' is being used in the sense of an
objective ontological reference, there is still no surety that the term
is being used in synonymous ways. One has to ask whether the
various experiences of 'nothingness' are similar or dissimilar experiences of the *same* phenomenon, i.e. 'nothingness', or different experiences of *different* phenomena, i.e. 'nothingness' is a term which is
used to cover alternative ontic realities. In this latter instance,
which seems to fit at least a substantial segment of the data of
mystical experience more adequately, the difference between cases
is a difference between *what* is experienced, not just *how* something
is experienced. The appropriateness of this second schema, i.e. that
the term is used to cover differing ontic 'states of affairs', recom-
mends itself because to hold that it is just a case of *how* one experiences a common reality, one would have to have a sufficiently
delimiting list of corresponding and agreed predicates that the experienced object possessed in both (or more) cases which are being
compared. This, however, is absent in at least many, if not most,
cases. Concrete cases of usage will assist us here. Stace, for
example, finds the use of 'nothingness' to be a near-universal
feature of mystical experience, which he takes to be another valuable support for his universalistic 'core' thesis. Thus he compares
the use of the term as found in a Hasidic tale with that found
elsewhere in eastern and western mystical reports. Unfortunately
Stace's comparison is facile, being based on an ignorance of the
Hasidic–Kabbalistic context, which gives the term its peculiarly
Hasidic meaning. The term 'nothing' or 'nothingness' in this
Jewish intellectual environment does *not* mean, as Stace erroneously believes, a reference to an introvertive experience of mystical
unity of the monistic sort which Stace favours.[72] Stace, working
from translations rather than the original Hebrew texts, fails to
appreciate that the term in this setting is a translation of the term
Ayin which is used in Kabbalistic literature as a name of God
relating to his first acts of self-revelation from his self-contained
mysteriousness as *Eyn Sof* (God as He is in Himself) and yet still
prior to his manifestation as the first Sefirah *Keter*. In the late-

thirteenth-century work *Masoret ha-Berit* the following understanding of the term *Ayin* is given: 'having more being than any other being in the world, but since it is simple, and all other simple things are complex when compared with its simplicity, so in comparison it is called "nothing" ["Ayin"]'.[73] As *Ayin*, 'nothingness', God, as the term is meant to indicate, is still beyond any and all human understanding of experience. As *Ayin*, God is still alone. No human experience *ever* achieves relation with this dimension of God's nature. Stace's comments on this notion, therefore, can be seen to be a case of eisegesis which is totally *out of context* and without any meaning in the original kabbalistic sources and Hasidic mystical report.

Alternatively, the term 'nothingness' also is prominent in Buddhist texts. *Mu*, the Chinese and Japanese Buddhist term for 'nothingness' and 'non-being', for example, is not a referent to God as he is in himself or in his first stages of self-revelation, but rather refers to the absolute ontological condition of emptiness or *śūnyatā* which transcends all being, all predication, all substantiality. And here, of course, the understanding of *śūnyatā* becomes the subject of fierce debate between competing schools of Buddhism, being especially important to the Mahāyānists. Again, it is often, but in my view erroneously, argued that the Christian mystical tradition of Dionysius the Areopagite[74] and his heirs which talks of 'nothingness', as *nichts* in Eckhart's language, is the same as the Buddhist *Mu*, for the Christian mystic such as Eckhart seeks the re-birth of his soul now purified through its immersion into the *Gottheit*, whereas the Buddhist seeks *śūnyatā* as the transcendence or liberation from all selfhood. We note too that the elusive concept of the 'self', obviously central to this discussion, needs close scrutiny in its eastern and western and Buddhist Christian contexts, if these comparisons are to make sense. Merely adding to the list of terms used in all traditions that of the 'self', without thorough exploration and analysis of its meaning, is to compound the confusion respective to clarifying, for example, the notion of 'nothingness'.[75]

In like fashion, Stace also argues that Islamic mysticism manifests similar universal features to those found in Buddhism, Hinduism, Judaism, and the like. However, close attention to the ultimate Islamic mystical state of *fana fi-Allah* will reveal that, for example, it is not the same as, say, *nirvāṇa*, and likewise, when the Islamic mystic talks of the 'nothingness' of his experience he does *not* mean the same thing as does the Chinese Master when he talks of *Mu*, or the Hinayanist and Mahayanist when they talk of *śūn-*

yatā. Involved in the 'nothingness' of *fana* is not only loss of identity – the similarity which Stace fastens on to make his erroneous comparison – but also *baqa* (lit. subsistence), everlasting life in *Allah*. However, in Buddhist doctrine there is no entity or state comparable to *baqa*, as there is no God or God-like being in Buddhism. It is precisely this merging into Allah in the sense of *baqa* that, for example, the Sufi Abu Ali of Sind describes when he writes of his experience of *fana*:

> Creatures are subject to changing 'states' but the gnostic has no 'state', because his vestiges are effaced and *his essence annihilated by the essence of another, and his traces are lost in another's traces*.[76]

Again, Baba Krihi of Shiraz gives precise sense to this Islamic use of 'nothingness' when he discusses his experience:

> But when I looked with Allah's eyes – only Allah I saw. I passed away into nothingness, I vanished, and lo, I was the all-living – only Allah I saw.[77]

Related to the linguistic-cum-ontological confusion just discussed, there is also a substantial logical issue which we briefly referred to earlier and which now calls for more sustained discussion. This issue relates to the claim that mystical language is defined by its 'ineffability' and its 'paradoxicality'. These two features are standard elements in all phenomenological descriptions of mystical experience and are taken to be grounds for their comparability; but do they actually support this position? Do these elements logically allow for the inquiry into the possible identity of mystical experiences and their attempted comparability, especially their claimed equivalence or similarity? What leads me to ask these questions is the following argument: the terms 'paradox' and 'ineffable' do not function as terms that inform us about the context of experience, or any given ontological 'state of affairs'. Rather they function to cloak experience from investigation and to hold mysterious whatever ontological commitments one has. As a consequence, the use of the terms 'paradox' and 'ineffable' do not provide *data* for comparability, rather they eliminate the logical possibility of the comparability of experience altogether. Consider the following example: (1) mystic A claims experience *x* is paradoxical and ineffable; while (2) mystic B claims experience *y* is paradoxical and ineffable. The only logically permissible conclusion one can draw in this situation is that both mystic A and mystic B claim their experience is paradoxical; *nothing* can be said about the content of their respective experiences x and y for there is no way to give content to experiences x or y in such a manner as to learn anything about them, apart, as we have said, from their both being paradoxical, which could then serve as the basis of a reasonable comparison. To assume, as James, Huxley, Stace, and many others do, that, because both mystics claim that their experiences are paradoxical, they are describing like experiences is a *non sequitur*.

Another way of getting at this issue is by asking the question: 'What ontological or logical reason demands that there be only one experience that is ineffable or paradoxical?' What emerges in answer to this question is that if mystical experience(s) are being accurately described when they are said to be paradoxical and ineffable, then these experiences are actually being removed from all possibility of definition, description, pointing to, and thus also, of comparability. One could express this position regarding the claims and consequences of the claims relative to the mystical experience thus: 'Every mystical experience x is P and I, where P = paradoxical and I = ineffable', thus 'any statement regarding the internal character of x will be paradoxical and ineffable'. Given this position, one has no reasonable grounds for making the assertion that any two mystical experiences x are the same. That is to say: in Case (i), 'x is PI' could logically refer to an experience containing attributes or elements a, b, c . . .; while in Case (ii), 'x is PI' could logically refer to an experience containing attributes or elements d, e, f. And the same in every additional case, i.e. Case (iii), 'x is PI' could logically refer to an experience containing attributes or elements g, h, k, and so on. As there is no way to get behind the expression 'x is PI' in each respective case, this in fact being the logical force of the expression 'x is PI', there is no way to evaluate Cases (i), (ii), (iii) in order to ascertain whether they are the same – even if they were the same. Once one has introduced *per definitionem* the features of paradox and ineffability, no other result can follow. Moreover, not only is there now no possibility of comparing different mystical experiences, but the perplexing question about the status and intelligibility of the other elements in mystical reports also opens up. How strongly can any of the elements in a mystical report be taken as evidence for a phenomenology or typology of mysticism in so far as these statements are associated with the basic notion that mystical experience is ineffable and paradoxical? If the terms 'paradoxical' and 'ineffable' mean anything, do they not cancel out all other descriptive claims, thus undermining any and all attempts at a phenomenological typology of mystical experience based on post-experiential reports? There is certainly something logically and lin-guistically odd at work here that is almost always ignored and which needs careful critical scrutiny. *A fortiori* it would appear that to take the mystic's claim seriously, i.e. that his proposition '*x* is PI' is a true description, turns out to have the damaging implication that one cannot make any reasonable or even intelligible claim for any mystical proposition. The proposition '*x* is PI' has the curious logical result that a serious interpretation of the proposition neither makes the experience *x* intelligible nor informs us in any way about *x*, but rather cancels *x* out of our language – which, of course, is what most mystics claim they want. This, however, is no founda-tion for a phenomenology of mysticism or a typology of compar-ative mystical experience, for there are a wide variety of mutually exclusive ontological 'states of affairs' which can thus be ruled out. At this juncture, it genuinely is a case of 'where you cannot speak be silent'.[78]

Going one step further, it should also be noted that there is a complex issue operating in the identification of the object of mystical experience which is usually ignored. The issue to which I refer is the fact that writers on mysticism seem to take the terms 'God', *nirvāṇa*, etc., more as names than as descriptions, i.e. they are handled as if they were arbitrary labels of some underlying common reality. This, however, is an error, for 'God' and *nirvāṇa* or even 'Being' or *Urgrund* are not only or even primarily names but are, rather, descriptions, or at least disguised descriptions, and carry a meaning relative to some ontological structure. Thus, the term 'God' carries with it ontological characteristics, perfection characteristics, i.e. all the *omni* words we attribute necessarily to God, and 'personality' characteristics, etc. Alternatively, *Atman* car-ries some of the same, but also some considerably different ontic, metaphysical, and 'personality' characteristics and the same, but even more radically apposite, assertion is required when we refer to *nirvāṇa*. Substituting what seem to be more neutral terms such as 'Being' also proves less helpful than at first appears because 'Being' too is not a free-floating bit of ontological information, but part of the flotsam and jetsam of specific meaning-systems. When Plato speaks of 'Being', his meaning is different from that intended when the term finds its way into the philosophical vocabulary of Spinoza and Schelling, or Sartre and Heidegger, to say nothing of Zen or Taoism.

These remarks lead us back again to the foundations of the basic claim being advanced in this paper, namely that mystical experience is <u>contextual</u>. A suggestive place to pick up the thread of the argument is in the context of the oft made and oft repeated statement that mysticism, in one sense or another, aims at assisting the self to 'transcend' his situation. Thus, in all traditions we have practices that function in the role of asceticism – yoga, meditation, and the like which are aimed at freeing the 'self' from its 'conditioned existence', whatever the given experiential, socio-historical and religious ideological 'conditions' might happen to be. These processes of 'liberation' *appear*, on the face of it, as movements which lead the 'self' from states of 'conditioned' to 'unconditioned' consciousness, from 'contextual' to 'non-contextual' awareness. Moreover, this is the usual way of evaluating them, especially by those seeking some variety of the *philosophia perennis*, the universal common mystical experience. For they argue, behind or above the limitations placed upon our consciousness by our conditioned historical, socio-ideological situation there is a shared universal vision of the commonality of reality which is had by those who know how to transcend these arbitrary sociological and historical determinations, the evidence for this being the claimed similarity of mystical experience across cultures and historical epochs. Those who advocate this position, however, are misled by appearances. For it is in appearance only that such activities as yoga produce the desired state of 'pure' consciousness. Properly understood, yoga, for example, is *not* an *un*conditioning or *de*conditioning of consciousness, but rather it is a *re*conditioning of consciousness, i.e. a substituting of one form of conditioned and/or contextual consciousness for another, albeit a new, unusual, and perhaps altogether more interesting form of conditioned-contextual consciousness.

There is no substantive evidence to suggest that there is any pure consciousness *per se* achieved by these various, common mystical practices, e.g. fasting, yoga, and the like. This point is well illustrated through consideration of the widely practised art of yoga. Yoga is found in all the major oriental religions, yet the goal of yoga, and even the meaning of yoga,[79] differs from particular tradition to particular tradition. Thus, for example, in Upanishadic Hinduism yoga is practised in order to purify and unify the individual 'soul' and then to unite it with Brahman or, as later represented in the Bhagavad Gita, with Krishna. However, even within Hinduism, yoga combines with other metaphysical systems which claim to provide the 'way' and define the 'goal', *samādhi*, differently. The Sāṃkhya tradition, for example, understands the goal to be the perfection of

the soul which does not lead to any form of *unio mystica* but rather
to a splendid self-identity which, like God's perfection, is self-
contained and isolated.[80] Alternatively, Buddhism also inherited
yoga practices as a central element but now as central to a radically
different metaphysical schema which recognized neither the existence of a personal God – or even an impersonal one – nor the
substantiality of individual souls (*ātman* or *perusha*). Instead
Buddhism views yoga as a technique for overcoming its metaphysical *raison d'être*, suffering and the corollary liberation from all
illusions of substantiality. Yoga is now put at the service of 'emptiness', remembering that emptiness is not a 'something' and that
one must not reify emptiness into a thing as, for example,
Heidegger does with 'nothing'.[81] It must also be noted that in
Buddhism, as in Hinduism, the proper metaphysics also becomes
the subject of debate and schism, creating alternative Buddhist
schools[82] with their differing analyses of the nature and purpose of
yoga. Without going into further detail, let it suffice to note also
that yoga is also practised in Jainism and other oriental traditions
which take still other views than those found in Hinduism or
Buddhism regarding the nature of the soul, ultimate reality, and the
purpose of life. This variety of dogmatic doctrinal belief is not
something to be dismissed as merely marginal or preparatory, nor
can one, recognizing the complexity of the circumstances, talk
about yoga in the abstract, for yoga in that circumstance will then
certainly become just an empty abstraction. Moreover, the significance of the contextual element becomes all the more pressing when
one realizes that for Indian systems metaphysics *is* soteriology.
What one believes does affect one's salvation – and 'salvation',
differingly understood from tradition to tradition, is the respective
goal(s) of each. The experience that the mystic or yoga has is the
experience he seeks as a consequence of the shared beliefs he holds
through his metaphysical doctrinal commitments.

Closely allied to the erroneous contention that we can achieve a
state of pure consciousness is the oft used notion of the 'given' or
the 'suchness' or the 'real' to describe the pure state of mystical
experience which transcends all contextual epistemological colour-
ing. But what sense do these terms have? What is the 'given' or the
'suchness' or even the 'real'?[83] Analysis of these terms indicates
their relativity; they are applied to a variety of alternative and even
mutually exclusive 'states of affairs' and 'states of no-affairs'. This
variety itself should alert us to the real danger and arbitrariness
involved in this gambit. Phenomenologists seem especially prone to

this fruitless naivety – all intuit the 'given' but their intuitions differ significantly. It can fairly be said that no attempt to state clearly or individuate the 'given' has succeeded. Indeed, talk of the 'given' seems to be a move made to short-circuit the very sort of epistemological inquiry here being engaged in, but such a move fails because there is no evidence that there is any 'given' which can be disclosed without the imposition of the mediating conditions of the knower. All 'givens' are also the product of the processes of 'choosing', 'shaping', and 'receiving'. That is, the 'given' is appropriated through acts which shape it into forms which we can make intelligible to ourselves given our conceptual constitution, and which structure it in order to respond to the specific contextual needs and mechanisms of consciousness of the receiver. This description of the epistemic activity, even the epistemic activity involved in mystical experience, of course requires what in the Kantian idiom, though not in Kant's own manner, would be called a 'transcendental deduction',[84] i.e. an argument which reveals *both* conditions of knowing in general as well as the grounds of its own operation and which is thematized according to specific possibilities – and this seems both appropriate and necessary, though its structure cannot even be outlined here. There seems no other way to get at the issue that would be philosophically satisfactory and which would satisfy our interest in the legitimation of the conditions of our knowledge, mystical knowledge included. This means that the mystic *even* in his state of reconditioned consciousness is also a shaper of his experience; that he is not a *tabula rasa* on which the 'ultimate' or the 'given' simply impinges itself – whatever ultimate he happens to be seeking and happens to find. This much is certain: the mystical experience must be mediated by the kind of beings we are. And the kind of beings we are require that experience be not only instantaneous and discontinuous, but that it also involve memory, apprehension, expectation, language, accumulation of prior experience, concepts, and expectations, with each experience being built on the back of all these elements and being shaped anew by each fresh experience. Thus experience of x – be x God or *nirvāṇa* – is conditioned both linguistically and cognitively by a variety of factors *including the expectation of what will be experienced*. Related to these expectations are also future directed activities such as meditation, fasting, ritual ablutions, self-mortification, and so on, which create further expectations about what the future and future states of consciousness will be like. There is obviously a self-fulfilling prophetic aspect to this sort of activity.

The creative role of the self in his experience is not analogous to the passive role of the tape-recorder or camera. Even in mystical experience, there seems to be epistemological activity of the sort we know as discrimination and integration and, in certain cases at least, of further mental activities such as relating the present experience to past and future experience, as well as traditional theological claims and metaphysics. Take, for example, Jan van Ruysbroeck's descriptions given in his *The Adornment of the Spiritual Marriage*:

When the inward and God-seeing man has thus attained to his eternal Image, and in this clearness, through the Son, has entered into the bosom of the Father: then he is enlightened by Divine truth, and he receives anew, every moment, the Eternal Birth, and he goes forth according to the way of the light in a Divine contemplation. And here there begins the fourth and last point; namely, a loving meeting, in which, above all else, our highest blessedness consists.

You should know that the heavenly Father, as a living ground, with all that lives in Him, is actively turned towards His Son, as to His own Eternal Wisdom. And that same Wisdom, with all that lives in It, is actively turned back towards the Father, that is, towards that very ground from which It comes forth. And in this meeting, there comes forth the third Person, between the Father and the Son; that is the Holy Ghost, Their mutual Love, who is one with them Both in the same nature. And he enfolds and drenches through both in action and fruition the Father and the Son, and all that lives in Both, with such great riches and such joy that as to this all creatures must eternally be silent; for the incomprehensible wonder of this love eternally transcends the understanding of all creatures. Wonder is understood and tasted without amazement, there the spirit dwells above itself, and in one with the Spirit of God; and tastes and sees without measure, even as God, the riches which are the spirit itself in the unity of the living ground, where it possesses itself according to the way of its uncreated essence.

Now this rapturous meeting is incessantly and actively renewed in us, according to the way of God; for the Father gives Himself in the Son, and the Son gives Himself in the Father, in an eternal content and a loving embrace; and this renews itself every moment within the bonds of love. For like as the Father incessantly beholds all things in the birth of His Son, so all things are loved anew by the Father and the Son in the outpouring of the Holy Ghost. And this is the active meeting of the Father and of the Son, in which we are lovingly embraced by the Holy Ghost in eternal love.[85]

Ruysbroeck then goes on to describe the 'unity' man may achieve in God which I quote *in extenso*:

And after this there follows the union without distinction. For you must apprehend the Love of God not only as an outpouring with all good, and as drawing back again into the Unity; but it is also, above all distinction, an essential fruition in the bare Essence of the Godhead. And in consequence of this enlightened men have found within themselves an essential contemplation which is above reason and without reason, and a fruitive tendency which pierces through every condition and all being, and through which they immerse themselves in a wayless abyss of fathomless beatitude, where the Trinity of the Divine Persons possess Their Nature in the essential Unity. Behold, this beatitude is so onefold and so wayless that in it every essential gazing, tendency, and creaturely distinction cease and pass away. For by this fruition, all uplifted spirits are melted and noughted in the Essence of God, Which is the superessence of all essence. There they fall from themselves into a solitude and an ignorance which are fathomless; there all light is turned to darkness; there the three Persons give place to the Essential Unity, and abide without distinction in fruition of essential blessedness. This blessedness is essential to God, and superessential to all creatures; for no created essence can become one with God's Essence and pass away from its own substance. For so the creature would become God, which is impossible; for the Divine Essence can neither wax nor wane, nor can anything be added to It or taken from It. Yet all loving spirits are one fruition and one blessedness with God without distinction; for that beatific state, which is the fruition of God and of all His beloved, is so simple and onefold that therein neither Father, nor Son, nor Holy Ghost, is distinct according to the Persons, neither is any creature. But all enlightened spirits are here lifted up above themselves into a wayless fruition, which is an abundance beyond all the fullness that any creature has ever received or shall ever receive. For there all uplifted spirits are, in their superessence, one fruition and one beatitude with God without distinction; and there this beatitude is so onefold that no distinction can enter into it. And this was prayed for by Christ when He besought His Father in heaven that all His beloved might be made perfect in one, even as He is one with the Father through the Holy Spirit . . .[86]

Though this description may appear, on first reading, epistemologically, theologically, or metaphysically neutral, closer inspection will reveal a myriad of epistemological, theological and metaphysical assumptions or doctrines which colour the account both *before* and *after* it occurs.

Moreover, in almost all cases, if not in all, mystical experience knows, as we have shown, what end it seeks from the inception of its traversal along the 'mystic's way'. Thus the Sufi *tariq*, the Taoist *Tao*, the Buddhist *dharma* and the Christian *via mystica* are all 'intentional', i.e. intend some final state of being or non-being, some goal of union or communion, some sense of release, exaltation, blessedness, or joy. And the *tariq*, the *Tao*, and the *via mystica* seek different goals because their initial, generative, problems are different. The Sufi and Christian mystic begin with the 'problems' of finitude, sin, and distance from God, while the Buddhist begins with the problem of suffering and *anitya* or impermanence and, again, the Taoist starts from a positive appreciation of the self and world and seeks to protract spiritual life by the victory of the *yang* over *yen*. The respective 'generating' problems at the heart of each tradition suggest their respective alternative answers involving, as they do, differing mental and epistemological constructs, ontological commitments, and metaphysical superstructures which order experience in differing ways. The mind can be seen to contribute both the problem and the means of its overcoming: it defines the origin, the way, and the goal, shaping experience accordingly. The Buddhist experience of *nirvāna*, the Jewish of *devekuth*, and the Christian of *unio mystica*, the Sufi of *fana*, the Taoist of *Tao* are the *result*, at least in part, of specific conceptual influences, i.e. the 'starting problems' of each doctrinal, theological system. We are each a unitary consciousness and each of us connects the 'problem' and its 'answer' through forms of connection, synthesis, and objectivity which are integral to our consciousness as conscious agents of the sort we are. Indeed, it appears that the different states of experience which go by the names *nirvāna*, *devekuth*, *fana*, etc., are not the ground but the *outcome* of the complex epistemological activity which is set in motion by the integrating character of self-consciousness employed in the specifically mystical modality. These synthetic operations of the mind are in fact the fundamental conditions under which, and under which alone, mystical experience, as all experience, takes place. These constructive conditions of consciousness produce the grounds on which mystical experience is possible at all.

This entire area of the 'intentionality' of experience and the language of experience as it relates to mysticism is a rich area for further study. By way of only introducing the significance of this topic for our concerns, I will merely suggest that, if one looks closely at the language of mystics, as well as at mystical devotion, practices, and literature, one will find that much of it is 'intentional' in the sense suggested by Husserl and Brentano. Though I am no great admirer of either with regard to their more general metaphysical positions, their discussion of 'intentional language' *per se* is instructive, for it calls to our attention that certain terms such as 'expects', 'believes', 'hopes', 'seeks', 'searches', 'desires', 'wants', 'finds', 'looks for', involve, as Brentano said, 'an object in themselves'. We must heed the warning that linguistic intentionality does not generate or guarantee the existence of the 'intentional object', but we must also recognize the epistemologically formative character of intentional language mirroring as it does intentional acts of consciousness. Using the language modern phenomenologists favour we might say that 'intentionality' means to describe a 'datum as meant', i.e. to be aware that an action includes a reach for some specific meaning or meaningful content.

The value of recognizing the intentional quality of much mystical theory and practice can be brought out by reflecting on the intentionality involved in yoga and like mystical behaviour. Thus, we need only ask the mystic the quite proper question: 'Why are you doing such and such?' To this question the *yogi*, for example, would answer that he takes up his gruelling practice because he holds to a specific metaphysic of self and suffering (differing in Hinduism and Buddhism and even within each broad tradition) and believes that, in the words of the *Śiva Samhitā*: 'Through [yoga] practice (*abhyasa*) success is obtained, through practice one gains liberation.'[87] The Sufi mystic would answer likewise that he practises the ritual acts of *dhikr* (recollection of the divine names), the breathing exercises, the fasting, and the prayer regimens because, as Ibn Ata Allah notes: 'Recollection of God (*dhikr*) . . . is the very prop upon which the Way (*tariqa*) (to unity with God, i.e. *tawhid*) rests.'[88] The same sort of replies and intentional reasoning (though of course giving different intentions) can be found in most mystical traditions, and certainly in those of Judaism, Christianity, Islam, Buddhism, Taoism, and Hinduism.

Though we have concentrated on the active role of the knowing self in the epistemological process for the most part in this paper as a corrective to the traditional way in which mystical experience is approached it also has to be recognized, at the same time, that this experiential situation also needs to be turned round. That is to say, lest my readers gain a misapprehension of my view, or of the complexity of the epistemological process involved in mystical experience a few words about the 'known' aspect of mystical experience are called for. To get the conditions of mystical experience properly set and in proper perspective, it is imperative to notice that in any experiential situation like that claimed by and for the mystics the full content of the concept of experience needs to be appreciated. When Smith says 'I experience x' he is not only involved in the sorts of epistemological procedures that we have just discussed, i.e. that the mind is active in constructing x as experienced, but he is also asserting that there is an x to be experienced. In other words, mystics and students of mysticism have to recognize that mystical experience is not (putatively) solely the product of the conditioned act of experience as constituted from the side of the experiencer, but is also constituted and conditioned by what the *object* or 'state of affairs' is that the mystic (believes he) 'encounters' or experiences. To say, 'Smith experiences x' is also to recognize that this experience is in part dependent on what x is. But here is the rub – this recognition also requires the additional awareness of the complexity of the situation in that what 'x is' is itself, at least partly, determined by a contextual consciousness. To clarify this point, consider this example: to say, 'Smith has a mystical experience of God' means in terms of our foregoing discussion, not only to assert that Smith conditions the situation in structured ways, but also that the constitution of his experience depends on the cognizance of the putative reality of the object of his experience, i.e. God. Yet the complexity is compounded by the recognition that the existence of 'God' is itself, at least in part, contributed to experience. One might express this dialectic more clearly as follows: 'Smith experiences God' entails, given the strong sense of experience the mystics intend, both (*a*) 'Smith consciously constitutes "God"' as well as (*b*) ' "God" makes himself known to Smith' – recognizing that here too, 'God' has also been, at least partially, conditioned for Smith. For Smith, as for all of us, only knows things as they 'appear' to him.

Another way of revealing these different elements in the mystical (and other) experience is to recognize what language has to teach us through the use of the two quite different locutions: (*a*) 'Smith experiences God' and (*b*) 'God is given to Smith in experience'. Locution (*a*) suggests something of the recognition of the independence of the object of experience, though this too is regulated by structures of consciousness and experience, while locution (*b*) points towards the situational, i.e. the fact that our experience of God belongs to an experiential context which is, at least partially, regulative and determinative of the content of the experience. In this way, we can again see clearly how it is that mystical experiences differ from tradition to tradition. The Jewish mystic 'experiences God' and 'God is given to the Jew in his experience,' whereas the Buddhist mystic, in contradistinction, recognizes the 'objectivity' of *nirvāṇa* and both 'experiences *nirvāṇa*' and has '*nirvāṇa* given to him' (make itself present) in his experience. Moreover, to take account of the differing objects of experience is to recognize of necessity the difference of the experiences themselves – even if these differences are themselves at least partially contributed to 'reality' at an earlier or parallel stage.

IV

Our discussion, though somewhat lengthy, has only begun to touch upon some of the more fundamental issues relating to a proper philosophical and phenomenological study of mysticism. Our primary aim has been to mark out a new way of approaching the data, concentrating especially on disabusing scholars of the preconceived notion that all mystical experience is the same or similar. If mystical experience is always the same or similar in essence, as is so often claimed, then this has to be demonstrated by recourse to, and accurate handling of, the evidence, convincing logical argument, and coherent epistemological procedures. It cannot be shown to be the case merely by supported and/or unsupportable assertions to this effect, no matter how passionately these are advanced, nor again can it be demonstrated by *a priori* assumptions on the matter which 'prove' their case in what is essentially circular fashion.

Hopefully it has been made clear that we do not hold one mystical tradition to be superior or 'normative' as, for example, did Stace and Zaehner (and in opposite directions, one might add, with Stace favouring monism and Zaehner theism). Nor have we any particular dogmatic position to defend in this discussion. Our sole concern has been to try and see, recognizing the contextuality of our own understanding, what *the mystical evidence* will allow in the way of legitimate philosophical reflection. Our investigation suggests what it suggests – a wide variety of mystical experiences which are, at least in respect of some determinative aspects, culturally and ideologically grounded. Yet having argued for this position, we are aware that two things have to continue to be done: (1) further careful, expert, study of specific mystical traditions has to be undertaken to uncover what their characteristics are and especially how they relate to the larger theological milieu out of which they emerge; and (2) further fundamental epistemological research into the conditions of mystical experience has to be undertaken in order to lay bare the skeleton of such experience in so far as this is possible. This latter enterprise is especially important and, yet, is all the more neglected.

One final word about the use of the available evidence and the construction of a theory to account for it. A strong supporting element in favour of our pluralistic account is found in the fact that our position is able to accommodate *all* the evidence which is accounted for by non-pluralistic accounts without being reductionistic, i.e. it 's able to do more justice to the specificity of the evidence and its inherent distinctions and disjunctions than can the alternative approaches. That is to say, our account neither (*a*) overlooks any evidence, nor (*b*) has any need to simplify the available evidence to make it fit into comparative or comparable categories, nor (*c*) does it begin with *a priori* assumptions about the nature of ultimate reality – whatever particular traditional theological form this metaphysical assumption takes (such *a priori* assumptions are common to almost all the non-pluralistic accounts). As a consequence of these hermeneutical advantages, one is in a position to respect the richness of the experiential and conceptual data involved in this area of concern: 'God' can be 'God', 'Brahman' can be 'Brahman' and *nirvāṇa* can be *nirvāṇa* without any reductionist attempt to equate the concept 'God' with that of 'Brahman', or 'Brahman' with *nirvāṇa*. This respect for the relevant evidence, both experiential and conceptual, is an essential element in the study of mysticism which is disregarded only at the philosopher's peril.

NOTES

1   For a complete defence of this position, see my forthcoming paper on 'Mystical Experience and Theological Truth'.
2   See Ninian Smart's essay 'Interpretation and Mystical Experience' in *Religious Studies*, vol. 1, no. 1 (1965).

3   See, for example, R. Panikkar's *The Unknown Christ of Hinduism* (London, 1964) and *Kultmysterium in Hinduismus und Christentum* (Munich, 1964).

4   See Aldous Huxley, *The Perennial Philosophy* (London, 1946) and Fritjof Schuuon, *The Transcendental Unity of Religions* (New York, 1953).

5   See, for example, A. Leonard, 'Studies on the Phenomena of Mystical Experience' in *Mystery and Mysticism* (London, 1956); R. Otto's *Mysticism East and West* (New York, 1957), and D. T. Suzuki's, *Mysticism Christian and Buddhist* (London, 1957). See also F. Heiler, *Prayer* (London, 1933); J. Maréchal, *Studies in the Psychology of the Mystics* (London, 1927); William Johnston, *The Still Point* (New York, 1970); James Pratt, *The Religious Consciousness* (New York, 1930); E. Underhill, *Mysticism* (London, 1911).

6   R. C. Zaehner's three major studies of mysticism are *Hindu and Muslim Mysticism* (London, 1960); *Mysticism, Sacred and Profane* (London, 1957; New York, 1961); and *Concordant Discord* (London, 1970). See also his *Our Savage God* (London, 1974).

7   W. T. Stace's two major contributions to the study of mysticism are *The Teachings of the Mystics* (New York, 1960); and *Mysticism and Philosophy* (Philadelphia, 1960; London, 1961).

8   Ninian Smart's major contributions to the study of mysticism are *Reasons and Faiths* (London, 1958); *The Philosophy of Religion* (New York, 1970); 'Interpretation and Mystical Experience' in *Religious Studies*, vol. 1, no. 1 (1965); 'Mystical Experience' in W. H. Capitan and D. Merrill (eds.) *Art, Mind and Religion* (Pittsburgh, 1967), pp. 133–58; 'Mystical Experience' in *Sophia*, I (1962), pp. 19–25; 'History of Mysticism' in P. Edwards (ed.), *Encyclopedia of Philosophy* (New York), Vol. 5. See also the essay by Prof. Smart in the present volume.

9   For criticism of Zaehner see below pages 30–32.

10 For criticism of Stace see below pages 27–30. It is also important to recognize Stace's fundamental bias in favour of a monistic account of mysticism which sees the monistic as the most authentic form of mysticism. This bias corrupts much of his handling of evidence and the nature of his arguments and judgements. See also W. J. Wainwright, 'Stace and Mysticism', in *Journal of Religion*, 50 (1970), pp. 139–54.

11 Smart's studies are problematic on this crucial point and at times he even lapses into holding what we have called Thesis II. Thus, for example, in summarizing the results of his critique of Zaehner in his paper on 'Interpretation and Mystical Experience' in *Religious Studies*, vol. 1, No. 1 (1965) he writes: 'To put the possibility which I am canvassing in a simple form, it can be reduced to the following theses: 1. Phenomenologically, mysticism is everywhere the same. 2. Different flavours, however, accrue to the experiences of mystics

because of their different ways of life and modes of auto-interpretation.

3. The truth of interpretation depends in large measure on factors extrinsic to the mystical experience itself.'

12   We shall critically consider these phenomenological typologies, however, later in this paper in light of our more general thesis about the nature of mystical experience.

13   I have read every major study of this subject known to me and in my reading the only two students of the subject who seem *sufficiently* to recognize the full meaning and implications of this issue in a systematic way for the study of mysticism are R. C. Zaehner and Ninian Smart. Yet even they do very little with it. The point is also recognized in a narrow context by H. P. Owen in his article on 'Christian Mysticism' in *Religious Studies* 7 (1971), pp. 31–42.

14   For a technical discussion of the Buddhist doctrine of *nirvāna* see D. Kalupahana, *Buddhist Philosophy* (Hawaii, 1976), pp. 69–90; C. Prebish (ed.), *Buddhism: A Modern Perspective* (Pennsylvania, 1975); L. de la Vallée Poussin, *Nirvana* (Paris, 1923); I. B. Horner, *The Early Buddhist Theory of Man Perfected* (London, 1936); R. Johansson, *The Psychology of Nirvana* (New York, 1970); T. Stcherbatsky, *The Buddhist Conception of Nirvana* (Leningrad, 1927); G. R. Welbon, *The Buddhist Nirvana and Its Western Interpreters* (Chicago, 1968).

15   R. C. Zaehner, for example, claims to identify four distinct types of mysticism in Hinduism. See his *Concordant Discord* (London, 1970), p. 204 ff.

16   W. T. Stace, *Mysticism and Philosophy*, pp. 31–8.

17   W. T. Stace, *Mysticism and Philosophy*, p. 31.

18   W. T. Stace, *Mysticism and Philosophy*, p. 31 f.

19   W. T. Stace, *Mysticism and Philosophy*, p. 34.

20   W. T. Stace, *Mysticism and Philosophy*, p. 36.

21   For more details of this sort of phenomenon in artistic perception, see E. H. Gombrich, *Art and Illusion* (London, 1960). See also Gombrich's essay 'The Evidence of Images' in C. S. Singleton (ed.), *Interpretation* (Baltimore, 1969), pp. 35–104.

22   See the Introduction to Zaehner's *Mysticism, Sacred and Profane* where he refers to his own youthful, natural, mystical experience undergone at age 20 (pp. xii f.). See also his *Our Savage God* (London, 1974), pp. 209–10.

23   Though Stace divides mystical experience into two types, 'introvertive' and 'extrovertive', he holds that both are really forms of a more ultimate absorptive pattern of a monistic sort. Thus this division is really only heuristic and preliminary.

24   R. C. Zaehner, *Concordant Discord*, p. 194.

25 R. C. Zaehner, *Concordant Discord*, p. 194.

26 R. C. Zaehner, *Concordant Discord*, p. 194.

27 See R. C. Zaehner, *Hindu and Muslim Mysticism* (London, 1960), p. 188.

28 See for this quite bizarre discussion R. C. Zaehner, *Mysticism, Sacred and Profane* (London, 1957; New York, 1961), pp. 191–2. For a critical discussion of Zaehner's position see N. Smart, 'Interpretation and Mystical Experience', *Religious Studies*, vol. 1, No. 1 (1965); F. Staal, *Exploring Mysticism* (London, 1975). See also N. Pike's criticism of Smart, 'Comments', in W. H. Capitan and D. D. Merrill (eds.), *Art, Mind and Religion* (Pittsburgh, 1967), pp. 144–50.

29 See for an extended discussion of this point to which I am indebted, N. Smart, 'Interpretation and Mystical Experience' in *Religious Studies*, vol. 1, No. 1 (1965), pp. 81–4.

30 For further material on the Jewish tradition see S. Katz, *Jewish Concepts* (New York, 1977); E. Urbach, *The Sages* (Jerusalem, 1975); S. Schecter, *Some Aspects of Rabbinic Theology* (New York, 1961); H. Donin, *To Be a Jew* (New York, 1972); G. F. Moore, *Judaism* (New York, 1973); M. Steinberg, *Basic Judaism* (New York, 1947).

31 See G. Scholem's *Kabbalah* (New York, 1974) and his *On the Kabbalah and its Symbolism* (New York, 1965).

31A For more on 'Devekuth' see G. Scholem's *Kabbalah* (New York, 1974); *Major Trends in Jewish Mysticism* (New York, 1954); and his essay 'Devekuth' in his *The Messianic Idea in Judaism* (New York, 1972), pp. 203–26. For additional material of importance, and a disagreement with Scholem's view see I. Tishby's *Mishnat Ha-Zohar* [in Hebrew] (Jerusalem, 1961), Vol. 2, pp. 287ff. Scholem's position, however, appears to me to be the substantially correct one.

32 Ninian Smart's view as stated in his article 'Interpretation and Mystical Experience', in *Religious Studies*, vol. 1, No. 1 (1965), seems to me also to be mistaken on this issue. His position is too close to that of Stace's in stressing the distinction between 'experience' and its 'interpretation' and fails, I believe, to see the essential importance of the pre-conditioning of the mystic's experience. He writes: 'This seems to me a clear indication that the monistic and theistic experiences are essentially similar; and that it is the correct interpretation of them which is at issue' (p. 85).

33 This account generally follows the excellent summary of the Buddhist position in C. Prebish (ed.), *Buddhism: A Modern Perspective* (Pennsylvania, 1975), pp. 29–35. See also E. Conze, *Buddhism: Its Essence and Development* (London, 1974; New York, 1965); R. Robinson, *The Buddhist Religion* (California, 1970); W. Rahula, *What the Buddha Taught* (New York, 1962); D. Rhys, *Buddhism* (London, 1914).

34   C. Prebish (ed.), *Buddhism: A Modern Perspective*, p. 34.

35   On *nirvāna*, see sources cited in note 14 above.

36   In addition to the sources cited above in note 33, see N. Smart, *Doctrine and Argument in Indian Philosophy* (London, 1964); S. Radhakrishnan, *Indian Philosophy* (London, 1941); K. N. Jayatilleka, *Early Buddhist Theory of Knowledge* (London, 1963); D. Kalupahana, *Causality: The Central Philosophy of Buddhism* (Hawaii, 1975); E. Conze, *Buddhist Thought in India* (Michigan, 1967); K. N. Jayatilleka, *Survival and Karma in Buddhist Perspective* (Kandy, 1969).

37   L. Wittgenstein, *Philosophical Investigations* (Oxford, 1958), section 304.

38   John Ruysbroeck, 'Regnum Deum Amantium', ch. 22, cited by E. Underhill, *Mysticism* (London, 1911), p. 425.

39   Meister Eckhart, *Mystische Schriften* (Berlin, 1903), p. 122.

40   For more on Plotinus, see A. H. Armstrong, *Plotinus* (London, 1953); W. R. Inge, *The Philosophy of Plotinus*, 2 vols. (London, 1918); E. Underhill, *Mysticism* (London, 1911); A. H. Armstrong, 'Plotinus', in A. H. Armstrong (ed.), *Cambridge History of Later Greek and Early Medieval Philosophy* (Cambridge, 1967), pp. 195–271; E. Brehier, *La Philosophie de Plotin* (Paris, 1961); J. M. Rist, *Plotinus: The Road to Reality* (Cambridge, 1967). This work also includes a full Bibliography for further research.

41   Plotinus, *Enneads*, VI, 7:34 in Creuzer (ed.), *Plotini Opera Omnia* (Oxford, 1835).

42   On the fascinating history of Sabbatianism see G. Scholem, *Sabbatai Sevi* (Princeton, 1973). For a shorter résumé of Scholem's research, see ch. 8 of his *Major Trends in Jewish Mysticism* (New York, 1954) and his *Kabbalah* (New York, 1974).

43   On the Frankist movement, see G. Scholem, *Major Trends*, ch. 8.

44   For more details of the Zoharic system, see G. Scholem's *Kabbalah* (includes a complete Bibliography for further research); and his *On The Kabbalah and Its Symbolism* (New York, 1965). There is also a translation of the major part of the Zohar in English by H. Sperling and M. Simon (London, 1931–4), 5 vols.

45   On Lurianic Kabbalah, see G. Scholem, *Major Trends*, ch. 7; see also the relevant sections of Scholem's *Kabbalah*.

46   On the mystical school of Safed, which included Isaac Luria, Moses Cordovero, and Joseph Karo, among others, see S. Schechter, 'Safed in the Sixteenth Century' in his *Studies in Judaism*, 2nd Series (Philadelphia, 1908), pp. 202–306. See also R. J. Z. Werblowsky, *Joseph Karo* (Oxford, 1962).

47   R. Robinson, *The Buddhist Religion* (California, 1970), p. 33.

48 On Buddhist monasticism see C. Prebish, *Buddhist Monastic Orders* (Pennsylvania, 1975). See also N. Dutt, *Early Monastic Buddhism* (Calcutta, 1960); S. Dutt, *Buddhist Monks and Monasteries of India* (London, 1962); I. B. Horner, trans., *The Book of Discipline*, 6 vols. (London, 1938–66); G. De, *Democracy in Early Buddhist Sangha* (Calcutta, 1955).

49 For more on Zen Buddhism, see Shoku Watanabe, *Japanese Buddhism* (Tokyo, 1968); H. Dumoulin, *A History of Zen Buddhism* (London and New York, 1963); D. T. Suzuki, *Introduction to Zen Buddhism* (New York, 1964; London, 1969); J. Kitagawa, *Religion in Japanese History* (New York, 1966); D. T. Suzuki, *Essays in Zen Buddhism*, 3 vols. (London, 1949–53).

50 See on Sufi monasticism and the Sufi orders, the excellent work by J. Spencer Trimingham entitled *Sufi Orders* (Oxford, 1971). See also A. Schimmel, *Mystical Dimensions of Islam* (North Carolina, 1975); R. Gramlich, *Die schutischen Derwischorden Persiens* (Wiesbaden, 1965).

51 See F. Staal, *Exploring Mysticism* (London, 1975).

52 This is the name of Carlos Castaneda's Mexican Indian teacher. See Castaneda's trilogy *Teachings of Don Juan: A Yaqui Way of Knowledge* (Berkeley, 1970); *A Separate Reality: Further Conversations with Don Juan* (New York, 1971); and *Journey to Ixtlan* (New York, 1972).

53 For Zen sources on 'testing' *nirvāna* or *satori* see the discussion of the Zen koan and other procedures which take place between a Zen Master and his disciples. Some discussion of this matter can be found in, for example, H. Dumoulin, *A History of Zen Buddhism* (London and New York, 1963); P. Kapleau, *The Three Pillars of Zen* (Boston, 1967); Guy Welbon, *The Buddhist Nirvana and its Western Interpreters* (Chicago, 1968); E. Lamotte, *Histoire du Buddhisme indien* (Paris, 1967); D. T. Suzuki, *Introduction to Zen Buddhism* (Kyoto, 1934); *Zen Comments on the Mumonkan* (New York, 1974).

54 For details see Hakuin's autobiography, 'The Itsu-made-gusa' in *Hakuin Oshō Zenshū*, I, pp. 149–230 (Tokyo, 1935). See also his more extended treatment of this topic in his 'Orategama' in *Hakuin Oshō Zenshū*, V, pp. 105–246. See also the chronicle of Hakuin's life prepared by his disciple Enji Torei entitled 'Shinki – dokumyo Zenzi nempuingyokaku' (Chronicle of Hakuin) in *Hakuin Oshō Zenshū*, I, pp. 1–78. For a brief, helpful discussion of these events see H. Dumoulin, *A History of Zen Buddhism* (London and New York, 1963), pp. 247–55.

55 See W. T. Stace, *Mysticism and Philosophy*, pp. 106–7.

56 See W. T. Stace, *Mysticism and Philosophy*, p. 109.

57 William James, *The Varieties of Religious Experience* (New York, 1958), Lecture XVI, pp. 292–3.

58   William James, *The Varieties of Religious Experience*, p. 293.

59   M. Buber, *I and Thou* (New York, 1970; London, 1971), p. 159.

60   On Kafka, see his *Collected Complete Stories* ed. N. Glatzer (New York, 1971). See also his classic tales, *The Castle*, *The Penal Colony*, and *The Trial*.

61   See M. Buber, *I and Thou*, pp. 158–9.

62   From R. H. Blyth, *Zen and Zen Classics*, vol. I (Japan, 1960), pp. 114–15. Cited by Ben-Ami Scharfstein, *Mystical Experience*, p. 168.

63   William James, *The Varieties of Religious Experience*, p. 293.

64   W. T. Stace, *Mysticism and Philosophy*, pp. 131–2.

65   W. T. Stace, *Mysticism and Philosophy*, p. 132.

66   W. T. Stace, *Mysticism and Philosophy*, p. 132.

67   For more on Richard Jefferies' nature-mysticism, see his *The Story of My Heart* (London, 1912). For a brief discussion of Jefferies' life and thought, see R. C. Zaehner, *Mysticism, Sacred and Profane*, pp. 45–9.

68   Henry Suso, *Little Book of the Eternal* (London, 1953), p. 185.

69   *Brihadāranyka Upanishad*, I:4:10.

70   See the *Samyutta Nikāya*, IV:360.

71   A full critical discussion of the problems inherent in a variety of the most important phenomenological typologies of mystical experience will appear in my forthcoming paper entitled 'Phenomenology, Description, and Mystical Experience'.

72   W. T. Stace, *Mysticism and Philosophy*, pp. 133 ff.

73   See David ben Abraham ha-Lavan, *Masoret ha-Berit*, cited by G. Scholem, *Kabbalah* (New York, 1974), p. 95. See Scholem's entire discussion of this term in his *Kabbalah*, pp. 94–5.

74   For more on Dionysius the Areopagite see J. Vanneste, *Le Mystère de Dieu* (Brussels, 1959); E. Underhill, *Mysticism* (London, 1911); H. Koch, *Pseudo-Dionysius Areopagita* (Mainz, 1900); H. F. Muller, *Dionysius, Proclus, Plotinus* (Münster, 1918); I. P. Sheldon-Williams, 'The Greek Christian Platonist Tradition' in *The Cambridge History of Later Greek and Early Medieval Philosophy*, ed. A. H. Armstrong (Cambridge, 1967), pp. 457–72. This work includes a Bibliography for further research.

75   See Masao Abe, 'Non-Being and Mu' in *Religious Studies* 11, No. 2 (June 1975), pp. 181–92. See also F. Sontag, 'Freedom and God' in *Religious Studies*, 11, No. 4 (December 1975), pp. 421–32.

76   Cited in R. A. Nicholson, *The Mystics of Islam* (London, 1914), p. 17.

77   Cited in R. A. Nicholson, *The Mystics of Islam* (London, 1914), p. 59.

78   L. Wittgenstein; *Tractatus Logico-philosophicus* (London, 1961), section 7. On the subject of paradoxical language in mystical reports see

also W. Alston, 'Ineffability' in the *Philosophical Review*, 65 (1956); Paul Henle, 'Mysticism and Semantics' in *Philosophy and Phenomenological Research*, vol. iii (1949), pp. 416–22; B. Russell, *Mysticism and Logic* (London, 1917); G. K. Pletcher, 'Mysticism, Contradiction and Ineffability' in *American Philosophical Quarterly*, vol. x (1973), pp. 201–11; B. Williams, 'Tertullian's Paradox' in A. Flew and A. McIntyre (eds.), *New Essays in Philosophical Theology* (New York, 1955; London, 1972); (Mysticism and Sense Perception', *Religious Studies*, Vol. 9 (1975), pp. 257–78; Peter Moore's paper, 'Mystical Experience, Mystical Doctrine, Mystical Technique' in this volume, pp. 105–7; S. Katz, 'The Language and Logic of Mystery' in S. Sykes and J. Clayton (eds.), *Christ, Faith and History* (Cambridge, 1972), pp. 239–62; Richard Gale, 'Mysticism and Philosophy' in *The Journal of Philosophy*, 57 (1960); J. N. Horsburgh, 'The Claims of Religious Experience', *The Australasian Journal of Philosophy*, Vol. 35 (1957), pp. 186–200.

79 On the wide variety of possible meanings of the term 'yoga', see, for example, E. W. Hopkins, 'Yoga technique in the Great Epic [Mahabharata]' in *JAOS*, vol. xxii (1901), pp. 333–79. See also the exhaustive study of yoga by Mircea Eliade, *Yoga* (London, 1958; New Jersey, 1969[2]); and J. H. Wood, *The Yoga-system of Pantanjali* (Cambridge, Mass., 1914).

80 For more on this, see R. C. Zaehner, *Hinduism* (New York, 1962; Oxford, 1966), pp. 94 ff.

81 See, for example, F. Streng, *Emptiness* (Nashville, 1967); see also R. Robinson, *The Buddhist Religion*, pp. 52–3. On some of the logical issues raised by this topic, see S. Katz, 'The Logic and Language of Mystery' in S. Sykes and J. Clayton (eds.), *Christ, Faith and History* (Cambridge, 1972), pp. 239–62.

82 See C. Prebish (ed.), *Buddhism: A Modern Perspective*; see also David Kalupahana, *Buddhist Philosophy* (Hawaii, 1976), especially ch. 12; M. Eliade, *Yoga* (London, 1958; New Jersey, 1969[2]); T. Nanaponika, *The Heart of Buddhist Meditation* (New York, 1962).

83 For an interesting discussion of several senses of the term 'real', see J. Bennett, 'Real' in K. T. Fann (ed.), *Symposium on J. L. Austin* (London, 1969), pp. 267–83.

84 Kant defined transcendental knowledge as follows: 'I call *transcendental* all knowledge which is occupied not so much with objects as with the mode of our knowledge of objects in general in so far as this mode of knowledge is to be possible *a priori*', *Critique of Pure Reason*, B25. See also Kant's *Critique of Judgement*, 'Introduction'. On the contemporary discussion of what is involved in trying to frame such a 'transcendental deduction', see W. van O. Quine's *Word and Object* (Cambridge, Mass., 1960) as well as his *Ontological Relativity and Other Essays* (New York, 1969). See also P. F. Strawson, *Individuals*

(London, 1959) and his *Bounds of Sense* (London, 1966). Of the recent journal literature see M. S. Gram, 'Transcendental Arguments', *Nous* 5 (1971), pp. 5–26; and Gram again in: 'Hintikka and Spurious Transcendentalism' in *Nous* 8 (1974); 'Categories and Transcendental Arguments', in *Man and World* 6 (1973); 'Must Transcendental Arguments be Spurious?' in *Kant-Studien* 65 (1974). See also J. Hintikka 'Transcendental Arguments' in *Nous* 6 (1972), pp. 274–81. The back issues of *Kant-Studien* have many other papers of interest and relevance on this theme too numerous to list separately here.

85   Jan van Ruysbroeck, *The Adornment of the Spiritual Marriage* (London, 1916), pp. 176 ff.

86   Jan van Ruysbroeck, *The Adornment of the Spiritual Marriage* (London, 1916), pp. 245 ff.

87   *Śiva Samhitā*, iv, 9–11, cited in M. Eliade, *Yoga* (London, 1958; New York, 1969), p. 40.

88   Ibn 'Ata' Allah, *Miftaḥ al-Falah* cited in J. S. Trimingham, *Sufi Orders*, p. 198.

STEVEN T. KATZ (editor): Ph.D. (Cambridge University). In addition to editing the present volume Dr Katz's other works include: *Jewish Philosophers* (1975); *Jewish Concepts* (1977); and *Martin Buber and Hasidism* (1978). He is also a member of the editorial team of the *Cambridge History of Judaism* and *The History of Nineteenth Century Religious Thought* being published by the Cambridge University Press. He has also published several dozen articles and reviews in such leading philosophical and religious journals as *Religious Studies, Scottish Journal of Theology, Religion, Tradition, Jewish Social Studies*, as well as the *Encyclopedia Judaica* and the *Encyclopedia of Hasidism*. He held the Burney Studentship in the Philosophy of Religion at Cambridge University from 1970 to 1972 and has been a visiting Professor at the Hebrew University of Jerusalem, King's College, University of London, and the University of Lancaster. At present he is Associate Professor of Religion at Dartmouth College, Hanover, N.H., U.S.A.

Mystical Literature

CARL A. KELLER

1. The Presuppositions of comparison between Mystical Writings of Divergent Religions

'Mysticism' is a phenomenological concept coined by western scholars. The way the term is generally used nowadays results from a rather bold assumption (which underlies the whole effort of the phenomenology of religion): that the things we find in one religion – types of experience, goals of spiritual life, practices, etc. – are found also in others, as well as outside the realm of religion.[1] There is of course some truth in this assumption, but it may nevertheless be asked whether the problems involved in comparative study of phenomena pertaining to different cultures are always taken into consideration. As far as the comparative study of 'mysticism' is concerned, this is decidedly not the case.

In the context of Christian theology, the words 'mystical', 'mystic' have a precise meaning: they designate the highest stage of Christian *gnōsis* or religious knowledge, conceptualized as 'union' with God and the perfection of man. Thus, for example, Niketas Stethatos of Studios, a disciple of Symeon the New Theologian (eleventh century), says in his 'Chapters about Gnōsis' (III, 41):[2]

> There are three degrees among those who are engaged on the ascent towards perfection: purificatory, illuminatory, mystical, which is also the one making perfect; the first is of beginners, the second of those who are at half-way, the third of those who have reached the end, perfection.

'Mystical theology' is, then, the final knowledge of the mysteries of God, the highest knowledge mortal men may hope to achieve.[3]

It would be quite rewarding to probe the history of the concept of 'mysticism' and to show how the terms of Christian theology have come to be applied to similar experiences or aspirations in non-Christian religions. This process was based on certain philosophical and anthropological presuppositions which have undoubtedly determined to a very great extent the direction in which investigation of the matter was going to develop. Among such presuppositions we should have to mention the conviction that there is a similarity or even identity of human experience in all cultures, that trans-cultural understanding and even identification is possible, and that ideological and language constructs are only a garb which can easily be discarded in order to lay bare the common substance. The axiom is that man is able to comprehend the inner experience of any of his fellow human beings because this inner experience is alike in all cultures. Talk about 'mysticism' in the sense of 'universal mysticism' is indeed legitimate only if the inner experience of others is properly understood by the investigator.

This axiom however is too readily admitted by writers on mysticism. We even come across the theory that comparative study of mystical experience is more likely to meet with success than comparative study of religious doctrines. To put it in the words of R. C. Zaehner:

> Whereas the comparison between the orthodoxies of religions of Semitic origin on the one hand and the orthodoxies or predominant trends in Indian religions on the other are often forced or inapplicable, comparisons between mystical writings of quite divergent religions are at least comparisons between like and like.[4]

This means that there are two kinds of religious writings: on the one hand, doctrinal statements where the differences of language and thought patterns defy comparison, and on the other, mystical writings which might differ in tone and in vocabulary but which nevertheless have something in common, something apparently quite essential which makes comparison between them possible. This common basis which, according to Zaehner, underlies mystical writings of all religions would presumably be the mystical experience itself. To be sure, Zaehner admits that there are various types of mystical experiences, sacred or even profane,[5] but these are only varieties of one unique species called 'mysticism'.

But how are we to know what mystical experience is like, and how are we to jump to the conclusion that it is fundamentally the same throughout the world, even if allowance is made for individual elaborations here and there? The nature of the experience cannot, at any rate, be directly inferred from our documents: in studying mysticism, we are dealing with texts, generally written texts and occasionally oral statements. Even Zaehner would agree that on the level of linguistic formulation the differences between the texts are sometimes enormous: a prose treatise in Arabic on the subject of *taṣawwuf* has another vocabulary and other modes of thought than a Tamil Shaiva hymn or a sermon in medieval German. Mystical texts are very unlike one another, and yet Zaehner says that 'comparison between them is at least comparison between like and like'!

There are two questions which ought to be clarified first before affirmations of this sort can be made:

(i) What do we understand by 'mystical writings'? Are there definite criteria by which the mystical character of a given text may be ascertained?

(ii) What is the relationship between mystical writings, and the mystical experience of which they are supposed to give account? Is there a straight passage from the text to the underlying experience?

It goes without saying that these two questions are intimately linked, for we would label as 'mystical' a text which is about mystical experience, and this latter, we think, is well known to us because it is minutely described in the very texts which we consider as 'mystical'!

2. *A working Definition of 'Mystical Writings'*

In the present study, the first of the two questions will be dealt with in a rather cursory way. In order to arrive at a working definition of mystical literature, we propose to fall back upon the meaning the term 'mystical' has in traditional Christian theology. There it denotes, as we said above, the highest and the most intimate, the most personal knowledge a believer may hope to attain. This knowledge concerns God the Father, the Son, and the Holy Spirit, i.e. the sacred Trinity understood as ultimate Reality and ultimate Truth, and it consists in immediate apprehension of this ultimate Truth. It is thus ultimate knowledge, knowledge which comprehends totally the things beyond which there is nothing to be known.

'Mystical writings' are texts which deal with ultimate knowledge: with its nature, its modalities, its conditions, its methods, and also with secondary insights which might be granted to a seeker in the course of the pursuit of his task. Every religion posits something as its ultimate truth and reality: a God, or some Absolute of one kind or another, and in every religion men try to attain and to perceive in the most intimate conceivable way the ultimate truth which their particular tradition proclaims. 'Mystical writings' are thus texts which discuss the path towards realization of the ultimate knowledge which each particular religion has to offer, and which contain statements about the nature of such knowledge.

This definition of mystical writings is quite empirical and it will not always allow us to decide with certainty whether or not a particular text has to be regarded as mystical. It is, however, useful as a broad basis for selecting the materials we are going to analyse in the present study. Thus we can take into account the great diversity of religious constructs without judging *a priori* the identity, or similarity, or comparableness of 'mystical' experiences.

3. *Language and Experience: a Literary Approach*

Our second question asks: how are we to evaluate the relationship between such writings and the actual realization of the ultimate knowledge which constitutes their subject-matter? Are these writings the outcome of ultimate knowledge, i.e. have they been composed under the inspiration and guidance of ultimate knowledge as realized by the author? Are they based on actual experience? Do mystical writings exist because their authors have realized and experienced, in their personal lives, the ultimate knowledge which their religion confesses? Do mystical authors talk about the truth which has broken through their own innermost existence? In other words, are mystical authors mystics? And what is their mystical experience like?

This raises a large, intricate problem: how is writing in general related to experience? Obviously there is not always and not necessarily such a relationship. Language is a very polyvalent tool with which things can be imagined and built up which have never been experienced in actual life. What is at stake is thus the philosophical, psychological, sociological, and linguistic problem of the relationship between language and experience. This problem has many dimensions and it requires specialists in all of these disciplines to arrive at a satisfactory answer. In the context of the present study such a broad inquiry cannot be attempted. We must limit ourselves to one particular approach.

I propose to approach the problem of the relationship between mystical writings and mystical experience through an *analysis of the varieties of mystical writings,* i.e. *of the literary genres indulged in by mystical authors*. I fully agree with P. G. Moore who, in an article summarizing 'Recent Studies of Mysticism', comes to the conclusion that the study of mysticism

> should be based upon a careful study of mystical language . . .
> Ideally this should take the form of a detailed phenomenology,
> history, and sociology of the varieties of mystical language.[6]

Universal mysticism – according to our definition, the search, proper to each religion and carried out within each religion by some of its adepts, after full apprehension of what that religion defines as the highest and most intimate knowledge available to its adherents – expresses itself in a number of literary genres among which it is possible to identify at least the following: aphorisms, biographies, reports on visions, commentaries, dialogues, instructions, prayers, religious poetry, and fiction. Each of these genres has a specific background in social life and each might be characterized, in very general sociological categories, according to the particular social situation which has occasioned it. Thus, for instance, in all societies and religious communities certain people are likely to have visions or, as some would prefer to put it, hallucinatory states. Normally they would talk to others about what they see and hear. The circumstances of such communication may change from one society to another. Whereas in some societies vision is more or less institutionalized as a regular means of access to an invisible world – invisible to all except the chosen ones, i.e. the visionaries – in others it is considered either as only a preliminary stage on the path to ultimate knowledge, or as a pathological symptom. But visions there would be, and the visionary experience would be reported to others. The formal social framework is everywhere the same: someone sees things hidden to ordinary men, and he tells what he sees or has seen.

'Instructions' occur in all communities and societies, although the concrete circumstances in which this happens may vary: 'instructions' may take the form of sermons pronounced regularly and publicly during ritual performances, or of private counselling from master to disciple, or of theoretical and practical teaching imparted by a knowledgeable person to a group of seekers. But always there is someone who has authority to pass his knowledge on to others who are eager to learn. Likewise, all the other literary genres have their specific social background whose formal structure remains constant throughout all societies and communities.

Given, then, the general structure of social life which determines them – the situation of teaching, praying, producing lyrical poetry, etc. – how do the various literary genres relate to experience? We propose to examine one by one the literary genres mentioned above and to try and assess the likelihood of their being an accurate account of the author's personal experience.

4. *Analysis of Literary Genres found in Mystical Writings*

(*a*) *Aphorisms*.   The saying, prose or poetry, is the most elementary and perhaps the most authentic form of mystical literature. Such sayings share the characteristics of gnomic literature all over the world: they state not only how things are but how they ought to be. They are always didactic, giving terse expression to a moral or a religious truth. Their subject-matter and their language are traditional, with some new flash of insight every now and then. It seems that the authors of aphorisms concentrated their effort on refining the formulation of their statements: the themes of traditional thought are taken up, resolved into their elements, discussed, enriched by references to texts and to information derived from various sources, and finally couched in precise language. Aphorisms are the product of intellectual activity at its very best.

Some examples chosen more or less at random from various religious traditions are likely to suggest that mystical aphorisms represent tradition rather than individual mystical achievement.

In Christianity, aphoristic literature has been produced right from the beginning of the mystical quest, as can be seen, for example, from the *Apophthegmata Patrum*, collections of pithy summaries of spiritual truths attributed to the anchorites and monks of the Egyptian and Syrian deserts. In later centuries most of the Fathers of orthodox mysticism couched their teachings in short 'chapters' (*kephalaia*), aphoristic summaries of mystical doctrine and practice:

> They say that the task of 'practical philosophy' is to purify the intellect by ridding it from all manifestations of passion; that the task of 'contemplation of nature' is to show that the intellect is capable of having all knowledge about the truth of existing things and of the reasons why they do exist; that the task of 'theological initiation' ('mystagogy') is to make the intellect similar to God and, as far as possible, to make it coincide with grace, remembering nothing besides God above Whom there is nothing to be known.[7]

In this 'chapter', Maximus the Confessor (d. 662) admits that he is merely formulating traditional thought ('they say . . .'), but this aphorism can be considered as representative of a great many others whose traditional character is not explicitly mentioned. It gives a short summary of the three stages of the mystical ascension as it is taught in Christian mysticism: *praxis, theôria, theologia,* i.e. purification of the intellect, contemplation of the universe by means of thorough knowledge of the noetical world, and union with God through progressive incorporation into his saving grace: *via purgativa, via contemplativa* or *illuminativa, via unitiva.* As in most of Maximus' 'chapters', the analysis of these three stages (which ultimately stem from non-Christian sources) is here combined with Biblical language and exegesis ('God', 'grace', etc.).

The aphoristic style of Christian monks was perpetuated by early Islamic masters whose sayings have been collected by the first Arabic writers on taṣawwuf.[8] Here is an example chosen from the sayings of Abu Sa'īd al-Kharrāz (d. 899):

> The first stage for that one who has found the knowledge of 'unification' (i.e. of proclamation of the 'unity' of God) and the realization of that, is that there passes from his heart the remembrance of all things and he becomes alone with God Most High.
>
> Moreover, he said: The first sign of 'unification' is that the servant gives up everything and returns all things to Him to Whom they belong and that He is in control of them and makes them subject to Himself. Thus He hides them in them from them; within them He reduces them to nought and thus He makes them fit unto Himself. This is the beginning of 'entering into unification', as far as constant unification is concerned.[9]

These are sayings which apparently describe a Muslim mystic's first experiences on the mystical path. They seem to be culled from actual experience. On closer scrutiny, however, one discovers that they are based on two key terms of traditional Islamic theology: *tawḥīd,* 'unification' or proclamation of the unity and unicity of God, and *dhikr,* 'mentioning', 'uttering', or 'remembering' God's name and revelation. Abu Sa'īd al-Kharrāz insists that 'unification' must 'be found', 'realized', 'entered into'; not content with merely repeating the liturgical formula 'God is one and there is none besides him' (*lā ilāh illā 'llāh*), he pushes its meaning to its logical conclusions: if God is really one and alone, then nothing can exist besides him, and such things as seem to exist are in fact entirely dependent on him. Therefore, 'uttering' the truth of God's unity must lead to the *experience* of God's unity: the one who goes on reciting the sacred formula is bound to become oblivious of everything except God, including his own empirical being. In this way he 'realizes' true *tawḥīd*, i.e. the true confession of Islamic faith. The aphorism, then, could properly be understood as a purely theoretical deduction from the main tenets of Islamic theology.

In some of his celebrated aphorisms (*ḥikam*), the Egyptian Sufi master Ibn Atā Allāh (d. 1309) dwells on the ambiguities of language. According to him, mystical language is always coloured by the total personality ('the heart') of the speaker:

> Every utterance [*kalām*: theological and mystical teaching] that comes forth does so with the vestment of the heart from which it emerged.

It is not possible to know the nature of a Sufi's experience by merely listening to his talk, unless there is a direct transmission of that experience from master to disciple:

> Whoever has been given permission to speak out [i.e. who has the authority of a true master] will have his expression understood by his listeners, and his symbolic allusion will be clear to them.
> Sometimes the lights of inner realities will appear eclipsed when you have not been given permission to give expression to them [i.e. language is inadequate as long as the master has no inner authority to hand on the knowledge].

Therefore, Sufi language is always ambiguous. It is either the ecstatic babble of people who have not yet realized the Truth, or the pragmatic teaching of a master who tells his disciples what they are to do:

> Their [the Sufis'] expression is either because of the overflow of ecstasy or for the purpose of guiding a disciple. The former case is that of those who are still on the way (*as-sālikūn*); the latter case is that of those who possess a function and have realization [i.e. of authoritative and recognized teachers].[10]

In these aphorisms, Ibn Atā Allāh's language is specifically Islamic, nurtured by Arabic psychology and theology (note terms like 'heart', 'to give permission', 'expression', 'to give expression', 'allusion', 'inner realities', etc.). It is the language of a particular tradition and must be understood in the context of that tradition. The sentences are concise and artistically wrought. Ibn Atā Allāh is a fine author, but whoever wishes to study the nature of his 'mysticism' is well advised not to discard lightheartedly his warnings as to the gap between experience and expression!

If we turn to India, we find the aphoristic style right at the start of mystical thought and teaching. The late Paul Horsch has shown convincingly that the *gāthās* and *ślokas* interspersed in Vedic literature and in the poetic sections of the Tipitaka, short sayings which can be isolated from their context and studied as literary documents in their own right, have been composed by saints and seekers who did not always submit to the brahmins' claim to spiritual leadership.[11] An example taken from the Bṛhad-Araṇyaka-Upanishad may serve as an illustration:

> About this there is the following *śloka*:
> When all the desires that abide in the heart are dissolved,
> Then mortal man becomes immortal; in this life he attains Brahma.[12]

Here the author of the Upanishad quotes and then interprets an aphorism which was already current in the circles for which he wrote his treatise. This aphorism (coined by an unknown sage) offered an alternative to the brahmins' official claims. Brahma was admittedly the ultimate reality functioning at the base of the universe. But whereas the brahmanical priests pretended to handle Brahma and thus to assure happiness and longevity for themselves and for the whole commuinty, the aphorism teaches a method by which mortal men may attain Brahma itself; and whereas the priests promised their clients fulfilment of all desires, the aphorism insists that in order to reach the highest goal all earthly desires must be stilled. The aphorism (which antedates Yajnavalkya who in the Upanished is only its expounder) is strongly anti-brahmanical but it is understandable only against the background of brahmanical ideology.

Medieval India too has had its authors of aphorisms. We may mention here the vacana-tradition of the Virashaivas. 'Vacanas' are delicately carved prose sentences dealing with various aspects of the Virashaivas' religious life and containing usually the signet of the author in the form of a particular name of Shiva. They are personal, especially because they

> describe the devotee's state directly and the god only by implication; the concern is with the subject rather than the object of worship.[13]

Despite this personal character, however, the authors constantly use traditional symbols, images, concepts, and even phrases, as A. K. Ramanujan has shown in his stylistic analysis of Virashaiva vacanas.[14] Thus, Basavaṇṇa, the founder (or reformer) of the

Virashaiva religion (twelfth century), makes apparently a statement about his own innermost experience in the following vacana:

> After the King has made me come unto His bed and lain with
> me,
> Should I still fear?
> I am a woman more honoured than any!
> After the touch of the alchemic stone
> Would iron still be iron?
> But if the Lord-of-the-Meeting-Rivers should spurn me, should I
> not die?[15]

In fact, the author expresses his relationship to Shiva in traditional or even universal metaphors (in South Indian literatures the lover is usually represented as a king), and it would be rather hazardous to deduce from this aphorism a psychological analysis of the author's mystical experience.

In conclusion, we may stress again the traditional, artistic, and very often intellectual character of the mystical aphorisms. It is evidently exceedingly difficult to assess the experiential value of such sayings. How are we to isolate the author's personal practice and experience from the religious and intellectual tradition of the community within which he lives and works and from which he has derived most of his skill and knowledge? Further, how are we to distinguish the cumulative mystical experience of many generations of seekers laid down in traditional thought and doctrine, from what is merely speculation, theory, abstract elaboration – or poetical conjuration – of things one hopes some time to experience? Aphorisms are mostly normative utterances, and normative utterances are not necessarily prompted by actual experience.

(b) *Biographies,* collections of typical sayings and anecdotes, and full-length lives of holy men and mystics, are very popular in all religious traditions.[16] This literature, however, raises problems of accuracy and historicity too well known to need discussion: biographies of holy men are mostly 'legendary', they are projections of the community's aspirations, hopes, and expectations with regard to outstanding religious leaders, they reflect the society's collective ideas concerning a man whom it supposes to be constantly in touch with the symbols of its ultimate values. The ideal portrait of the holy man lingers always in what anthropologists call the society's 'myth-dream'; that body of notions derived from a variety of sources such as rumours, personal experiences, desires, conflicts, and ideas about the total environment which find expression in myths, dreams, popular stories, and anecdotes.[17]

It necessarily comprises ideas about the manner in which a person representing ultimate value should live. The society's myth-dream shapes the language and thought of all its members, including authors of biographies, and so the biography of a mystic is a spontaneous expression of the society's ultimate certitudes, its rational and irrational longings, pinned on a historical figure in which it recognizes a faithful defender of its highest goals.

To be sure, some writers of mystical biographies have critical pretensions. They sift the materials of popular tradition, they examine the evidence in the light of the reliability of the informers, and finally they limit themselves to mere reporting of sayings attributed to the hero, and of incidents from his life which they deem well attested. Such is the method employed by the first biographers of early Muslim mystics. But the very selection of the items reported reveals the biographer's own theoretical stance rather than the historical experience of the mystic, and this stance again is largely conditioned by the cultural environment in which the author has been brought up.

This does not mean, of course, that there are no 'mystics', nor that there is no such thing as 'mystical experience'. It is only a reminder that biographical literature should not be considered uncritically as a true picture of it and that it cannot be used naively as a faithful presentation of a mystic's inner life. Some sort of mystical experience may even be one of the sources of a community's myth-dream, but we are far from knowing exactly what it is like.

(c) *Reports on Visions.* Hallucinatory states and visions are common to all mystical traditions. In mystical literature we find three categories of texts dealing with visionary experiences:

(i) Stories about visions which have been granted to holy men; these fall under the category of biographical and hagiographical writings which have just been discussed, and they partake of the same ambiguities and shortcomings.

(ii) Manuals of visionary experience, such as the *Fawā'iḥ al-jamāl wa fawātiḥ al-jalāl* of Najm ad-Dīn al-Kubrā (d. 1221), or the Manual of Buddhist visionary experience edited by D. Schlingloff.[18]

Here we find descriptions of objects perceived by the vision-aries, or of objects which, according to the 'orthodoxy' of the respective traditions, ought to be perceived. Stress, however, is placed on the interpretation of such symbols as may appear to the eye of the ecstatic, and such interpretation is always in accordance with the doctrinal tenets of the tradition.

(iii) Reports on visions made by the visionaries themselves. This literature offers an immense field for future research, as very little has been done in this area so far. Ernst Benz rightly insists on the need for a 'zukünftige Philologie des visionären Schrifttums'.[19] The few studies that do exist concerning visionary experience in Christianity, Islam, and Ancient India[20] tend to prove that there is a close relationship between the acquired language and thought habits of the human subject, and the contents of the visions he may have. Visions are a kind of language which runs parallel to the spoken language and to the conceptual framework of the vision-ary's daily life. In brief, the Christian sees Christian symbols: the Cross, Christ, the Virgin, and so forth; the Muslim perceives Arabic letters and non-figurative designs; the Buddhist contemplates Buddhas sitting on lotus thrones. Visions appear, then, as interior projections or visualizations of the respective community's myth-dream which the subject has chosen, consciously or unconsciously, as his own personal myth-dream.

This does not mean that mystics do not have visions at all; visionary experiences and hallucinatory states are a reality about which psychologists and physicians give us ample scientific infor-mation. But as far as investigation of mystical experience and the comparative study of mysticism are concerned, the analysis of reports on visionary phenomena does not lead beyond the compari-son of divergent myth-dreams.

The following two examples, culled from early Christian mystical tradition, tend to show to what considerable extent the contents of visions are voluntarily determined by the doctrinal foundations of the mystical quest – in this case the Bible and its presentation of the heavenly world on the one hand, and the Platonic dichotomy: phenomenal world/noetical world, on the other:

On another occasion he told us this story: 'Having perfected every kind of life that I desired, then I had another desire. I desired to keep my mind for five days only undistracted from [the contemplation] of God. And, having determined this, I barred the cell and enclosure, so as not to have to answer to any man, and I took my stand, beginning at the second hour. So I gave this commandment to my mind: "Do not descend from heaven, there you have angels, archangels, the powers on high, the God of all; do not descend below heaven."

And having lasted out two days and two nights, I exasperated the demon so that he became a flame of fire and burned up all the things in the cell, so that even the little mat on which I stood was consumed with fire and I thought I was being all burned up. Finally stricken with fear, I left off on the third day, being unable to keep my mind free from distraction, but I descended to contemplation of the world lest vanity be imputed to me.'[21]

That such 'contemplation' is indeed considered as a visionary experience becomes clear from the following example:

So great a knowledge had he of the Holy Scriptures and the divine precepts that even at the very meals of the brethren he would have periods of absent-mindedness and remain silent. And, being urged to tell the details of his ecstasy, he would say: 'I went away in thought on a journey, seized by contemplation.' For my part, I often knew him weep at table and, when I asked the cause of the tears, I heard him say: 'I shrink from partaking of irrational [i.e. material] food, being myself rational and destined to live in a paradise of delight owing to the power given us by Christ.'[22]

(d) Commentaries. A great deal of mystical writing consists of interpretations of work done by forerunners. Many a fundamental passage of the ancient Upanishad seems to be a simple comment on the *gāthās* and *slokas* analysed by Horsch.[23] In the Bṛhad-Aranyaka-Upanishad, for instance, Yajnavalkya offers the following interpretation of the *sloka* quoted above ('When all desires are dissolved, then mortal man becomes immortal'):

Just as the lifeless slough of a snake lies, cast off in the ant-hill, even so lies this body. Then this bodiless, immortal Life-Breath (*prāṇa*) is truly Brahma, it is verily Light.[24]

The work of subsequent Indian thinkers, beginning with Bādarāyana, the presumed author of the famous *Brahmasutras*, followed by a host of renowned philosophers such as Shankara, Rāmānuja, Madhva, and others, may be understood as a gigantic effort to interpret key passages of the Upanishads. A similar process of ongoing commentation can be observed in Buddhist texts. The same holds true of the Islamic world. P. Nwyia has shown how the language of the Sufis has grown out of the Qur'ān, there being constant interaction between their 'mystical' quest and the sacred text which they tried to elucidate.[25] Al-Junaid (d. 910) was the first to comment on the *saṭhiyyāt*, inspired, mystical utterances, of Abū Yazīd Bistāmī (d. 875), and he has been imitated by many after him. In his *Kitāb al-luma'*, al-Sarrāj (d. 988) makes the following comment on Abu Sa'īd al-Kharrāz's aphorism quoted above ('the first stage for one who has found knowledge of unification . . .'):

> The meaning of this is that the remembrance of things passes away by *dhikr*, i.e. the 'remembrance' of God. The phrase 'giving up everything' means that the servant relates nothing to himself nor to his powers or abilities, but he perceives truly that things have their sustenance only in God and not in themselves. The phrase 'He is in control of them and makes them subject to himself' points to the fact that God is the Master of his servants as well as of the true experience of 'unification' which gets hold of them, so that finally they may perceive that things are sustained by God. As someone has said:
>
> > In every thing there is a witness
> > Attesting that he is one.
>
> The phrase 'makes them subject to himself' means that [the Sufi] is not affected by the things which he contemplates because all things have their sustenance in God alone. Finally, when [Abu Sa'īd al-Kharrāz] says 'He hides them in them from them; within them He reduces them to naught', his meaning is: the servants have no sensorial perceptions, nor do they give heed to physical or psychological excitations which may be felt in a state of true knowledge, because they realize immediately that things are wiped out by the power of God and by the saving mediation of his will.[26]

Later in time, Ibn 'Arabī (d. 1240) interpreted the *masā'il* of Tirmidhī (ninth century), a catalogue of 157 fundamental questions concerning the spiritual and mystical life.[27] His own works have been interpreted by himself (in the *Tarjumān al-'ašwāq*, an esoteric commentary on a series of love-songs) and by many others (particularly the *Fuṣūṣ al-hikam*[28] and the *Futūḥāt al-makkiyya*[29]). Anṣārī's (d. 1089) *Manāzil as-sā'irīn*, a very complete and systematic presentation of one hundred stages of the mystical progression, and Ibn Atā Allāh's *Ḥikam*, have been commented upon a number of times.[30] The great texts of Jewish mysticism, most prominently its *magnum opus*, the splendid *Zohar*, are but commentaries on the Tora. The outstanding Christian mystics, from Maximus the Confessor (d. 662) to Eckhart (d. 1328) and John of the Cross (1542–91) have been devout readers and expounders of the Bible: their works are understood only if the Biblical background is constantly kept in mind.

Ancient texts and the experience they describe – whatever their original nature – have come to be regarded as normative; they have been studied, pondered, adapted to new conditions, compared, combined, expanded, internalized, and thus handed on to later generations as the treasure-house from which the mystical quest might be sustained.

A commentator tries to explain tradition, and even if modern standards of 'objective' historical exposition are not yet applied and the traditional commentator reads his own theology into the text he explains, he performs an act of intellectual investigation. As to the nature of his own mystical achievements which may or may not lie behind it – or ahead of it – we would hardly dare to assess it on the basis of his expository output. In this type of literature, the mystical quest appears as a continuous effort to understand and to teach a doctrine which had been received from others, the doctrinal and purely theoretical element being indeed of paramount importance.

(e) *Dialogues.* The literary form of dialogue is very common in mystical literature. There are dialogues between teacher and disciple, as for instance in the prose part of Shankara's *Upadeshasāhasrī* which is entirely composed in this way:

Disciple: Venerable, if (as you tell me) I am absolutely changeless like one in deep sleep, how then do you account for the states of dream and waking?

Guru: But do you constantly experience them?

Disciple: I do certainly experience them, but alternatively and intermittently, not constantly.

Guru: So these two states are accidental and do not arise from your true Self (which is the True Reality on which the states are superimposed).[31]

Thus by dialogue and close reasoning, the *guru* endeavours to lead his disciple to realization of the Absolute. A famous Buddhist example of the same type of dialogue is found in the *Milindapanha*,

'The questions of King Milinda', where all the questions a disciple might ask are examined and resolved in the most effective manner.

Other dialogues are of the type of 'contest literature': the teacher argues with an opponent and tries to defeat him. Such, for example, is the method usually employed by Indian philosophical and theological authors who begin their demonstrations with an exposition of the '*pūrvapaksha*', i.e. the adversary's point of view which is then demolished and superseded by the author's own theories. Very often, too, mystical doctrines are presented as the answer given by a sage to an inquirer (Buddhist *Suttas*, Hindu *Purāṇas*, etc.).

This literary device suggests the following remarks: (i) Dialogues usually betray the author's desire to lead the reader along a certain path and to conduct his reasoning in such a way that in the end he submits to the author's views. The element of reasoning is thus of prime importance. (ii) This form undoubtedly reflects real-life situations, it has a clearly defined *Sitz im Leben*: the classroom, the lecture hall, the master's *āshram*. Sometimes, such life situations are vividly described in the dialogues themselves, as in the following passage taken from one of the works of the Persian mystic Jalāl ad-Dīn Rūmī (d. 1273) which incidentally touches upon the problem of language:

> The Master said: I was speaking one day amongst a group of people, and a party of non-Muslims was present. In the middle of my address they began to weep and to register emotion and ecstasy.

> Someone asked: What do they understand and what do they know? Only one Muslim in a thousand understands this kind of talk. What did they understand that they should weep?

> The Master answered: It is not necessary that they should understand the inner spirit of these words. The root of the matter is the words themselves, and that they do understand. After all, every one acknowledges the Oneness of God, that he is Creator and Provider, that he controls every thing, that to him all things shall return, and that it is he who punishes and forgives. When anyone hears these words . . ., a universal commotion and ecstatic passion supervenes, since out of these words comes the scent of their Beloved and their Quest.[32]

This text attests the Semitic belief in the creative power of words. The opposite attitude, i.e. total disregard for words and meanings, is expressed in a Zen-dialogue which is in fact the radical negation of the value of dialogue:

A monk said to Chao Chou: I have just entered the monastery; I beg the master to teach me.

Chao Chou said: Have you eaten yet?

The monk said: I have eaten.

Chao Chou said: Then go wash your bowl.

And the monk understood.

Comment. Whenever Chao Chou opens his mouth, you can see his gall bladder, he shows his heart and liver. The monk did not really understand anything: he thought a bell was a pot.[33]

This dialogue too has grown out of a real-life situation, but Islam and Zen are worlds apart . . .

How are writings such as these related to the experience of the hero or of the author? Only indirectly, it would seem: experience may linger somewhere at the back of the disputator's mind, or it may be aimed at as the final goal of the discussion, but its nature can hardly be ascertained.

(*f*) *Instructions.* These are very common and may assume various forms: sermons, discourses and treatises on special topics, summaries of philosophical and theological systems. Here again the element of personal experience is rather irrelevant in comparison with the exposition and transmission of a doctrine which is primarily an intellectual construction. It may be admitted that mystical teaching is effective only in so far as the teacher incarnates in his life the things he tries to convey to others; that he is accepted as a true master only if he is himself engaged in the mystical quest. Teachers in all spheres of existential, practical learning teach more effectively when they teach 'what they are', rather than 'what they say', and this holds true particularly of teachers in mystical 'experience'. In that sense authors of instructions deemed useful and worthy of inclusion in the list of theoretical works regarded as authoritative by a certain mystical tradition were probably themselves authentically walking along the 'path'. But it is quite feasible also to expound 'mystical' doctrine without in the least having been granted the corresponding experience. At any rate it is impossible to draw a neat dividing line between experience and doctrinal elaboration. The ongoing discussion of whether Eckhart was a mystic who taught what he had himself experienced, or whether he was simply teaching doctrines which he had found in the Neoplatonic and Christian traditions, without having himself experienced the 'Godhead' beyond 'God', is a very striking case in point.

(g) *Prayers.*   Prayers, both prose and poetry, are frequently met with in mystical literature. In prayer, ultimate Reality is addressed as a partner in life or as an object of worship which faces the worshipper. The contents of prayers vary considerably within one and the same mystical tradition, ranging from contemplation of God's manifestations in nature and history (for instance in the worshipper's personal life-history, as in Augustine's *Confessions*), to requests for spiritual gifts.

As an example of the first category we may quote a prayer of a Muslim, al-Ḥallāj (d. 922):

> I saw my Lord with the eye of my heart.
>   He said, 'Who are you?' I said, I am You.
> You are He Who fills all place
>   But place does not know where You are.
> In my subsistence is my annihilation;
>   In my annihilation, I remain You.[34]

This is a sort of visionary dialogue with God where despite the affirmation of identity the distinctiveness of God and worshipper is maintained. This dialogue surely contains prayer but it is exceedingly difficult to decide whether it is based on actual experience or whether it is theoretical conceptualization of a *desire* and *longing* for identity-in-diversity.

Here are some more prayers by a Muslim (Ibn Atā Allāh):

> My God, from the diversity of created things and the changes of states, I know that it is your desire to make yourself known to me in everything so that I will not ignore you in anything.

> O God, your penetrating decision and your conquering will have left no speech to the articulate nor any state to him who has a state.

> My God, how often has your justice destroyed the dependence I built on obedience or the state I erected! Yet, it was your grace that freed me from them.[35]

These prayers betray characteristically Muslim attitudes: through creation and the various states men undergo during their mystical career, God makes himself known to the adepts; he has a will; he condemns men's improper commitment to things of human creation; he dispenses his grace to men; men can only abandon themselves totally to God's guidance.

Alternatively, a characteristically Hindu attitude is found in Māṇikkavācagar's hymns to Shiva (eighth century):

My bonds Thou loosedst, mad'st me Thine! And all
The loving saints – who ashes gave – beheld.
Thou didst exalt, within the temple court,
Ev'n me Thou didst exalt, who knew not anything.

Thou Only-Wise! Ambrosia! me, a servile cur,
When Thou didst take and make Thine own, was I then wise?
Thou saw'st my ignorance that day Thou mad'st me Thine!
Ah, Lord of grace, was I then wise? was I then strong?[26]

Māṇikkavācagar does not contemplate Shiva's revelation in creation and history (although he considers like most Hindus the universe as a form of God): Shiva has no will to mould a world outside him and to conduct the destinies of men according to a preestablished plan. He is only the 'beyond' of the world (and the stuff out of which it evolves), and so there exists an antithesis between 'knowledge' of Shiva, i.e. 'being his own', and ignorance, i.e. the abasing existence in a world which in itself is ignorance and bondage. Whereas the Muslim in prayer and adoration looks back on God's meaningful and purposeful activity in nature and history (doing so in conformity with traditional Islamic theology), the Hindu praises the One who is Knowledge, and he remembers with horror the state and the world of ignorance where he was before (doing so in perfect agreement with the general pattern of Hindu thought).

The other category of prayers (requests for spiritual gifts) may be briefly illustrated by an example from the Islamic mystic Dhu-'l-Nūn Miṣrī, one of the most prayerful figures of the Sufi tradition:

O God, my inmost being is unveiled in thy sight, and I am distressed before thee; when sin has led me astray, the remembrance of thee (*dhikr*) brings me back to thy fellowship, knowing that the control of all affairs is in thy hand and that they originate from thy decrees. O God, who is more merciful than thyself to all my shortcomings, for thou hast created me weak? And who is more forgiving than thou, for thy knowledge of me was from aforetime? Thy command to me is all-embracing; I have resisted thee only by thy permission, and thou hast reproached me therewith. I have disobeyed thee, and thou wast aware of it and hast proved me in the wrong. I ask thee for the mercy that I need, and the acceptance of my plea . . ., that thou wilt forgive me my sins, both deed and thought.[37]

and by one from the Hindu tradition, Māṇikkavācagar again:

Thy loving ones have gained 'cessation' absolute; but here
My spirit ever melts, outside I lie – base dog – and mourn!
O Master mine, I would attain true love's vast sea of bliss,
That change, surcease, oblivion, sev'rance, thought, bound,
    death knows not!

They've seen the sea-like bliss, have seized it, and enjoy! Is't meet
That I, low dog, with added pains and pining sore should bide?
Master, do thou thyself give grace, I pray! I faint! I fail!
Cut short thy work! O light, let darkness flee before thy mercy's
    beam![38]

The difference in tone and in theological outlook needs no comment.

Prayers always give voice to a deep sense of God's presence, but they are formulated in traditional religious and theological language, and the praying believer never separates himself from the solid conceptual framework of his spiritual life. Comparing prayers coming from various religious traditions is tantamount to comparing the religious traditions in their entirety. If there is some experiential background to prayer, prayer is not in itself 'mystical' experience.

(h) *Religious poetry and fiction.*   In mystical literature we very often come across works of poetical and religious imagination: Hindu Purāṇas, Mahāyāna Sūtras, collections of religious poetry like the *Devāram* of the Tamil Shaivas and the *Divya Prabandham* of the Tamil Vaishnavas, all in India; the mystical works of the great poets of Persia, Aṭṭār, Rūmī, and others; Ibn al-Fāriḍ, numerous works of Ibn 'Arabī in Arabic; most of Christian religious poetry – to mention only some of the more outstanding works from the various traditions. The modes of poetical inspiration are manifold and mysterious and subject to psychological investigation, but it should be clear that we cannot take these products of creative invention at their face value as expressions of personal mystical experience – unless we postulate that poetical inspiration as such is identical with mystical experience.[39] Such a broad application of the term 'mysticism' would, however, go beyond our initial definition of mystical literature and make the term 'mystical' so broad as to be of little value.

5. Conclusion:
The true nature of the study of mysticism

This rapid survey of mystical literary genres demonstrates how narrow are the limits of our ability to know the essence of mystical experience. Our knowledge of mysticism is based on the study of texts. The analysis attempted in the present paper has shown that texts do not necessarily reflect experience, and even if they do, it is impossible to chart the passage from the text to the experience. So we must concentrate our efforts on the study of mystical language. The study of mysticism is primarily, if not exclusively, a philological and an exegetical enterprise, and as such it partakes of all the hermeneutical problems involved in exegesis and interpretation. As to the mystical experience itself, in its purity, scholarly work must be conscious of the gap which separates linguistic expression from experience. None of the literary genres which we have examined gives an unbroken and direct account of the experience and of its nature.

When we turn from literary form to content, i.e. to the language of the texts, to the terminology employed and to the ideas set forth, we see at once that they vary considerably from one religious tradition to the other. The terminology and ideology of *bhakti* are completely Hindu and totally different from the terminology and ideology of *tasawwuf* which are decidedly Muslim, and both are different from the terminology and ideology of Christian *gnōsis* and *theōsis*. In each tradition, the language is specific and non-interchangeable; what the underlying experience is like, we do not know: we are dealing with languages, and with languages alone.

In the light of all this, we cannot help feeling how far R. C. Zaehner was from the target when he pretended that

> comparisons between mystical writings of quite divergent religions are at least comparisons between like and like.[40]

In reality, when we compare mystical texts, we are comparing doctrinal systems or, in other words, total myth-dreams of societies, communities and individuals. Zaehner's affirmation proceeds from a series of unconscious axioms such as: 'mystics pass beyond the level of rational consciousness to absolute consciousness'; 'absolute consciousness is but one, and as such, universal'; 'divergent forms of mystical experience are but forms of absolute consciousness'.

These axioms are indeed implied in Zaehner's definition of 'mysticism'. According to him, mysticism is

> the realization of a union or a unity with or in (or of) something that is enormously, if not infinitely, greater than the empirical self.[41]

In Zaehner's mind, this definition is ontological, not phenomenological: the 'something infinitely greater than the empirical self' does exist and in mysticism 'union or unity with or in (or of) it' is truly 'realized'. This 'something', Zaehner himself would call 'God'. In various ways, mystics from all religious traditions have 'realized' union with 'God'; this is why comparisons between their writings are 'at least comparisons between like and like'. Zaehner's stance is determined by the Catholic doctrine of 'natural mysticism'.

We do not deny *a priori* the legitimacy of a theological approach to mystical literature. After all, it might be true that mystics from all religions have realized union with God, and the monotheistic creed which proclaims one God as the Creator, Sustainer, and Saviour of all men, whatever their religion and 'myth-dream', might equally be true. The atheistic creed of modern rationalism is not the last word about TRUTH. But even if a theological approach is admitted, the student of mysticism cannot reach beyond his own personal experience. He may be a mystic himself and follow his own mystical path to the end realizing union with God, or with Shiva, or realizing the unity of the Absolute, or extinguishing his desires in nirvāṇa: it will always be his own personal experience, and if he studies the writings of others, he is confronted with all the perplexities which we have mentioned. We know perhaps – more or less – what our own personal experience is, but we shall never know the nature of 'mystical experience' in general, particularly if we pass from our personal environment to other religions.

In order to avoid misunderstandings, it would perhaps be wise to avoid speaking of 'mysticism' at all. There is only one thing we know for certain: that there were in each of the great traditions men and women who were not satisfied with the ritual aspect of religion, but who tried to live totally the meaning of their faith, not only on the level of outward behaviour, but on the level of deep psychological or spiritual experience, on the level of their innermost being. They extended their religious practice to the realm of the inner dimensions of human existence. They neither practised nor propagated 'mysticism': 'mysticism' is an abstract concept. It is a word devoid of concrete meaning. The famous question of the

Muslim 'mystics': *mā al-taṣawwuf?* does not mean, as some attempt to translate, 'what is mysticism?' but simply: 'what is *taṣawwuf?*', i.e. 'what is that particular trend in Islamic religious life – and there only, not elsewhere – which is called *taṣawwuf?*' The so-called Muslim 'mystic', the *mutaṣawwif,* or *murīd*, or Sufi, did not practise 'mysticism': he tried to internalize the fundamental tenets of Muslim faith, *tawḥīd*, the unity of God. Similarly, the Hindu *sanyāsi* and the Hindu *bhakta* did not hanker after 'mysticism': they were seeking *brahmajñāna*, 'knowledge of Brahma', or *Shiva-anubhava*, *Shiva-bhoga*, total experience of Shiva, or *sāyujya*, union with the particular form of the deity they preferred to others. Nor did the Christian monk study 'mysticism': he was after the *basileia tou theou*, the Kingdom of God which he discovered in his heart, and he strove for *gnōsis* and *theōsis*, for ultimate knowledge and union with God.

'Mysticism' is a purely formal concept; the term is a reminder that a religion is not only outward performance but also, for some of its adherents at least, a never-ending quest after its own perfection, the perfection which is inherent in its specific structure, a perfection to be realized on the level of the spiritual, the interior, dimension of man.

NOTES

1 Thus, Ben-Ami Scharfstein, *Mystical Experience* (Oxford and Baltimore, 1973) has chapters on 'Everyday Mysticism', 'Creator's Mysticism', 'Psychotic Mysticism'; 'mysticism' is taken as a type of experience which 'characterizes every intense effort to create' and which 'we find not only in religion and philosophy, but, obviously, in art and literature, and, less obviously, in science' (p. 2).

2 Niketas Stethatos of Studios, *Chapters about Practice, Physics and Gnosis*, III, 41; translated from *Philokalia tôn hierôn nêptikôn*, vol. 3 (Athens, 1960), p. 335 f.

3 Niketas Stethatos says, op. cit., I, 45 (*Philokalia*, p. 283) that those who practise 'mystical theology' enter, with the aid of the Holy Spirit, into the 'knowledge of the mysteries of God'.

4 R. C. Zaehner, *Hindu and Muslim Mysticism* (London, 1960), p. 2.

5 Cf. R. C. Zaehner, *Mysticism Sacred and Profane* (Oxford, 1957). More recently, B. Scharfstein, op. cit.

6 P. G. Moore, 'Recent Studies of Mysticism', in: *Religion, Journal of Religion and Religions*, vol. 3 (1973), p. 146–56; quot. p. 152.

7 Maximus the Confessor, *Chapters about Theology*, VII, 94; translated from *Philokalia*, vol. 2 (Athens, 1958), p. 185.

8 Cf. for instance: Al-Sarrāj (d. 988), *Kitāb al-luma' fī 'l-taṣawwuf*; Sulamī (d. 1021), *Tabaqāt al-ṣūfīya*; Abū Nu'aim (d. 1038), *Ḥilya al-awliyā'*; al-Qušairī (d. 1072), *Risāla*.

9 Al-Sarrāj, *Kitāb al-luma'* (Cairo, 1960), p. 53; translation partly by M. Smith, *Readings from the Mystics of Islam* (London, 1958), p. 31 f.

10 Ibn Atā Allāh's *Ṣufi Aphorisms*, tr. Victor Danner (Leiden, 1973), p. 50, nos. 183–6; text in Paul Nwyia, *Ibn Atā Allāh et la naissance de la confrérie śādilite* (Beirut, 1972), p. 159, nos. 170–3.

11 Paul Horsch, *Die vedische Gāthā-und Śloka-Literatur* (Bern, 1966).

12 *Bṛhad-Aranyaka-Upanishad*, 4.4.7. Translation partly based on: *The Bṛhad-āranyaka Upaniṣad*, Ramakrishna Math (Madras, 1951), p. 363.

13 A. K. Ramanujan, *Speaking of Shiva*, Penguin Books (London, 1973), p. 53.

14 In his Introduction to the *Virashaiva Vacanas*, cf. n. 13.

15 *Basvaṇṇavara Ṣaṭsthaḷada Vacanagaḷu*, ed. Dharwar, 1954, no. 738; translation based on: *Vacanas of Basavaṇṇa*, ed. H. Deveerappa (Sirigere, 1967), p. 243.

16 To mention only a few classics: cf. the Arabic works mentioned above in n. 8, and later Persian biographies such as Aṭṭār's (d. 1220, or 1229/34) *Tadhkirat-al-'awliyā'*; in Sanskrit Aśvaghoṣa's *Buddhacarita*; anonymous lives of Shankara, Ramanuja, and others; in Tamil the remarkable and unfortunately little known Periyapurāṇam; the Mahratti lives of Mahratti mystics; in Christianity, the *Legenda aurea*, and a host of other works.

17 K. D. L. Burridge, *Mambu, A Melanesian Millennium* (London, 1960), p. 27.

18 Fritz Meier, *Die fawāiḥ al-ǧamāl wa-fawātiḥ al-ǧalāl des Najm al-Dīn al-Kubrā* (Wiesbaden, 1957); Dieter Schlingloff, *Ein buddhistisches Yogalehrbuch* (Sanskrittexte aus den Turfanfunden VII) (Berlin, 1964).

19 Ernst Benz, *Die Vision: Erfahrungsformen und Bilderwelt* (Stuttgart, 1969), p. 648.

20 Ernst Benz, op. cit. (n. 19); Violet Macdermot, *The Cult of the Seer in the Ancient Near East* (London, 1971); Fritz Meier, op. cit. (n. 18); Jan Gonda, *The Vision of the Vedic Poets* (The Hague, 1963); Dieter Schlingloff, op. cit (n. 18).

21 Violet Macdermot, op. cit. (n. 20), p. 356.

22 Ibid., p. 363. Both examples are from the Lausiac History of Palladius.

23 Cf. above, n. 11.

24 *Bṛhad-Aranyaka-Upanishad* 4,4,7.

25 Paul Nwyia, *Exégèse coranique et langage mystique: Nouvel esssai sur le lexique technique des mystiques musulmans* (Beirut, 1970).

26 Translated from al-Sarrāj, *Kitāb al-luma'* (Cairo, 1960), p. 53.

27 Al-Tirmidī's questions, along with the two series of answers written by Ibn 'Arabī, have been conveniently edited by Osmān I. Yaḥyā; Al-Tirmidī, *Kitāb ḥatm al-'awliyā'* (Beirut, 1965), pp. 142–362.

28 Osmān I. Yaḥya, *Histoire et classification de l'œuvre d'Ibn Arabi* (Damascus, 1964), pp. 241–56, lists 120 commentaries, including an introduction written by Ibn 'Arabī himself!

29 Osmān Yaḥya, op cit., p. 232–4, gives a list of 15 (or 14) commentaries.

30 Helmut Ritter, 'Philologika', in: *Der Islam*, vol. 22 (1934), pp. 90–3, mentions ten commentaries on Anṣarī's *Manāzil;* another one (the oldest extant) was published by S. Laugier de Beaurecueil in 1954, and a more recent one appeared in Cairo in 1969. For commentaries on Ibn Atā Allāh's *ḥikam*, cf. Victor Danner, op. cit. (n. 10), p. 16.

31 Translated from the critical edition of the *Upadeśasāhasrī*, by Sengaku Nayeda (Tokyo, 1973), p. 210 (*Gadyabandha* II, 86–9); for other translations cf. Swami Jagadānanda, *A Thousand Teachings* (Madras, 1943), p. 53 f.; Paul Hacker, *Upadeshasāhasrī von Meister Shankara* (Bonn, 1949), p. 42.

32 A. J. Arberry (trans.), *Discourses of Rūmī* (London, 1961), p. 108.

33 Stephan Beyer, *The Buddhist Experience, Sources and Interpretations.* (Encino and Belmount, California, 1974), p. 264. A most vivid picture of such dialogues emerges from Lin Tsi: *Entretiens*, tr. P. Demiéville (Paris, 1974).

34 Tr. David R. Blumenthal, *The Commentary of R. Ḥōter Ben Shlōmō to the Thirteen Principles of Maimonides* (Leiden, 1974), p. 65; the various Arabic texts ibid., p. 338; the commentary ibid., p. 204 f.

35 Tr. Victor Danner (n. 10), p. 65 (nos. 11, 14, 15); text in: Paul Nwyia (n. 10), pp. 213 ff. (nos. 8, 11, 12).

36 G. U. Pope, *The Tiruvāçagam or 'Sacred Utterances' of Māṇikka-Vāçagar* (Oxford, 1900), p. 65.

37 Al-Sarrāj, *Kitāb al-luma'* (Cairo, 1960), p. 328 f.; tr. Margaret Smith, *Studies in Early Mysticism in the Near and Middle East* (London, 1931) (re-edited Amsterdam, 1973), p. 231.

38 G. U. Pope, *The Tiruvāçagam* (n. 36), p. 270 f.

39 As would be done, for instance, by B. Scharfstein, cf., op. cit. (n. 1), pp. 71–6.

40 See above, n. 4.

41 R. C. Zaehner, *At Sundry Times* (London, 1958), p. 171; see also Zaehner's *Hindu and Muslim Mysticism* (London, 1960), p. 5.

CARL A. KELLER, D.D. (University of Basel). Among Professor Keller's numerous publications are *Das Wort* OTH. *als 'Offenbarungszeichen Gottes'* (1946);

Die Vedantaphilosophie und die Christusbotschaft (1953); *Commentaire des petits prophètes*, Vols. I, 11 (1965/71). In addition he has contributed numerous articles to a wide variety of continental scholarly journals dealing with such varied subjects as Hindu, especially Tamil, mysticism, Sufism, and Biblical Studies. After lecturing in India from 1946–52 he returned to Switzerland, becoming first Professor of Old Testament at the University of Lausanne in 1956, and then moving over to occupy the chair in the History of Religions in 1966.

Mystical Experience, Mystical Doctrine, Mystical Technique

PETER MOORE

The philosophical analysis of mysticism comprises two overlapping lines of inquiry: on the one hand the identification and classification of the phenomenological characteristics of mystical experience, and on the other the investigation of the epistemological and ontological status of this experience. The first line of inquiry is generally focused on the question whether the mystical experiences reported in different cultures and religious traditions are basically of the same type or whether there are significantly different types. The second line of inquiry centres on the question whether mystical experiences are purely subjective phenomena or whether they have the kind of objective validity and metaphysical significance that mystics and others claim for them. Now the fact that these questions continue to be answered in such diverse and conflicting ways inevitably raises two further and more fundamental questions: first, do the data on which the philosophical analysis of mysticism draws really constitute an adequate basis for the kinds of inquiry proposed? Secondly, are the methods and theoretical presuppositions of these inquiries properly tuned to the subtlety and complexity of the subject-matter? In this article I shall explore these methodological questions, and in so doing clarify the ways in which satisfactory answers to the two original questions might be found.

It often seems to be forgotten that the immediate data of the philosophical analysis of mysticism are not mystical experiences themselves, but the mystics' accounts of these experiences. It follows that the fruitfulness of philosophical analysis primarily depends on the extent to which these accounts render accessible to non-mystical investigation the experiences to which they refer. Now a number of philosophers have argued that the mystics' accounts of their experiences do not render the latter accessible to rational inquiry. For them the limit of rational inquiry is the discovery that, at least so far as the non-mystic is concerned, mystical experience is ineffable. Arguments about the ineffability of mystical experience provide a convenient starting-point for an examination of the nature of mystical language and literature.

The arguments in question take their cue both from explicit references to ineffability in mystical writing and from features of mystical language which suggest or imply ineffability. Now the first question that arguments about ineffability must answer is this: why, if mystical experience is ineffable, do mystics in fact write so much about it? The most radical solution put forward has been that mystical writings should be regarded not as descriptive accounts, but rather as mainly theological or devotional in purpose, or as concerned with giving practical advice and encouragement to aspiring mystics.[1] The fact that mystics have motives for writing other than the desire to communicate information about their experiences certainly requires emphasis in the context of philosophical analysis, where there is a tendency to treat mystical writings as if they were intended as clinical reports of experience. But the argument that mystical writing is mainly non-descriptive in character simply cannot be sustained. In the first place the non-descriptive uses of language are parasitic upon its descriptive uses and occur typically in the context of the latter. Interpreting the meaning of an experience, expressing one's response to it, or recommending others to cultivate such experience for themselves are all linguistic operations which require at least a minimum description of what it is that is being interpreted, responded to or recommended. Secondly, it is quite clear that a great deal of mystical writing is in fact mainly descriptive in intent. This is true not only of the accounts of those whose experiences, because they occur independently of any religious practice, may be called 'natural' mystical experience, but also of the writings of mystics who, because their experiences are 'cultivated' within the disciplines of a particular religious tradition, obviously do have motives for writing other than the desire to describe their experiences. That is to say, although these writings have in the main a theological, devotional, or practical purpose, they none the less contain – in addition to the inevitable descriptive minimum and notwithstanding the tendency among religious mystics to refrain from giving much detail regarding their own experiences in particular – a substantial amount of detailed description of experience, much of it highly sophisticated even by modern psychological and scientific standards. Thus, if mystical writing is recognized as being at least substantially descriptive in character, the argument about ineffability is essentially this: that mystics, whether or not they acknowledge the fact, are failing fundamentally in their attempts to communicate their experiences to non-mystics. What I want to suggest is that there is no real evidence for this extreme view.

In think it is important to distinguish three basic categories of mystical writings: (i) Autobiographical reports of specific instances or types of mystical experience.[2] (ii) Impersonal accounts, not necessarily based exclusively upon the writer's own experiences, in which mystical experience tends to be described in generalized and abstract terms.[3] A sub-category here would be the stereotyped or conventionalized accounts of mystical experience which occur within sacred scriptures and which often are not even the work of a single writer or of known authorship.[4] (iii) Accounts of a mainly theological or liturgical kind which although referring to some mystical object or reality do not refer, unless very obliquely, to mystical experience itself.[5] These three categories of mystical writing I shall call the first-order, second-order, and third-order categories respectively. Now clearly it is, only first- and second-order writing which is relevant to the philosophical analysis of mystical experience (and, incidentally, second-order writing should not be regarded as inferior to first-order writing, for it can involve insights and perspectives of a kind which are not necessarily to be found in autobiographical writing). What makes it all the more important to distinguish between these three categories of writing is that a single text may contain writing from more than one category.

A large proportion of the statements cited in support of the radical ineffability argument must in fact be discounted because they come from third-order writing. Furthermore, of the ineffability statements taken from the relevant first-order and second-order categories, many refer to types of ineffability which have no direct bearing on the argument that mystics are failing to communicate information about their experiences. Two such types are worth identifying here. First there is what might be called the 'emotional' type of ineffability. Here the trivial and normally accepted sense in which no experience can be literally 'shared' with or 'conveyed' to another becomes an acutely frustrating limitation for one who wishes to communicate some deeply felt and profoundly valued experience (e.g. of gratitude, love, beauty, or religious experience). St Teresa of Avila writes on one context:

> I have only said what is necessary to explain the kind of vision and favour which God bestows on the soul; but I cannot describe the soul's feelings when the Lord grants it an understanding of His secrets and wonders – a joy so far above all joys attainable on earth that it fills us with a just contempt for the joys of life, all of which are but dung.[6]

This sense of ineffability – probably the type most frequently expressed in first- and second-order mystical writing – if anything stimulates the writer to greater efforts of communication and perhaps to greater successes therein. A second type of ineffability might be called the 'causal' type, where a mystic states that he cannot understand whence or how some experience has arisen, or what the underlying conditions of the experience are. But this type of ineffability does not necessarily affect the mystic's ability to describe the actual contents of the experience. 'The way in which this that we call union comes, and the nature of it, I do not know how to explain,'[7] writes St Teresa; and yet she has a great deal to say here and elsewhere about the structure, contents, and effects of this type of experience.

Once these largely irrelevant senses of ineffability have been excluded, we are in a position to evaluate the extent of the problem posed by what may now be identified as the descriptive type of ineffability. And it soon becomes clear that statements about descriptive ineffability do not support the argument that mystical experience is radically ineffable. Compared with third-order ineffability statements, which are typically comprehensive and uncompromising in their reference ('Brahman is not this, not that', etc.), descriptive ineffability statements are usually partial and qualified in their reference. For one thing, rarely is the experience as a whole said to be beyond description. Again, there are different *aspects* and – at least in the case of cultivated mysticism – different *stages* of experience, and these vary considerably in the degree to which they are communicable. Not only do mystics affirm that there is no difficulty about describing their experiences to fellow mystics; it is also clear that they believe that their experiences can be described in some measure even to non-mystics. Thus of one of the lower stages of her contemplative experience St Teresa of Avila writes: 'This will be easily understood by anyone to whom Our Lord has granted it, but anyone else cannot fail to need a great many words and comparisons.'[8] This need for a great many words and comparisons is, one would have thought, a principal reason for the copiousness of much mystical writing. Of a higher stage of her experience, however, St Teresa writes: 'I do not know if I have conveyed any impression of the nature of rapture: to give a full idea of it, as I have said, is impossible.'[9] If mystics in some contexts suggest that an experience is describable and in others that it is beyond description, this is evidence not of uncertainty or inconsistency but very probably of the fact that a different stage or aspect of experience is being referred to (though doubtless it is true also that mystics differ in their skill with words and in their optimism regarding the ability of non-mystics to comprehend what they say). Furthermore, even those aspects or stages of mystical experience acknowledged as difficult or impossible to describe are not necessarily beyond all possibility of communication. For if mystics are using language at all responsibly then even what they say about the indescribable types or aspects of experience may at least serve to define them in relation to a known class of experiences. Thus when St John of the Cross calls ineffable the experience of 'the touch of the substance of God in the substance of the soul',[10] he is none the less communicating something of the experience by defining it in terms of the categories 'substance', 'touch', and so on. Similarly, his statement that the delicacy of delight felt in this experience is 'impossible of description', in so far as it is not a case of 'emotional' ineffability, at least defines the experience within the class of 'delights impossible of description', which is far from being empty or meaningless to non-mystics.

It is well known that mystics use a great deal of figurative and symbolic language to back up their literal statements. The power of such language to evoke or communicate experience is clearly very great in non-mystical contexts, and there is no reason to suppose that mystics do not use it equally effectively. In some contexts of course the mystical use of imagery and symbolism may be no more hopeful or helpful than the attempt to convey an idea of the colour red to one who cannot discriminate it by saying that it is 'warm and loud to the eyes'. The point is that the success of both figurative and literal language is dependent on some continuity of experience and vocabulary between writer and reader. Now mystics in fact write as if this sort of continuity existed. In this case the relationship of the mystic to the non-mystic is not, as is often assumed, like the relationship of the sighted to the blind, but more like that of the sighted to those with at least a glimmering of sight. Mystics do not belong to a class of persons cut off from non-mystics; it must be remembered that they were once non-mystics themselves. In writing as they do, therefore, they must surely be aware of both the limitations and the possibilities of their attempts to communicate their experiences to non-mystics.

Despite the foregoing observations, it might still be argued that, however skilful the mystic's attempts to communicate his experiences, what is most essential in them ever eludes rational conceptualization. One feature of mystical language commonly identified as evidence for this is the use of paradox. There are of course various ways of showing that paradox is not literally intended. But the argument is that such theories do not fit the mystical paradox. What mystics are trying to describe cannot be described without their falling into contradiction, even though one might envisage other language systems in which the experience could be described without such contradiction.[11] The only alternative would be to adopt the somewhat eccentric theory that mystical paradox represents the accurate description of an experience which is literally self-contradictory.[12]

But before the need to choose a theory of mystical paradox comes a more fundamental task – namely, that of establishing the truth of the widely held view that, as one proponent confidently asserts,

> the mystic's paradoxes are central to his experience, and con-
> tradictory descriptions are one of the most striking characteris-
> tics of his attempts to say what his experience was like. Worse
> still, it is evident that the mystic not only feels that the experience
> was of a contradictory sort, but . . . that the object of his experi-
> ence has contradictory properties.

The same writer quotes as an example the following lines from the Hindu *Isha Upanishad*:

> That One, though never stirring, is swifter than thought . . .
> Though standing still, it overtakes those who are running . . .
> It stirs and it stirs not.
> It is far, and likewise near.
> It is inside all this, and it is outside all this.[13]

This is typical of the evidence adduced for the ubiquity and insolubility of mystical paradox. Yet there is no question of such passages being descriptions of a contradictory sort of experience, for the simple reason that they are not descriptions of experiences of any sort at all. In fact the passage quoted belongs squarely in the third-order category of mystical writing. The kind of paradox it contains is easily explained, once its immediate and its wider contexts are taken into account, as a rhetorical juxtaposition of complementary insights concerning the immanence and transcendence of Brahman.[14]

Now a detailed survey of mystical writing would show that while paradox is fairly common in third-order writing, it is much less in evidence in second-order contexts, while in first-order writing it appears hardly at all. Not only does this mean that paradox cannot after all be treated as a major obstacle to the philosophical analysis of mystical experience; it also suggests a way of explaining paradox wherever it does occur in mystical writing. For if it is true that the less straightforwardly descriptive the context the more likely the appearance of paradox, it would seem a reasonable assumption that paradox itself is not straightforwardly descriptive, and that this is the case even when it does crop up in straightforwardly descriptive contexts. In other words, mystical paradox is most plausibly explained according to the same kinds of theory whereby paradox is explained in non-mystical contexts. Indeed most mystical paradoxes need but little prodding before their real meaning falls out, while many of the figurative expressions used by mystics – as in talk of being blinded through excess of light or wounded with the sweet pains of love – can scarcely be regarded as even superficially paradoxical. There is, in short, no evidence that mystics are forced by their experiences to break the law of non-contradiction in their writings. And even where the real meaning of a paradox remains obscure, it would seem reasonable to assume that the paradox is not literally intended unless the mystic asserts as much independently of his use of the paradox itself. If mystics really did have literally contradictory experiences of the kind suggested one would expect to hear much more about them in addition to the mere presence of paradox in their writings. In mysticism as in other contexts the use of paradox appears to be an example not of the failure of language but of its effective application. Indeed, the term 'paradox' in strict English usage means 'a contradictory statement not literally intended'.

Mystics make no secret of their difficulties with language, and the nature of these difficulties must not be underestimated. But I do not think that there is any evidence, either in the forms of mystical language itself or in what mystics say in commenting on their writing, to lend support to the view that mystical experience is inaccessible to a substantial degree of comprehension and critical analysis by non-mystics. No one who is acquainted with mystical writing can fail to be impressed by the care and subtlety with which many mystics write about their experiences. And in particular there is no evidence to suggest that mystics do not observe the same rules of language and logic that apply in non-mystical writing. The reason why mystical writing so often seems obscure is that it has not been adequately analysed in relation to the doctrines, practices, and institutions which form its wider frame of reference.

If mystical experience is accessible to philosophical analysis, then the principal methodological requirement of this analysis is a proper understanding of the distinction between mystical experience and the modes of its interpretation. Unfortunately this crucial distinction has often been over-simplified and its wider ramifications ignored. The writer whose work has probably exercised the greatest influence on the study of mysticism in recent years defines interpretation as 'anything which the conceptual intellect adds to the experience for the purpose of understanding it, whether what is added is only classificatory concepts, or a logical inference, or an explanatory hypothesis', and his search for a 'universal core' of mystical experience is conceived as an attempt 'to penetrate through the mantle of words to the body of experiences which it clothes'.[15] The basic inadequacy of this understanding of the distinction is scarcely mitigated by conceding that experience and interpretation are 'distinguishable though not completely separable',[16] or that the distinction is not clear-cut in practice but only in principle, or that it is impossible to provide a description of mystical experience completely free of interpretation. For the point is that in mysticism as in other contexts 'experience' and 'interpretation' are not even in principle mutually exclusive epistemological categories. Many of the disagreements about the variety or otherwise of mystical experience stem from a failure in the theoretical analysis and methodological application of this complex distinction – or, rather, relationship – between experience and interpretation.

The complexities of the distinction are best explored in the context of the mystical writing which forms the immediate data of the philosophical analysis of mysticism. I suggest that these accounts are likely to comprise as many as four theoretically distinct elements:

(i) References to doctrinal interpretations formulated after the experience is over. These constitute what I call *retrospective interpretation*.

(ii) References to interpretation spontaneously formulated either during the experience itself or immediately afterwards. These are elements of *reflexive interpretation*.

(iii) References to features of experience which have been caused or conditioned by a mystic's prior beliefs, expectations and intentions. These I call *incorporated interpretation*.[17] Two types of it seem likely:

(*a*) ideas and images reflected in an experience in the form of visions and locutions and so forth (*reflected interpretation*);

(*b*) features of experience moulded into what might be termed phenomenological analogues of some belief or doctrine (*assimilated interpretation*).

(iv) References to features of experience unaffected by the mystic's prior beliefs, expectations, or intentions. These constitute *raw experience* (a less tendentious term than 'pure' experience).

This scheme of the relationship between experience and interpretation is both consistent with general principles of psychology and epistemology, and compatible with any theory of the origins and significance of mysticism. In particular it is worth stressing that the scheme in no way implies a reductionist account of mystical experience (though, again, it would be consistent with any reductionist account put forward). The category of raw experience leaves open all the important questions regarding the ultimate source and significance of mystical experience. Not even the most supernaturalist Roman Catholic mystical theologian would dispute the presence in mystical experience of what I have defined as incorporated interpretation. Nor would any doctor of the Theravādin *Abhidhamma* find the scheme incompatible with his own analysis of higher states of consciousness. The main problem of course is that of actually discriminating between the different elements in any given account of mystical experience. And yet, unless the attempt is made, even if only in a speculative and provisional way, there is little chance of coming anywhere near valid conclusions concerning either the phenomenology or the epistemology of mystical experience. Moreover, if the analysis of a given text is to be successful it must be viewed in relation to the doctrines, practices, and institutions which are likely to have influenced both the experience itself and the way in which the experience has been recollected and described. And the influences in question include not only *interpretation* but also *selection*; for a mystic is likely to be selective not only in what he remembers of his experience, but also – especially in second-order writing – in what remembered details of his experience he considers worth recording. I shall consider in turn the kinds of influence that might be expected from each of the sources mentioned above, before proceeding to some observations about the nature of mystical experience as such.

Those who imagine that the distinction between experience and interpretation is at least in principle clear-cut by the same token tend to treat the doctrinal elements in an account as factors irrelevant, if not actually obstructive, to the phenomenological analysis of the experience in question. Yet to ignore the doctrinal elements in an account is to risk ignoring important features of the experience itself. For there is a complex interplay between experience and doctrine, both at the external level where doctrine affects the description of an experience, and at the internal level where doctrine may affect the substance of the experience itself. The suggestion that the doctrinal elements in an account obscure the real nature of the experience described makes about as much sense as saying that if we want to know what a chicken really looks like we must first pluck out all its feathers.

Consider first a point regarding the external interplay of experience and doctrine. Even to the extent that a clear distinction could be drawn between experience and interpretation (as in principle it can between raw experience and retrospective interpretation) the non-mystic, unlike the mystic himself, still would not be in a position to view the experience independently of the doctrinal categories whereby it is interpreted. For, as cannot be stressed too often, the non-mystic's source of data is the mystic's already interpreted account of his experience, and the non-mystic cannot check the latter against the original experience. The nearest he can get to this ideal is by comparing the account in question with other accounts by the same mystic or by other mystics from the same tradition. But the main point is that the doctrinal elements in an account may themselves mediate information about the phenomenological character of the experience and cannot therefore be discounted either as superfluous additions or as problematic obscurations. Thus, although in some accounts doctrinal elements and phenomenological elements may be juxtaposed, in others (particularly in second-order writing) they may be conflated. In some mystical writing, for example, doctrinal terms and scriptural quotations or allusions may be used as a kind of shorthand language in the description of mystical experience, so that an understanding of the terminology and scripture of a writer's tradition will often provide additional clues regarding the nature of the particular type or feature of experience in question. In short, doctrinal categories may themselves be patient of phenomenological analysis.

A second point relates to the internal interplay between experience and doctrine. Interpretation is often represented as if it were something simply added to, or superimposed upon, an existing or independent nucleus of experience. This may be roughly right in the case of some first-order accounts of 'natural' mystical experience, but it hardly suffices in the case of most reports of experience cultivated within a religious tradition, especially where the reports belong to the category of second-order writing. Indeed such a view of interpretation would not even apply to retrospective interpretation; for this may be developed over a period of time and in relation to a whole sequence of experiences, even though it may be attached to a particular experience described in a given account. The relationship of interpretation to experience is still more complex however; for just as interpretation may change or develop in response to new features of experience or in the light of new doctrinal understanding, so too may experience itself develop in accordance with changes in a mystic's beliefs, expectations, and intentions. This element within experience – which I have called incorporated interpretation – thus both reinforces and is reinforced by the mystic's beliefs, so that these beliefs may indeed be as much 'read off' from an experience as added to it (though not of course read off in the way that the naive supernaturalist supposes). And yet this mutually reinforcing cycle of experience and interpretation will not necessarily be a closed and unchanging one; new features of experience and interpretation will constantly be drawn in. Whether in the process of their complex interaction the experience becomes any more or any less profound or the interpretation any more or any less accurate are of course further questions.

It is sometimes suggested that religious doctrines constitute obstacles to the mystic's own understanding of his experience, the corollary being that the fewer doctrinal presuppositions a mystic has the more likely he is to understand the real nature of his experience and the more likely also to report it accurately. But while it is undoubtedly the case that a mystic's beliefs and expectations are likely to affect the nature both of his experience and his report of his experience, this constitutes no more of a problem in the case of mysticism than it does in the case of any other form of experience. The mystic's doctrinal background should, therefore, be seen as a key to his experience rather than a door which shuts us off from it. If a mystic's reports of his experiences appear obscure, this is often because the investigator has neglected to acquaint himself sufficiently with the nature of the tradition within which the mystic writes. There is a more fundamental point at issue however. Quite apart from the fact that it is a mystic's beliefs and intentions which motivate him to cultivate his experiences in the first place, it is probable that these beliefs and intentions not merely affect the experience in the form of incorporated interpretation but actually facilitate and literally 'educate' the experience as a whole. In this case the view that reports of 'natural' mystical experience must somehow be more informative concerning the real nature of mystical experience than reports of 'cultivated' experience are seriously mistaken. The lack of doctrinal presuppositions might prevent the mystic not only from understanding and describing his mystical states but even from experiencing the fullness of these states in the first place. The possession of what could be called a 'doctrinal vocabulary' might indeed serve to precipitate features of experience which would otherwise remain at the margin of consciousness if not actually beneath it. The fullest and most informative experiences might be those for which the subject was prepared beforehand – prepared, that is, in respect of some definite doctrinal background. Finally, if doctrines really were obstacles to the mystic's own understanding of his experience one would expect to find plenty of evidence for this in the mystical traditions; but the evidence is, on the contrary, that mystics find their doctrinal vocabularies a help rather than a hindrance in the cultivation and interpretation of their experiences.

I turn next to a consideration of the relationship between mystical experiences and the mystical techniques whereby they are induced. (The term 'induced' is appropriately ambiguous here, since it leaves open what in some contexts will be a crucial theological question: whether a particular experience has resulted exclusively from the practice of a certain set of techniques, or whether these latter have only prepared the way for its supervention through divine grace.) The tendency to neglect mystical techniques in the philosophical analysis of mystical experience is a further consequence of viewing this experience as if it were somehow a self-contained nucleus. And the associated argument that mystical techniques are surely irrelevant to an understanding of mystical experience as such is mistaken not simply because it involves the unwarranted assumption that the causal conditions of an experience exercise no significant effect upon this experience itself, but more radically because it implies that the causal conditions of an experience and the experience itself are mutually exclusive dimensions of mysticism. Furthermore, the principle of 'causal indifference' in the analysis of mystical experience, already questionable in itself, could easily lead to an indifference towards data or considerations which were relevant to the correct interpretation of this experience. This view of the relationship between mystical practice and mystical experience can only lead to a distorted and impoverished picture of the latter.

Any adequate account of mystical practices would have to include the whole programme of ethical, ascetical, and technical practices typically followed by mystics within religious traditions.[18] Here I shall confine my remarks to those more or less specialized techniques which constitute the immediate preconditions of mystical experience. These techniques fall into two main groups, which I shall call *meditation* on the one hand and *contemplation* on the other. Meditation involves the disciplined but creative application of the imagination and discursive thought to an often complex religious theme or subject-matter. Contemplation, although in some respects a development of meditation, in fact attempts to transcend the activities of imagination and intellect through an intuitive concentration on some simple object, image, or idea. It is during the activity of contemplation that mystical experience, when cultivated, typically arises. Neither type of technique can be regarded as peripheral to the study of mystical experience. Attention to the methods and subject-matter of systems of meditation is clearly relevant to the identification and understanding of reflected interpretation, since the deliberately created images and ideas of meditation appear to provide the material basis, so to say, of the objectively presented visions and locutions which often form an integral part of mystical consciousness. Nor is this surprising in view of the fact that for many mystics the work of meditation

will necessarily consist, in great part, in attending to, calling up, and, as far as may be, both fixing and ever-renovating certain few great dominant ideas, and in attempting by every means to saturate the imagination with images and figures, historical and symbolic, as so many incarnations of these great verities.[19]

Contemplation on the other hand is relevant to the understanding of assimilated interpretation, for at least during the lower stages of mystical experience the mystic continues to shape or control certain features of his experience. Indeed, no sharp division can be drawn between contemplation as an activity and contemplation as a state of consciousness, as is clear from the use of the word 'contemplation' itself, as well as of other, similar terms (e.g. the Sanskrit *samadhi*). It is noteworthy too that one of the terms most commonly used in the Christian tradition to denote states of mystical experience is 'prayer', which in non-mystical contexts usually has an exclusively active connotation. The names given to particular stages of prayer ('prayer of loving attention', 'prayer of quiet', and so on) thus suggest the active and intentional nature of experiences which might otherwise be thought of as purely passive states. Even in accounts of natural mystical experience there are indications that the experience has arisen in the context of an activity analogous to the formal religious techniques of meditation or contemplation. A good example is provided by the experience of R. M. Bucke made famous by William James.[20] This experience, though quite sudden and unexpected, significantly enough occurred when Bucke was in a calm and passive state of mind after an evening of discussing poetry and philosophy with friends. Again, there is some evidence that the ecstatic experiences of St Paul may have been less 'uncultivated' than is usually supposed.[21] Indeed, St Paul's momentous experience on the Damascus road appears to cut across several cherished classificatory divisions – mystical/numinous, natural/cultivated, individual/communal, and even Jewish/Christian.

Finally, it is necessary to consider the possible influences on mystical experience of a mystic's institutional and wider cultural background. These influences in many ways are but those of doctrine and technique writ large. Thus, with the view that mystics are somehow shackled by the doctrines of their tradition is often associated the claim that mystics are typically under pressure from ecclesiastical authorities to describe their experiences in orthodox terms, so that a mystic's account of his experience cannot always be trusted as an accurate rather than as a conventionalized description of his experience.[22] This is alleged mostly of theistic mystics, often because the investigator has made up his mind beforehand that theism and mysticism are somehow incompatible, or at least uneasy partners. In fact the mystics of a particular tradition show no more of a tendency to heterodoxy than do the non-mystics within that tradition. Indeed mystics are often notable for their defence of tradition against heterodox beliefs and practices. It is, however, implausible to suppose that mystics of any tradition should find their experiences incompatible with the doctrines of the institution in which their experiences have been cultivated; while the complex interaction of experience and interpretation noted earlier surely rules out any straightforward incompatibility between an 'experience' on the one hand and its 'interpretation' on the other.

One of the most important of the institutional and cultural influences on the description of mystical experience is the language used by mystics, especially the language of those who write from within an established tradition. I have already suggested that there is no evidence that mystics do not use language as carefully and responsibly as any other class of writer. But the possibility remains that the natural tendency of mystics to use concepts and images conventional within, and even hallowed by, their own traditions might work against the accuracy or reliability of their accounts. Although this possibility cannot be ignored, especially in the context of second-order writing, still there is no reason to suppose that mystics who draw upon a conventional vocabulary do not select only those words and images which fit the nature of their experience. Indeed it is surely because of its descriptive aptness that a conventional vocabulary becomes conventional in the first place. A more likely obstacle to the accurate communication of mystical experience arises where certain conventional words and images, which in themselves are perfectly suited to the description of some type or aspect of experience, eventually become misleading either because their impact has been blunted through over-use or because in the course of their use unfavourable associations have accrued to them.[23] Such terms are therefore liable to convey to the reader either the wrong impression or else no impression at all. Again, a concept or image may be effective only where the wider context of its usage is known. A mystic can be expected to choose words appropriate to the understanding of his readers only if he knows who his readers will be. But of course what a mystic cannot be expected to do is to write for the future or for cultures unknown to him. Now it is in fact the case that most of the mystical writing studied nowadays comes from past or relatively unfamiliar cultures. One of the reasons why the language of the mystics is frequently misinterpreted, or dismissed as obscure or even nonsensical, is that the investigator has not paid sufficient attention to the cultural and linguistic background of these accounts. For example, much of the mystical imagery often interpreted as evidence for the suppressed sexual character of mystical experience actually derives from conventional vocabularies of courtly love, chivalry, and so forth which have little to do with the kind of sexuality the modern reader has in mind.[24] The mystical language is here romantic rather than erotic, and this difference may be an important one even for the phenomenological analysis of the experiences in question. (And even where mystical language is in fact frankly sexual or erotic, a sensitive reading of the text and careful attention to the context generally reveals that the author, rather than displaying neurotic or pathological symptoms, is using such language in a deliberate and clearly conscious manner, often as part of a traditional symbolism.) Or again, what a mystic exactly means when he describes an experience as being above knowledge or understanding will depend in part on what concept and theory of knowledge is current in the age or culture to which he belongs. And so on.

Finally there is the possibility that institutional and cultural factors may affect not just the way in which a mystic reports his experience but also the nature of this experience itself. Such influences might include the conventions of language and iconography,[25] the shapes and rhythms of music and architecture, political and ecclesiastical structures, social manners and customs, and so on – all of which certainly permeate the world's mystical writings. These factors would be reflected in or assimilated into the substance of an experience in the same ways that I have suggested doctrines are reflected or assimilated. As a well-known social historian observes, 'even the way our senses report experiences to us may be structured by the conventions of language, art, and the like', so that 'while symbols are created by us, these creatures in a peculiar way come alive, turn upon us, and cause us and our experience to conform to their anatomy'.[26] But here again it must be emphasized that such influences do not imply the corruption of what would otherwise be a 'pure' experience. If an experience is not conditioned by one set of cultural factors then it will be conditioned by another, while if it were (or could be) free of all cultural conditioning whatsoever it might not be 'pure' so much as shapeless and undeveloped. In such a case, moreover, the subject of the experience would not only lack the means to communicate his experience coherently to others, but also find it difficult to represent it, reflexively or retrospectively, to his own understanding.

Apart from the influences exerted upon mystical experience by the particular conventions of language, art, and so on, there are no doubt less tangible and more general influences at work. The atmosphere and attitudes of society at large may affect in subtle ways the mystical experiences of its members. The incidence, intensity, and thereby even the contents of an experience are likely to vary according to whether there is a favourable or an unfavourable social stereotype of mystical experience (or of a particular type of mystical experience) and according to whether the latter is encouraged, discouraged, or simply treated with indifference.[27] In this context it is instructive (as well as amusing) to note a monograph published by a member of the Leningrad Pedagogical Institute which is devoted to an interdisciplinary study of (*a*) the reasons for the emergence and development of religious experiences, (*b*) their specific features and forms of manifestation, (*c*) the features characterizing religious experiences under the conditions of socialist society, and (*d*) ways of overcoming them.

And in another study the same author reveals a shrewd appreciation of at least one aspect of religious experience in his suggestion that

> to overcome religious emotional states, it is important for atheistic propaganda to be based on that 'fund of experiences of the person which has not yet taken on a religious cast and which under proper direction can crowd out religious experiences', since the psychological world of the believer involves a 'self-organizing and self-regulatory' system which is very hard to overcome directly.[28]

If a proper understanding of the relationship between experience and interpretation is the main prerequisite for the accurate phenomenological analysis of mystical experience, what is also required is an adequate descriptive vocabulary in which to contain without distortion the results of this analysis. Such a vocabulary must be consistent with the mystics' own descriptions of their experiences while remaining neutral in respect of their alleged metaphysical significance. For example, if a mystic reports an experience of the loss or transcendence of self interpreted in terms of a monistic metaphysics, the phenomenologist can go no further than classifying this type or feature of experience as a loss of the sense of self, or of self-awareness. A report of union with God, however, is likely to be more difficult to unravel phenomenologically; depending on the particular details of the claim and on clues given elsewhere in the account, any one of a variety of classifications might be appropriate. The experience might simply be one of the loss of the sense of self retrospectively interpreted as oneness or union with God. Or it might be a vivid experience of a numinous presence loosely (or presumptuously) interpreted as a union with that presence – the identification of the latter as 'God' being a theoretically separate item in the interpretation. Or again it might be clear from the account that the experience indeed involves phenomenologically a sense of contact or union with a personal presence felt as loving, powerful, and so on. And yet even examples of this last kind, while naturally they will be taken to support very strongly metaphysical claims concerning the existence and attributes of God (or a god), could never in themselves actually close the gap between phenomenology and metaphysics, since the term 'God' in any theistic tradition metaphysically implies much more than could be confirmed by the data of individual experiences or sets of experience. Mystics themselves would be the first to admit this.

Finally, despite the metaphysical neutrality of the descriptive vocabulary, this vocabulary will however contain references to metaphysical elements: namely, to those present in the experience through incorporated interpretation. For even where these elements can be identified as such they are still as much a part of the experience as the elements of raw experience, with which they are in any case intimately bound up. In most cases, however, it is a matter of doubt and speculation whether or not a given aspect of experience represents incorporated interpretation. All this poses a methodological dilemma as to how elements of incorporated interpretation are to be classified. One rough and ready method would be the following: where there is any doubt that a given feature of experience – call it x – is an example of incorporated interpretation, it is simply classified as 'x'; where it is almost certainly incorporated interpretation – for example, a vision of Christ in the style of Duccio – then it would be classified (x). But whatever the extent to which a given experience or aspect of experience may be bracketed as 'incorporated', the possibility nonetheless remains of its having a transcendent, i.e. non-subjective, source or reference. That is to say, we cannot rule out the possibility that an experience with a transcendent source or reference might yet be entirely 'adapted' to the mystic's familiar mental landscape. Incorporated interpretation must be 'bracketed', but not 'bracketed out'. The phenomenological analysis and classification of mystical experience is a far more complex task than many investigators have realized.

The considerable detail and subtlety of a great deal of mystical writing in fact demands a very complex and refined vocabulary of phenomenological analysis, so much so that an investigator is quite as likely to overlook certain details in an account as he is to read into it details which are not really there. On the other hand the possibility of making detailed discriminations entails the risk of failing to see the wood for the trees in the analysis of mystical writing. To guard against this a descriptive vocabulary should comprise terms which define the basic structure of an experience as well as terms which cover their specific contents. But by far the most serious error encountered in the philosophical analysis of mystical experience is the exclusion or neglect of certain features of experience – something that generally results either from the selection of features in accordance with some preconceived idea or theory of mysticism or from a failure to view mysticism in the context of the doctrines, techniques, and institutions with which it is organically bound up. Two important examples are worth briefly reviewing here.

One category of experience frequently excluded from serious consideration is that of visions, which are the most obvious examples of the 'reflected' type of incorporated interpretation. The reason typically given for their exclusion is that visions are psychic and sensory phenomena 'accidental' to the main substance of mystical experience and are moreover so regarded by the mystics themselves.[29] Now to exclude visions, locutions, and similar phenomena from the philosophical study of mystical experience on grounds such as this makes about as much sense as it would to exclude from a study of human psychology all considerations of dreams on the grounds that these do not constitute an essential part of the structure of the mind and are in any case dismissed as trivial or insignificant by most of the people who have them. Visions as a matter of fact have played rather an important role in the individual lives of many mystics, while in some mystical traditions they have been the focal phenomena and thus deliberately cultivated.[30] (Indeed dreams themselves, in so far as they are distinguishable from visions as a separate category of experience, have been an important mode of experience, including religious experience, in many cultures.)[31] Descriptions of the different types and diverse contents of visionary experience account for a large part of mystical writing, and for this reason alone such experiences surely deserve serious attention in the philosophical study of mysticism. It is true that mystics, by virtue of long introspection of their experiences, have generally taken a much more critical and sceptical view of their visions than is popularly supposed. But if it is easy to see why mystics are virtually unanimous in rejecting as being of inferior content and of dubious value the external or 'corporeal' type of vision, it is equally clear why it is impossible for them not to take seriously and value very highly some of the subtler kinds of vision – those of the 'imaginal' and especially the 'intellectual' types. Since these often form so integral a part of mystical consciousness, there is no reason why they should not be given prominent consideration both in the phenomenological analysis of mystical experience and in the philosophical evaluation of mystical claims. And finally, even

in the case of those visions (of whatever type) which may be
legitimately regarded as secondary or 'accidental' phenomena, it by
no means follows that they can throw no light upon the more
central features of mystical experience.[32]

The other common defect in the philosophical analysis of
mysticism is the tendency to ignore the fact that mystics in contemplative traditions typically report a series of phenomenologically
distinct stages of mystical experience.[33] Even where this fact is
recognized there is still a tendency to concentrate attention almost
exclusively upon the 'higher', i.e. more advanced stages of experience, the assumption being that these must be the most informative
concerning the nature and significance of mystical experience. Now
this assumption, although supported by a good deal of mystical
writing, cannot be regarded as universally valid, and even to the
extent that it is valid is certainly no justification for ignoring the
lower stages of mystical experience. Three considerations are per-
tinent here. In the first place, the lower stages involve features not
present at the higher stages, just as the higher stages may involve
features not present at the lower stages. This follows from the very
fact that there are stages of experience. For mystical experience not
only comprises static and constant features, in regard to which the
mystic remains passive; it has also a dynamic and developing character, sometimes carrying the subject along with it (as in the case of
ecstasy properly so-called), but often inviting his active response
and co-operation. In this way, as mystical experience passes from
one stage to another, some features of experience are suppressed or
disappear, while others are intensified and new ones arise.
Secondly, the higher stages of mystical experience are not always
described as richer or more informative in content. On the contrary
they may be described as having a negative character, either
because the mystic is no longer conscious or else because phenomenologically there is little or nothing to report – or at least
nothing regarded as significant.[34] Thirdly, and most importantly,
the nature of the higher stages of experience, regardless of how they
are described or evaluated within a particular tradition or by a
particular mystic, can only be understood when they are viewed in
relation to the lower stages of experience, of which they are the
development or culmination, just as the stages of mystical experience as a whole are only comprehensible when viewed in the light
of the techniques of meditation and contemplation whereby they
are induced and sustained. Failure to take into account the stages
of mystical experience easily leads to wrongly balanced compari-

sons between the mystical experiences of different traditions or between experiences reported by different mystics within the same tradition, while undue concentration on the higher stages of experience merely reinforces the one-sided picture of mystical experience as something essentially static, non-sensuous, undifferentiated, radically ineffable, and so on.

One thing that emerges from what has been said so far is that the classification of mystical experience must operate at three levels: the specific *contents* of an experience must be viewed in terms of its overall *structure*, and (where appropriate) its structure in terms of the different *stages* of experience cultivated within a particular tradition. This method of classification inevitably undermines the view that mystical experience consists of a series of disconnected mental images, intuitions, and feelings. For mystical experience is described as being a total and integral form of experience, involving the same range and complex co-ordination of features present in other modes of human experience: that is to say, cognitions, perceptions, conations, emotions, sensations, and so on, which are variously attributed (whether retrospectively or reflexively) to external data directly apprehended by the subject, to external causes lying beyond the subject's immediate apprehension, or to events or processes within the subject's own mind or body. Mystical experiences are not described by mystics as being purely 'mental' phenomena or 'disembodied' states of mind, but as involving tactile, substantial, and corporeal dimensions also. Likewise mystical doctrines and theories include a good deal about subtle bodies, psychic organs, and higher forms of existence interpenetrating (though sometimes reacting with) the ordinary world of things and persons.[35] Nor do these observations apply only to esoteric traditions such as the Hindu Tantra, the Jewish Kabbalah, or Chinese Taoism, but also to those mystical traditions more familiar and more readily accessible to philosophical analysis. Finally, and to anticipate a point to be made further on, the higher forms of existence referred to are experienced as being, if anything, more real and more stable than the world of ordinary experience. Thus one modern mystical writer stresses in particular

the intense reality and vivid objective presence of the higher states, utterly unlike the flat intangibility of self-centred imaginations. The higher states . . . are logically prior to the physical state, and consequently not to be interpreted in terms of physical phenomena posterior to them. Everything in such states, spatial characteristics included, is known as if in archetypal unchanging form, and is therefore startlingly more real (rationally-objective, ever-present) than the derivative and shifting forms of the physical world.[36]

Mystical experience, then, is reported by mystics as having the same dynamic structure and complexity of content characteristic of other modes of human experience. This structure and content philosophers, psychologists, and other investigators are only just beginning to analyse in any real depth and on a well-founded comparative basis.[37] To this extent, therefore, it is premature to expect any definitive answer to the question whether there are a number of phenomenologically distinct types of mystical experience or simply one basic type. On the other hand, the form of this question itself appears to be misleading, especially when framed in terms of different institutional contexts of mystical experience (e.g. Is Hindu mysticism different from Christian mysticism?). For the phenomenological distinctions that would define different types of experience are already apparent within traditions, whatever further distinctions emerge from comparisons between traditions. Again, while there are strong structural correspondences between the mystical experiences cultivated within different traditions, there are considerable variations in the more specific contents of these experiences. The answer might be, therefore, that the different traditions share a common variety of experiences, which assumes a particular pattern in a given tradition according to the several factors – including, of course, the possibility of 'supernatural' factors – at work within that tradition. Furthermore, the differences between experiences, even the minor and apparently insignificant differences, could turn out to be more important than the similarities. In this case the attempt to isolate the common features of mystical experience – whether in support of the thesis of the unity of mysticism or in order to provide a basis for the argument from unanimity – would be methodologically one-sided to say the least. The lists of common characteristics given in many studies, especially when based mainly on an analysis of the higher stages of mystical experience, serve usually to perpetuate the view of mysticism as a highly abstract and colourless dimension of human experience.

Clearly no phenomenological stone should be left unturned when it comes to assessing the epistemological and ontological status of mystical experience. But the starting point of this second line of philosophical inquiry should be a careful analysis of the various claims made by or on behalf of mystics concerning their experiences. Unfortunately the different kinds of claim are frequently mixed up or misunderstood, not least by those whose aim is to defend their validity or plausibility. Most typically the claims are framed in some form of the argument from religious experience, which is not one that is generally put forward by the mystics themselves; and even where this argument can be derived from claims that mystics do actually make, or shown to be consistent with them, it is scarcely representative of mystical claims as a whole. A crucial rule, therefore, is the following: claims made on behalf of mystics should always be checked against the claims made by the mystics themselves.

The first stage in the investigation of mystical claims – be it an investigation of the claims of a single mystic, or of a specific group of mystics, or of mystics in general – is the formulation of an accurate typology of the various claims implicit or explicit in the mystical accounts constituting the data. Here I shall simply identify four main categories into which the varieties of mystical claim can be sorted. First, there are the *subjective claims* made by mystics. These concern the relationship between mystical experience and changes in the subject's beliefs, understanding, personality, behaviour, creativity, and so on.[38] Claims in this category probably represent the bulk of the claims made by mystics. Secondly, there are *causal claims.* These relate on the one hand to the practical conditions which if fulfilled may lead to the supervention of mystical experience, and on the other to the alleged metaphysical causes and conditions of mystical experience. Thirdly, there are the *existential claims.* These essentially involve the assertion that mystical experience discloses or constitutes evidence for the existence or reality of some metaphysical entity (God, Brahman, etc.) independent of the empirical subject. Fourthly, mystics make a variety of *cognitive claims.* These fall into two groups: on the one hand claims that mystical experience reveals facts or truths about the nature or attributes of some metaphysical entity or reality, and on the other hand claims that mystical experience reveals facts or truths about the ordinary world of non-mystical experience. In either case the alleged facts or truths may be reported as part of the immediate data of an experience or as inferences made on the basis of the immediate data of the experience.

If a mystical claim is to be correctly understood and justly appraised, it must first be typologically identified and its logic and content analysed. This is particularly important in view of the fact that mystics often combine two or more theoretically separate claims in a single, complex claim, or make claims which presuppose or entail other claims. Furthermore, although a mystical claim must be analysed in formal terms, this does not mean that it can be properly evaluated without reference to the context and conditions of its original utterance. The variations in the conditions of a given claim will determine the comprehensibility of the claim in the first place, the seriousness with which the claim deserves to be treated, the methods appropriate to its testing, and so on. One of the most obvious variations in the conditions of a claim is in the amount of detail it contains. Another is in the degree of its universality: a claim may be made by a single mystic, by a number of mystics from the same tradition, or by mystics from different traditions. Again, the experiential basis on which claims are made varies greatly: a claim may be based on a single experience, on a group of experiences, or on a whole lifetime of mystical experience. And in this context special attention should be given to the ways in which mystics develop and modify their claims over a period, and even come to retract or contradict claims they have made previously. Finally, since few mystical claims are based exclusively on mystical experience, the assessment of a claim will typically involve a consideration of various non-mystical presuppositions and references.

The arguments both in criticism and in support of the non-subjective claims of mystics are well known and often rehearsed.[39] Here I want simply to focus attention on some basic methodological errors and misconceptions relating in particular to claims of the existential and cognitive types. The first point to be emphasized is that claims based on mystical experience, like those based on other forms of experience, are of both inferential and non-inferential kinds, so that clearly it is important not to confuse one kind with the other. Mystical experience is often treated as if it consisted of mental images which are then made the basis for unwarranted and unverifiable inferences concerning the existence of entities or realities not themselves the immediate objects of the experience. Not only does this kind of analysis not ring true when we turn to examine the writings of the mystics themselves; in addition it invents a difficulty for mystical claims where none exists, or at least raises objections which have no more force in the context of mysticism than they do in non-mystical contexts. To adduce universal problems of perception as the grounds for doubting the validity of the mystical claim in particular is a case of playing the same card twice over. For as one writer has pointed out, the mystic is not like one who infers the existence of fire from the appearance of smoke when he has no independent rule of inference justifying the link between the two, but like one who 'infers' smoke from the visual sensing of smoke – that is, like one who sees the smoke directly.[40] While it is certainly the case that some mystical claims are presented as inferences (valid or invalid as the case may be), others no less certainly refer to perceptions of objects or realities immediately apprehended.

The sense of immediacy or objectivity of what is apprehended in mystical experience comes across very strongly in mystical writing, and mystics stress that it persists long after the experience is over. Now to affirm this sense of immediacy or objectivity does not amount to a claim that mystical experience is self-authenticating; it does not imply certainty regarding the true status or correct interpretation of the experience. Indeed a mystic might insist that his experience was vividly real, and yet be unable to say anything much else either about its specific content or about its likely significance. Furthermore, the sense of objectivity on the one hand and the certainty which a mystic might or might not have regarding the significance of an experience on the other are both distinct from the doctrinal certitude which a mystic may possess on other grounds (i.e. through faith, reasoning, religious training, and so forth). The sense of immediacy or objectivity, certainty in regard to interpretation, and doctrinal certitude are, therefore, three logically distinct factors in mystical claims, however closely they may be related in actual accounts. One further point: philosophers sometimes complain that mystics too often seem unable to formulate the truths they claim to have received or apprehended during their experiences. As a matter of fact there are many mystics who have recorded very specific and elaborate claims or revelations regarding the contents or objects of their experience, and in these too philosophers have found much to complain about. There may, however, be good reasons for mystical uninformativeness where it does occur. Some non-mystical parallels are suggestive: one may know one has met a person and yet be unable to remember anything in particular about him; one may try to recall a tune, or a name, or a number one thought was fixed in one's mind; and so on. In some cases an experience may have been so brief, so unfamiliar, or so literally astonishing that little more is retained of it than a vivid sense of its objective reality and obvious importance.

The foregoing observations imply that mystical claims, whether inferential or non-inferential, are not self-authenticating in the sense normally understood by this term. Mystics indeed would be the first to insist on this. Often they admit to mistaking or misinterpreting their experiences,[41] they criticize other mystics for errors of interpretation,[42] they develop and modify their claims and interpretations in the light of new and more profound experiences, and so on. In other words, a mystic behaves in regard to his experiences in the same kind of ways in which, say, a naturalist or an astronomer behaves in regard to the specialized forms of experience relevant to his particular discipline, whether they are his own experiences or the experiences reported by others. Of course, where the objective validity or true interpretation of any form of non-mystical experience is in doubt, recourse can be had to a variety of tests and checking procedures, although these do not always settle doubts or disputes. But mystics too have their own equivalents of such tests and checking procedures for the assessment of mystical experience. These are comprised on the one hand in the advice and instructions given by mystics concerning the ethical, ascetical, and technical pre-conditions of mystical experience, and on the other hand in the detailed moral and psychological criteria used in mystical traditions to determine the authenticity and value of mystical states and revelations. There is nothing in principle to prevent philosophers from acquainting themselves with mystical experience at first hand by following the relevant procedures, or from applying the relevant criteria to whatever results are achieved. But in so far as mystical claims are to be evaluated at second hand, through the medium of mystical writing, the nearest one could get to testing these claims directly would be by collecting and examining the reports of individuals who in fact have taken the trouble to carry out the relevant tests and checking procedures. Now many such experimental reports of course exist – namely, in the writings of the mystics themselves. For a mystic is, precisely, one who has tested through his own experience the claims made by earlier generations of mystics. Finally, there is in mystical writing much evidence for the epistemological stability and hence objective validity of mystical experience: concordance among the reports of different mystics, refinement of observation, development of theory, improvement of technique, and so on. In sum, it could be argued that most if not all of the conditions which are met in the case of experiences known to have objective validity appear, from the accounts given by mystics, to obtain in the case of mystical experience too. But one could not expect confirmation of the veridical nature of mystical experience from mystical accounts alone, any more than one could expect confirmation of the veridical nature of any form of non-mystical experience if all one had to rely on were accounts of this experience.

Even if it were accepted that mystical experiences have objective validity, the questions remain concerning the wider metaphysical significance of these experiences. The claims made by mystics tie up with the doctrinal systems of religions whose relationship with any individual experience or set of experiences is bound to be an extremely complex one. But although doctrinal systems certainly cannot be regarded as mere extrapolations of religious experience, their ultimate justification must presumably lie in religious experience. Yet it is doubtful, in view of the historical and organic complexity of religion, whether the entire set of experiences necessary for the total validation (or otherwise) of a particular doctrinal system could ever be available to any single individual or even to any number of individuals at any given period. The relationship between mystical experience and doctrine appears to involve the continuous integration and co-ordination of new insights and experiences with the doctrines and practices received through tradition. And even in the most comprehensive of these systems there will always be areas of uncertainty and ambiguity, reflecting the uncertainty and ambiguity intrinsic in all human experience, including religious experience.

Finally there are the still wider issues of religious truth. For the religious systems with which mystical experiences are associated do not appear to be consistent with one another. Is this because each tradition feeds upon or fosters a different type or blend of religious experience from the total range of experiences available? Or are some religious traditions mystically more developed or profound than others? Could the study and practice of the mystical life help one to decide between the truth claims of different systems of belief? Or would such study and practice reveal instead the ultimate consistency of these apparently conflicting systems? The answers to these questions lie in the future – and perhaps they always will.

NOTES

1 See, for example, Troy Organ, 'The Language of Mysticism', *The Monist*, vol. 48 (1963), pp. 417–43.

2 Some of the best examples are to be found in the *Life* and *Spiritual Relations* of Teresa of Avila, the sixteenth-century Spanish mystic:

E. Allison Peers (ed. and tr.), *The Complete Works of St Teresa of Jesus* (London, 1946), vol. 1.

3   Accounts falling into this category form the bulk of the writings of St Teresa's great contemporary, St John of the Cross: E. Allison Peers (ed. and tr.), *The Complete Works of St John of the Cross* (London, 1934–5), 3 vols.

4   The accounts given in the Pali canon of Theravāda Buddhism of the successive levels of *jhāna* (transic concentration) and the various modes of *abhiññā* (superknowledge) provide good examples here.

5   Passages falling into this category occur in the Qur'ān, the Upanishads, the Psalms, and many other sacred texts.

6   Peers, *Complete Works of St Teresa*, vol. 1, p. 174.

7   Peers, *Complete Works of St Teresa*, vol. 1, p. 106.

8   Peers, *Complete Works of St Teresa*, vol. 1, p. 327.

9   Peers, *Complete Works of St Teresa*, vol. 2, p. 292.

10   Peers, *Complete Works of St John of the Cross*, vol. 3, p. 49.

11   See P. Henle, 'Mysticism and Semantics', *Philosophy and Phenomenological Research*, vol. 9 (1949), pp. 416–22; and G. K. Pletcher, 'Mysticism, Contradiction, and Ineffability', *American Philosophical Quarterly*, vol. 10 (1973), pp. 201–11.

12   As in W. T. Stace, *Mysticism and Philosophy* (London, 1961), ch. 5.

13   Pletcher, op. cit., p. 202.

14   For the appropriate kind of analysis see N. Smart, *Reasons and Faiths* (London, 1958), chs. 1–3.

15   Stace, op. cit., pp. 37, 94. For an example of a far more subtle and satisfactory analysis see B. Garside, 'Language and the Interpretation of Mystical Experience', *International Journal for Philosophy of Religion*, vol. 3 (1972), pp. 93–102.

16   Stace, op. cit., p. 31.

17   'Those symbols under which the mystic tends to approach the Absolute easily become objectivized, and present themselves to the consciousness as parts of experience, rather than as modes of interpretation' (Evelyn Underhill, *Mysticism*, London, 1930, p. 268).

18   Such programmes are expounded in works like Buddhaghosa's *Visuddhimagga* (tr. Bhikkhu Ñyānamoli, *The Path of Purification*, Colombo, 1964); Patanjali's *Yoga-sutras* and the commentaries thereon (tr. J. H. Wood, *The Yoga-System of Patañjali*, Cambridge, Mass., 1914/Delhi, 1966); St John Climacus' *Ladder of Divine Ascent* (tr. Archimandrite Lazarus Moore, London, 1959); St Teresa of Avila's *Way of Perfection* (Peers, *Complete Works of St Teresa*, vol. 2); and many others.

19   F. von Hügel, *The Mystical Element of Religion* (London, 1923), vol. 2, p. 41.

20 *The Varieties of Religious Experience* (Fontana Books, London, 1960), p. 385.

21 J. W. Bowker, '"Merkabah" Visions and the Visions of Paul', *Journal of Semitic Studies*, vol. 16 (1961), pp. 157–73.

22 Thus Stace, for instance, holds that western mystics are checked in their tendency to give a monistic interpretation of their experiences only 'by the menaces and pressure of the theologians and ecclesiastical authorities' (*Mysticism and Philosophy*, p. 232).

23 See, for example, R. E. Lerner, 'The Image of Mixed Liquids in Late Mediaeval Mystical Thought', *Church History*, vol. 40 (1971), pp. 397–411.

24 See E. Underhill, *Mysticism*, pp. 136–40; M. A. Ewer, *A Survey of Mystical Symbolism* (London, 1933), pp. 168–79; Denis de Rougemont, *Passion and Society* (London, 1956), pp. 141–70.

25 See, for example, S. Ringbom, 'Devotional Images and Imageless Devotions', *Gazette des Beaux Arts*, vol. 73 (1969), pp. 159–70; G. Henderson, *Gothic* (Harmondsworth, 1967), pp. 143–77. For a suggestive example from St Teresa, see *Spiritual Relations*, xxv (Peers, *Complete Works*, vol. 1, p. 346).

26 L. White, Jr, *Machina ex Deo: essays in the dynamism of Western culture* (Massachusetts, 1968), pp. 18–19.

27 On the sociology and in particular the institutionalization of mystical experience see C. Y. Glock and R. Stark, *Religion and Society in Tension* (Chicago, 1965), I. M. Lewis, *Ecstatic Religion* (Harmondsworth, 1971), and P. H. Ennis, 'Ecstasy and Everyday Life', *Journal for the Scientific Study of Religion*, vol. 6 (1967), pp. 40–8.

28 *Psychological Abstracts*, The American Psychological Association (Washington), vol. 44 (1970), p. 1668.

29 Stace, *Mysticism and Philosophy*, pp. 47–51.

30 See, for examples, G. G. Scholem, *Major Trends in Jewish Mysticism* (London, 1955), pp. 40–79; E. Underhill, *Mysticism*, pp. 266–97; M. Fakhry, 'Three Varieties of Mysticism in Islam', *International Journal for Philosophy of Religion*, vol. 2 (1971), pp. 193–207.

31 See, for example, E. R. Dodds, *Pagan and Christian in an Age of Anxiety* (Cambridge, 1965), pp. 38–53.

32 For balanced views of mystical visions, locutions, etc., see the discussion by Emily Herman in her undeservedly neglected study *The Meaning and Value of Mysticism* (London, 1925), pp. 45–68, and the more technical analysis of Karl Rahner in *Visions and Prophecies* (London, 1963). For the idea that visions, although subjectively 'adapted', can none the less represent objectively existent realities, see J. H. M. Whiteman, *The Mystical Life* (London, 1961) *passim*.

33 For detailed analyses of the successively cultivated levels or stages of mystical experience, see works such as Woods's *The Yoga-System of Patañjali*, Buddhaghosa's *Path of Purification*, and A. Poulain's *The Graces of Interior Prayer* (London, 1950).

34 For example, in the higher stages of Buddhist *jhāna* ideation and feeling are eliminated completely, these states of consciousness being valued for their subsequent effects rather than for any immediately experienced content (see Ñyānamoli, *Path of Purification*, pp. 354–71, 824–33).

35 On the psychic accompaniments and cosmological context of mystical experience see in particular the following: Ñyānamoli, *The Path of Purification* (esp. pp. 409–78); A. Farges, *Mystical Phenomena* (London, 1926); R. C. Johnson, *Watcher on the Hills* (London, 1959); R. Crookall, *The Interpretation of Cosmic and Mystical Experiences* (London, 1969); and J. H. M. Whiteman, *The Mystical Life*.

36 J. H. M. Whiteman, 'The Angelic Choirs', *The Hibbert Journal* (April 1954), p. 264.

37 The most substantial analytical study yet published is Ernst Arbman's three-volume *Ecstasy or Religious Trance in the experience of the ecstatics and from the psychological point of view*, Stockholm–Uppsala, 1963–70 (vol. 1 'Vision and Ecstasy'; vol. 2 'Essence and Forms of Ecstasy'; vol. 3 'Ecstasy and Psychopathological States'). This is a work deserving of much wider recognition and use than has hitherto been the case.

38 On the subjective validity of mystical experience, see H. N. Wieman, *Religious Experience and Scientific Method* (New York, 1926); M. Laski, *Ecstasy* (London, 1961); A. H. Maslow, *Religions, Values and Peak Experiences* (Columbus, Ohio, 1964); L. Schneiderman, 'Psychological Notes on the Nature of Mystical Experience', *Journal for the Scientific Study of Religion*, vol. 6 (1967), pp. 91–100; and J. Gilbert, 'Mystical Experience and Public Testability', *Sophia*, vol. 9 (1970), pp. 13–20.

39 For well-informed defences of existential and cognitive claims, see in particular H. J. N. Horsburgh, 'The Claims of Religious Experience', *The Australasian Journal of Philosophy*, vol. 35 (1957), pp. 186–200; G. K. Pletcher, 'Agreement among Mystics', *Sophia*, vol. 11 (1972), pp. 5–15; W. J. Wainwright, 'Mysticism and Sense Perception', *Religious Studies*, vol. 9 (1975), pp. 257–78; and D. Wiebe, 'The Religious Experience Argument', *Sophia*, vol. 14 (1975), pp. 19–28.

40 Pletcher, op. cit., p. 14.

41 A notable example is Martin Buber's revised interpretation of his experience of 'undivided unity', quoted and discussed in R. C. Zaehner, *Hindu and Muslim Mysticism* (London, 1960), pp. 17–19.

42 For example, the Islamic mystical theologian al-Ghazzāli criticizes

mystics who mistake an ecstatic loss of self-awareness for an actual identity with God, a case quoted and discussed in R. C. Zaehner, *Mysticism Sacred and Profane* (London, 1957), pp. 156–60.

PETER MOORE, Ph.D. (Lancaster). Dr Moore is Lecturer in Theology at the University of Kent at Canterbury with special research interests in oriental religions, the phenomenology of religion and religious experience. He has published articles in *Religion* among other journals, and is presently at work on a larger study of mysticism.

Some Epistemological
Reflections on Mystical Experience

DONALD M. MACKINNON

To one who has been for many years continually preoccupied by the problems of epistemology, the questions raised by mystical experience are inevitably among those that intrude themselves now in one way, now in another. Though often irritating, at the same time they continually furnish reminders of the richness and complexity of human experience. As I am myself totally without any personal familiarity with the world of the mystics, I must insist that the remarks which follow are grounded in an essentially second-hand acquaintance with writings that for their proper appreciation demand readers who themselves 'go along with' that of which they are reading, at least in order to understand what is being said.

For anyone steeped in the study of Kant's theory of knowledge, the mystics raise the question of the status of the sort of proleptic vision of the whole to which both the world which we experience and our experience of that world alike belong, which unquestionably some of the mystics claim. Their use of the term 'vision' in respect of their experience of this whole is, of course, metaphorical. The language of sight is preferred to that of hearing or touching because of its alleged greater immunity from any sort of subsequent correction. In everyday life seeing does not, of course, enjoy anything like a total immunity; we are all of us familiar with the experience of 'seeing things'; but if I suppose someone to be a long way distant and then think I hear his voice, I am more likely to think that I am 'hearing things' than I am to suppose myself deceived if I respond to a knock on the door and open it to see him before me. In such a case, sight shows my conviction of his absence to have been mistaken. Furthermore, we have to reckon with the powerful influence of the biblical contrast between sight and belief, the latter often regarded as a surrogate for the former.

But what is it to see a whole and what are we to say of the whole which allegedly we see? Here the investigations of Gestalt psychologists offer much that is suggestive in respect of the way in which we organize what impinges on our senses into wholes to which we respond as the wholes that they are. For instance, I am aware of the room in which this paper is being typed as a whole enduring in relative stability through a considerable period of time, reaching in both directions far beyond the very short period of my own acquaintance with it. Further, in responding to it as a whole, I take in the various items, themselves smaller wholes that make up its furniture. The movement from whole to part, from part to whole, in study of its detail is quite complex, even subtle. All the time the room as a whole provides the organizational context. And from this point we can go on to other examples of a rather different sort. For instance, we can consider what is involved in grasping as a whole a building of unusual richness and complexity, but still integrated by service of a defining purpose, e.g. a temple or a cathedral. There may be furnishings or features of exceptional beauty on which attention is concentrated; we all know churches where an overall mediocrity is partly redeemed by the presence of a picture or statue of commanding beauty. But we are also familiar with buildings which gather into the unity of an all-embracing design the very many items which they may contain, even to the extent of rendering us relatively indifferent to the strident individual blemishes we cannot help noticing in their adornment.

But such wholes are relative; they are not all-embracing. The same must certainly be said of the quite richest natural panorama of the sort one may occasionally enjoy from a hill top, for instance, in the Hebrides where from a very modest height one may enjoy an astonishingly comprehensive view of mainland and islands alike. One may be amazed by the extent of what enters the grasp of a single glance; but one well knows that, although it is the visually simultaneous presentation of a complex geographical whole and although one's understanding and imagination are all the time enriching the immediate deliverance of sight, what is attained to in the fullness of such an experience is fragmentary, both spatially and temporarily incomplete. In addition, before proceeding with the argument, it must be emphasized that in a full treatment of the relation of perception to the sorts of wholes I have mentioned, the interweaving of the elements of Kant's threefold synthesis of apprehension in intuition, of reproduction through imagination, and of recognition by concept, should receive extended treatment.

Although the experiences mentioned so far have been visual, the run of the argument has detached them from concentration on the visual element they contain, and we have been more concerned with the sort of wholeness they exemplify. It is now time to mention an example of a very different sort, namely the hope of those engaged in cosmological research to build up the map of the universe in time as well as in space. If such a map is achieved and comes to constitute a Gestalt in a sense akin (though vastly more complex) to those mentioned above, we can dimly imagine what it would be like for a master in this field to have such a map at his fingertips. It would not be a matter of sight in any ordinary sense. Rather it would be the ability to use an extraordinarily comprehensive frame of reference for the dating and locating of all events whatsoever. One could speak of the frontiers of human knowledge having been pressed back to their ultimate limit and one could regard such a man as in an intelligible sense a master of time and space alike. It is impossible for the mathematically ignorant to begin to imagine such a mastery; it lies beyond the reach of his understanding and any attempt to realize it in his own terms will distort its actuality by irrelevant metaphor. Thus even to speak of it as a seeing is to risk total misconception in representing an experience wherein the interpenetration of the conceptual and the observational is humanly unique.

Moreover, it might indeed be argued that, where the notion of a concept of wholeness is concerned here, we need to construe it much more in terms of a Gestalt than in the forms suggested by Kant's introductory treatment of discursive understanding by concepts in its formal purity in the 'Metaphysical Deduction of the Categories'. Here the significance of his obscure doctrine of schematism may be seen to extend beyond the field of the second synthesis, e.g. of reproduction in imagination. The transmogrification of *a priori* concepts through their schematization would seem to take the shape of representing to ourselves typical embodiments indicative of their organizational role in making objective perception possible. If Kant's treatment of the shape of the world about us points in the right direction, then the constructive activity must be carried through *as nearly as possible* to completion, if fragmentary and interrupted sense experience is to be read aright. And in this constructive, synthesizing activity, awareness of wholes as containing frames would seem to condition the reading or state. One could even speak significantly of this sort of mastery as dispositional.

Yet the transition from such an experience to the mystical involves a *metabasis eis allo genos*. In both alike, there is a transcending of familiar limits; but is there even an analogy between the two sorts of transcending involved? For in mystical experience it would seem that sometimes the claim is made to transcend the very point of view from which ordinary, even extraordinary, awareness is enjoyed, criticized, transformed, and a level to be reached in which that experience of often painful criticism and transformation is itself grasped for what it is. In this respect we have to reckon with a state of awareness which claims that the opposition of subjective and objective is overcome and the separation of an investigator's biography from the yield of his investigation obliterated without damage to either.

In the hymn to love that Paul includes in his first letter to the Corinthians, he speaks of a knowledge of ourselves 'even as we are known' that will one day be ours. It is clear that such knowledge is for him closely linked to the love which in this passage he esteems above faith and hope alike. This though it is clearer how he supposes the concept of such a knowledge to reveal the provisional character of faith and hope than how he supposes it to be related to the manner of that loving he portrays in exquisite detail. It would seem that he supposes the barriers between our own knowledge of ourselves in relation to our world and our knowledge of ourselves when we see ourselves (analogously) as God sees us, broken down proleptically in love, whether the love be of God or of neighbour. Where our love of God is concerned, it is for Paul always a love that is fundamentally responsive to one who first loved us and from whose creative love no destructive force is ever strong enough to withdraw us. To see ourselves as God sees us would seem to be for us to grasp in human terms what we are in God's love. Such a grasp is radically incomplete; it is arguably a matter of intermittent intrusive perception painfully achieved, shortly received, and quickly lost. It resists formulation not because it lacks the sort of objectivity necessarily involved in referential statement, but rather because it places before human beings the paradigm of an ultimate objectivity, an acceptance of things as they are, a presence to their actuality that is unbearable and terrifying. It is only a love that is perfect which casts out fear and such completed love is rare, and even when it occurs is intermittent, more quickly counterfeited than realized in its actuality.

In his second letter to the Corinthians, which is his most intimate apology for his life and work as an apostle, Paul speaks of having been 'caught up into the seventh heaven' and enabled to see the unutterable. Yet this experience carries little weight as a ground of his apostolic apology contrasted with the intrusive preoccupation of his imagination with the needs and failings of the many utterly second-rate human beings gathered in to the fellowship of the churches he had founded or whose welfare concerned him. Both the rapture and the disturbing claims of this love broke the ordinary pattern of his days and purposes. But while images might capture in part at least the overwhelming disclosure of a momentary experience, only his own clumsiness and continuing weakness availed to bode forth both to him and to his converts the mystery of God's love. So it is in his weakness that his strength is made complete.

In traditional accounts of the mystical path, we are familiar with the distinction between the way of purgation, the way of illumination, and the way of union. In anything that an epistemologist may write, it is on the way of purgation that his attention will fall. For it is at this stage in a course which might seem to involve all its three successive phases at one and the same time, that the irrelevant is stripped away and the pilgrim takes stock of what he cannot mean by what he claims to seek or by what he claims to seek him. Further, as we shall see, this stripping away of the irrelevant belongs as much to mystical experience that is focused on alleged visual images as to that for which images of every form are necessarily distractions from the sort of totally purified ultimate completeness of apprehension that beckons as a goal. So Paul was enabled to see that which he could not utter. It was no achievement won by the sort of combined moral and intellectual asceticism that wins for Plato's philosopher the vision of the 'Idea of the Good'; it is of God's own free giving that the apostle has had this experience. But to the extent to which it lends itself to representation in visual terms, it is a lesser communication of the divine presence than the one continually made to him in the pains and perplexities of his mission. So Isaiah learnt the fullness of the vision he enjoyed in the year of the King's death,[1] during and through the enterprise to which he was committed as a prophet through his experience of the Lord 'high and lifted up'. It is by way of discarding the particular experience that the authentic incommunicable is communicated. If mystical experience is properly spoken of as one in which the opposition of subject and object is overcome, it must also be characterized as an experience in which the object is so totally transparent that one must speak of the subject as reduced to the near *locus* of its transparency. Or (to use the metaphor favoured by Paul) the earthen vessel in which the treasure is contained and through which it is mediated is broken in pieces. All we see sometimes is the breaking, and the contrast afforded with its inexorable completeness, by the strange simplicity of the mystic's words. Yet this simplicity is one of the end rather than of the beginning and very few achieve it.

Where this whole world is concerned, the epistemologist stands on the sidelines, his only role that of tracing the way in which the language, for instance, of vision, of perception, of absolute wholeness is taken and twisted to serve in helping to articulate an experience that is the strange, wholly unique thing that it is because in it all conventional distinctions between far and near, familiar and strange, natural and transcendent are broken down. The visual image is crucially important here, if only because it is by identifying the image (and such images are very various) with the reality, even with the boding forth of the reality, that the mystic is betrayed. For what he communicates is not in his vision but in his life, and his language will inevitably be poetic rather than descriptive.

In conclusion I should like to interpret this point by reference to the *Revelations of Divine Love* of Mother Julian of Norwich. But first I must add a note on the very controversial question of the status of mental images. As a matter of empirical fact such images occur and they play an unquestionably important part in remembering the past. While a great deal of what we call memory is clearly dispositional and not actual, we have to reckon with occasional, often involuntary acts of recollection. Thus as I compose this paper, I may suddenly remember falling on the frosty pavement of the esplanade in the West Highland town of Oban two days before Christmas in 1925 when I was a boy of twelve. I may have, indeed I may know myself to have, an image of my body falling on the pavement. But what I remember is not this image; the accusative of my act of recollection is a great deal more complex and more precise than the image. Yet as the late Professor G. F. Stout pointed out very acutely, although the image is not the accusative of the act of recall, it has the function of directing attention on the thing or event I am recalling. If I treat the image as a representative copy of what I recall, I likewise know myself immediately to be in error. It is too vague and schematic to convey the object of recollection. Yet by its occurrence my attention is focused, in my example on the event of 23 December and not, for example, on the gifts I received two days later! To say that memory images function in this way is to affirm an empirical proposition and one whose conditions of verification it is not easy to specify. But it is defensible in that very many persons claim that this is a description of their own experience.

Now I am not suggesting for one moment that the visual experiences allegedly enjoyed by Mother Julian are to be regarded as memory-images. Indeed the sense in which a memory-image can itself be regarded as a visual experience is by no means entirely obvious; we are not even at ease in speaking of it as a dream might be spoken of as essentially visual. Yet such images (if they occur) are less unlike visual experiences than any other sort of experience. This though their vague and fleeting character makes it hard to allow them even the firmness of outline we find in the hardly recollected dream-experience. Yet there is in the visions Mother Julian claimed to enjoy of the suffering Christ a role in respect of her experience analogous to that fulfilled by memory images in Stout's analysis of recollection. She could describe what she saw; but such description was almost totally inappropriate to the revelation she claimed to have received. For this revelation touched the very relation of the temporal to the eternal, defined for a devout woman of the Middle Ages in terms of the unfathomable secret of Christ's incarnation. For her, the revelations of divine love to which she laid claim were revelations of the inwardness of Christ's passion. But they were so received as to enable her to realize, in a way at once spiritually profound and intellectually strenuous, what I can only call a new dimension of temporality. One is tempted to say that she wrote as if the future had already happened, indulging in every sort of paradox at once to affirm the reality of time and at the same time to deny its immunity to a certain sort of divine transcending. It is indeed in her attempt to frame through use the concept of this transcending that she makes her contribution to discussion of the metaphysical and theological problems of the status of time. It is a beginning and a beginning only to say that for her it is by seeking to read the secrets of Christ's passion that we may best hope to learn of time's relation to God and God's to time, and through learning what we can of these secrets, to penetrate in part the significance for us of the inexpugnable reality of our temporality.

The sort of experience of which Mother Julian's is an example would seem to be properly called intrusive. That is to say, it breaks in upon what we may call ordinary experience, demanding that for its articulation we take familiar conceptual orders and twist and turn them now in one direction, now in another so that in presenting to ourselves the whole spoken of at the beginning of these remarks we find ourselves involved in a sort of verbal or intellectual dance which while we are engaged in it, teaches us its own rhythm and its own steps, but which when we return to the walking pace of everyday life leaves us baffled concerning the shapes and styles of the steps we have so quickly made our own. Yet love remains, at least, the possibility of that total disinterestedness which is at the same time the complete engagement of ourselves. The greatest moralists have recognized in different ways Plato's wisdom in insisting that the incommunicable vision of the ultimate 'Idea of the Good' is only fulfilled by the return to the 'Cave' of those who have enjoyed it. What is theirs can only be possessed in communication, and communication is within the world of men. We are rightly critical of the unyielding authoritarianism of Plato's political philosophy; but we should not therefore lose sight of the clarity with which he grasped the problems of the relation of the lives of contemplative vision, of critical intellectual activity, and of human action. It was in the communication that the last involves (which we may see as love in a way in which he did not) that the problems of the relations of all three alike are not solved nor even dissolved, but given the context in which their deepest sense is shown. It is through the work of communication that the mystic's inclusive vision is defined, not once for all, but in the stumbling imperfection that demands continual correction, that indeed shows at the level of practice how hardly such frontiers as here conceived are crossed this side of the final horizon of death. Yet to grasp these frontiers for what they are and to let others know a little of what is involved in their passage, at once of the cost and of the glory, is not the least service that authentic mystics offer other men.

So it is too with Mother Julian; for while what she comes to know she is able to speak in a language of haunting simplicity, her attention and the attention of her readers is held fast by what she describes. Yet what she would reveal is not in the detail of her description. But that detail must be mentioned if we are not to forget that the ultimate secret which she dares to uncover had to have and continues to need to have flesh and blood expression. For if by language she reaches beyond the givenness of her visions, that language is still a human instrument and even as the image is inadequate to what it represents, so the language is inadequate to the hope it would convey, and it is only in the final human simplicity of the saint's life (of which her words are of course a part) that the hope she dares confess is effectively affirmed. Yet images and words alike are tools or ladders that human beings must use; for though the object must prevail over the subject, that prevailing must be acknowledged in relation to word and image as well as in the rough of everyday life, which of course provides the setting for the occurrence of the one and the criticism of the other.

NOTE

1   Isaiah VI. (The King was Uzziah.)

DONALD MACKINNON, M.A. (Oxon), D.D. Among Professor MacKinnon's numerous publications the most important are *Christian Faith and Communist Faith* (ed.) (1953); *A Study in Ethical Theory* (1957); *Borderlands of Theology* (1968); *The Stripping of the Altars* (1969); and *The Problem of Metaphysics* (his Gifford Lectures, 1974). He has also written widely in such major journals as *Philosophy, Journal of Theological Studies*, and the *Proceedings of the Aristotelian Society*. After teaching at Edinburgh and Oxford, from 1947 to 1960 he was Regius Professor of Moral Philosophy in the University of Aberdeen. Since 1960 he has been Norris-Hulse Professor of Divinity in the University of Cambridge and Fellow of Corpus Christi College, Cambridge. He has given the Gifford Lectures (1965–6); the Prideaux Lectures at Exeter University (1966); the Riddell Lectures at the University of Newcastle upon Tyne (1970); the D. Owen Evans Lectures at Aberystwyth (1973); and the Drummond Lectures at the University of Stirling (1977). He was president of the Aristotelian Society for 1976–7.

Language and Mystical Awareness

FREDERICK J. STRENG

Mystical awareness is often said to transcend the use of words, language, and thought. This has led to various claims about the non-verbal character of some or all mystical experiences. The concerns of this paper are to examine some basic assumptions about the use of language according to some mystics and philosophers of mysticism, to indicate that mystics interpret the function of language differently so that their understanding of the relation between the content of mystical experience and other human experiences itself will vary, and to show that different assumptions about the function of language contribute to different interpretations of the soteriological significance found in different sorts of mystical awareness. By showing that different mystics assume different functions of language resulting in different kinds of soteriological significance this essay will call into question two assumptions held by some philosophers of mysticism; these are (i) that the nature of ultimate reality assumed in (all) mysticism is an undifferentiated absolute Being, and (ii) that this Being is known through a special intuition that is radically – if not totally – different from everyday knowing.

There are several methodological assumptions which inform the following discussion. One of these is that, together with all the mystics considered here, I assume that there is a 'spiritual realm', ①
an ultimate context of value, or 'suchness' which cannot be totally comprehended by analyses which define it solely in terms of material energy or social functions. A second is that such a spiritual ②
realm is not conceived to be so radically different from conventional life and experiences that physical and social forces – including language – are irrelevant to its perception. Rather, the term 'spiritual realm' is a way of designating a character or dimension of existence that is manifested in some experiences and cultural forms more than others. A third assumption is that the function of this ③
analysis is to gain conceptual clarity about some of the possible relations betwen verbal expression and mystical experience. Whether or not it thereby serves to lay a foundation for spiritual

development in the reader depends on the way the analysis is used.

The term 'mysticism' has been used to refer to a variety of phenomena, including occult experience, trance, a vague sense of unaccountable uneasiness, sudden extraordinary visions and words of divine beings, or aesthetic sensitivity. For our purposes we will narrow the definition to: an interior illumination of reality that results in ultimate freedom. Ninian Smart has correctly distinguished mysticism in this sense from 'the experience of a dynamic external presence'.[1] Some elements found in all mystical awareness include: (i) the apprehension of ultimate reality, (ii) attainment of perfection through mental, emotional, and volitional purification, (iii) an attitude of serenity and total (transcendent) awareness, (iv) a sense of freedom from time–space conditions, and (v) expansion of consciousness and spontaneity through self-discipline. These may be combined with other religious aspects such as specific contemplative techniques; feelings of bliss or joy; ideas of the nature of self, the world, and ultimate reality; and an identification with a universal principle or perfect isolation from all action. The prime foci for specifying the nature of mystical awareness, however, are the elements found in all mystical awareness. This places mysticism in relation to, but distinct from, such religiously powerful experiences as 'creative imagination' which draws a person beyond himself or herself in poetic effulgence, or the personal life and devotion expressed in response to a numinous presence breaking into a decaying world.

Basic to mystic awareness is the claim that attitudinal purification is necessary for right perception. *What* one knows is closely related to *how* one knows. To see beyond the apparent, or superficial, world means a change in the mechanism of apprehension. We will see below that for some mystics this change is described as a radical rejection of all thought and particular conscious experiences; however, we want to point out in this paper that not all mystics define the change in this manner and that we need not assume a radical rejection of all thought in order to recognize that a fundamental change in apprehension takes place. Similarly, to affirm that mystics recognize that attitudes as well as ideas have to be expanded in order for them to be released from false assumptions about the nature of existence does not require a rejection of all logical forms, as suggested by R. Otto in *Mysticism: East and West*.[2] The unifying experience in mystical awareness may be radically different from conventional experience even if one does not appeal to a totally non-rational mode of experience.

A profound philosophical problem arises in the understanding of mysticism from the recognition that total consciousness – or 'total personality', which Plotinus called 'psyche' – is quite different from ego-consciousness or conventional experience. While total consciousness may be seen to have some relation to conventional consciousness, it is sufficiently different, according to the mystics, that it is not seen simply as an extension of the procedure or intensity of conventional experience. It is so different that there is a new consciousness of purpose based on a new threshold of awareness about themselves and the world. A total awareness represents a shift in how to look at oneself and the world so that the everyday contradictions and the anxieties resulting from internal or inner–outer conflicts are resolved. While conventional experience and even false perception is often reconciled within the comprehensiveness of a total consciousness, the richness of the awareness carries the mystic beyond the sense of a change in degree of awareness to the sense of a different kind of awareness.

If 'total awareness' in mystical experience is both significantly different from conventional thought but not – in all cases – regarded as totally unrelated, the question arises as to how one can account for this. The analysis here will attempt to show that one important aspect of this is that within the dynamics of human awareness a shift in the function of language helps to produce a catharsis in thinking and perceiving. The shift from conventional to mystical awareness, then, expresses a new attitude or temperament which is more than, but inclusive of, intellect or ideas. The nature of the total awareness can be defined in terms of its comprehensiveness and its total purity so that whatever is known (God, Brahman, Emptiness) also is known to have these qualities of totality and purity. These qualities are expressed, interpreted and to some degree developed through a use of language that must be aware of both its potential and its limitation. By reviewing the function of language in some Buddhist mystical literature and comparing it with the understanding of language found in some dominant *Budd/* western interpretations we will see how processes of knowledge are *West* closely related to the ontological claims made, especially in regard to the ontological assumptions implicit in the processes of knowing ultimate reality. This approach to understanding mystical awareness is therefore different from one which simply assumes a contrast between the mystical awareness and everyday perception in terms of either a divine revelation in contrast to human (perverted) thought or one which regards the mystical insight in principle to be an imaginative (if psychologically necessary) fantasy which is an epiphenomenon of physical and social forces.

In much discussion of the mystical awareness there is the assumption that the nature of mystical insight is a single type of consciousness; and the effort to understand this type swings to one of two conclusions: either such a consciousness is basically the elimination of form (conventional experience) or is an expression of the creative imagination. We need, rather, to begin with a different hypothesis: there may be a variety of distinct mystical structures of awareness. If we allow this, then there may also be the possibility that one or more of these structures include mental forms with quite different epistemological functions from those mental forms had when used in conventional experience. By focusing on the function of language in mystical awareness the following discussion will draw distinctions between types of mystical awareness which are not found if one simply compares the imagery of mysticism[3] or describes the psychological integration of the personality in mystical experience.[4] An analysis of the relation of language and conceptual awareness to mystical awareness is especially important when the mystical awareness is seen as more than a momentary experience and as a transformation of all subsequent conceptual and perceptual awareness. As we have indicated above, and as has been indicated by several notable scholars,[5] the mystical awareness is free from many conventional conceptual limitations. However, the conceptual framework is not totally suspended in all cases of mysticism. The assumption that the highest mystical awareness is a totally non-conceptual intuition is only one possible understanding of the nature of the mystical apprehension. The sensitivity of oneself and life that is more than 'mere intellectual understanding' may include a mindfulness of an 'empty' object of knowledge.

Through a comparison of the assumptions about the function of language in the Indian Mahayana Buddhist literature called *Perfection of Wisdom* (*Prajñāpāramitā*) with that which claims the mystical awareness generally to be a non-cognitive intuition of undifferentiated Being we hope to show that some of the key assumptions of the latter prevent it from being a comprehensive theoretical scheme for understanding mysticism. The claim that awareness is radically different from conventional experience is a prominent feature of mystical expression; the philosophical problem is how to understand the nature of the shift that occurs. In order to examine this problem we want to consider three interrelated factors: the nature of reality as perceived to be in a subjective apprehension or an objective reality, the correlation of the assumptions about the function of language with ontological assumptions, and the relation between various understandings of ③ mental processes and the kinds of ultimate apprehension depicted in different mystical experiences. These factors already have some exposure in the literature of recent philosophy of religion to which we will first turn.

Subjective and Objective Aspects of the Ineffable Character found in Mystic Experience

Both mystics and philosophers of mysticism commonly distinguish between the extraordinary character of mystical awareness and the conditioned, limited character of conventional apprehension. This distinction has been described in a variety of ways. Mystical awareness is described by terms such as 'total awareness', 'limitless awareness', 'ineffable', 'unique apprehension', 'non-conceptual gnosis', 'highest truth', 'absolute cognition', 'full knowledge', 'perfect insight', 'transcendent knowledge', and 'pure intuition'; it is contrasted with other terms such as 'limited awareness', 'conventional perceptions', 'apparent reality', 'everyday knowledge', 'formulation of positive predicates', and 'knowledge of sense objects'.

The dichotomy between mystical awareness and conventional knowledge is often explained in one of two ways. The first explanation locates the difference in a subjective mode of awareness; the second locates it in the 'objective' reality (Godhead, Brahman, *nirvāṇa*) with which the mystic 'unites' or which he or she 'attains'. With regard to the first alternative C. A. Bennett, for example, in his *A Philosophical Study of Mysticism: an Essay* contrasts the mystics' 'total-working' of consciousness with the 'part-working' of common, analytic awareness.[6] The characteristics of total-working consciousness include: it is synoptic, intuitive, noetic; it confers a knowledge that is inarticulate in conceptual terms but is suggested in a positive way by concepts.[7] Both total-working and part-working are important functions of the mind, but it is a post-analytical intuition which discerns the relation of wholeness to parts in a total-working apprehension; this is mystical intuition.[8] In this context the basic religious problem is the inability of the localized awareness to provide an integrated, and ultimately universal, intuition. Such an intuition takes place when a 'solving idea' dawns upon the perceiver, and the other data known in limited perceptions are reinterpreted in light of a new clue for making connections between the data.[9]

Another philosopher, W. T. Stace, in *Mysticism and Philosophy* also focuses on the mystical experience, and claims: 'The very essence of the experience is that it is undifferentiated, distinctionless, and destitute of all multiplicity.'[10] From a psychological perspective, E. Neumann argues that the encounter of the ego with archetypal mythical figures is an encounter with the unformed numinous within one's personality. For him, the mystical awareness expresses a transformation crisis of the personality in which the ego experiences at its extreme limits non-ego, an 'unconscious totality'. In this encounter, 'the creative numen as the plentitude of an increasingly formed outward and inward world'[11] stimulates the developing consciousness; this numinous transpersonal power forces a change in the person's momentary ego-form. The numinous, thus, takes shape in a unique utterance of the numen as it becomes manifest in the particular personality. Because the numinous reality is here seen as integral to the development of consciousness while being entirely different from the momentary ego-form it is recognized by Neumann to be a creative formless force whose presence results in a state beyond consciousness.

Here we should note that an emphasis on a subjective shift in modes of awareness does not require the affirmation of a separate and special organ or faculty of mystical knowledge. Students of mysticism, such as C. A. Bennett[12] and W. R. Inge[13] have pointed out that despite the declarations of some mystics who appeal to a special (sometimes a God-given) capacity to experience a transcendent insight or a unique 'third eye' of wisdom, this claim may be mistaken.

In contrast, the location of the distinctive character of mystical awareness in the objective reality, the 'Other', or the transcendent reality that overwhelms the individual stresses the disjunction of the true nature of reality and that found in everyday human experiences. (This view sometimes merges with a philosophical judgement about the limitation or perversity of human capacities as such.) Here the emphasis is placed on *what* the mystic perceives, rather than on the subjective modes of perception. For example, W. R. Inge writes that mystics 'are convinced that they are or have been in contact with objective reality, with the supreme spiritual Power behind the world of our surface consciousness'.[14] The activity and experience of contemplation, for him, is ontological.[15] The empirical ego is understood to be radically different from the universal Spirit that all people share with each other. While the inner experience of a person is radically changed in the mystical awareness, it is basically a confirmation that the soul has an affinity with 'the primal source of all reality'. He specifies his concern with a reality other than any found produced in the range of human consciousness when he writes:

> Psychologists have been at work upon these [mystical] experiences, and have brought in their favourite idea, 'the subconscious', or 'subliminal self'. There is a subconscious life, a storehouse of powers, instincts, intuitions, inhibitions, good and bad, which now and then come imperfectly into consciousness. But it seems to me very misleading to confound this with the inmost sanctuary of the soul in which the mystic is convinced that the Holy Spirit has His abode.[16]

Similarly, D. T. Suzuki, in his comparative analysis of Meister Eckhart's mysticism and his own personal interpretation of Zen Buddhism,[17] points out that when a mystic perceives Godhead or 'pure nothingness' as the ultimate condition of all phenomenal objects then the interpretation inevitably turns from psychology to metaphysics. For him eternity and 'absolute emptiness' transcend all relationships while making finitude what it is. There is no continuity between the comprehension of absolute emptiness and the discriminating mind in relative experience; we can know the former only by 'leaping or plunging into the silent valley of Absolute Emptiness'.[18]

The experience of a wholly-other ultimate reality as the deepest level of human sensitivity has led to a paradoxical notion. This is the mystics' claim that ultimate reality is different from common human thoughts and perceptions and yet is an expression of one's inmost self. The need to stop the conventional efforts and imaginings is seen, for example, in *Dialogues of the Supersensual Life* of Jacob Boehme, where the spiritual master tells his disciple:

> Blessed art thou ... if thou canst stand still from self-thinking and self-willing, and canst stop the wheel of thy imagination and senses; forasmuch as hereby thou mayest arrive at length to see the great Salvation of God, being made capable of all manner of divine sensations and heavenly communications. Since it is naught indeed but thine own hearing and willing that do hinder thee, so that thou dost not see and hear God.[19]

Here the individual is advised to refrain from one's own common thinking and willing in order to allow God's will and 'communication' to be known. In the Buddhist literature called *The Perfection of Wisdom* (*Prajñāramitā*) we also find the concern to stop conventional thought, or the attempt to grasp the reality termed 'Buddhahood' or 'Tathagatahood' with a concept. The Buddha says to his disciple Subhuti:

> Why is [perfect insight] an unthinkable enterprise? Because unthinkable are Tathagatahood, Buddhahood, Self-existence, and the state of all-knowledge. And on these one cannot reflect with one's thought, since they cannot be an object of thought, or of volition, or of any of the dharmas which constitute thought.[20]

It is important to note here that the nature of the restraint is different in the light of different assumptions about the nature of ultimate reality. For Boehme – as H. H. Brinton points out in *The Mystic Will*[21] – it is the unsearchable will of God which is the infinite reality in distinction to the individual person's will, which is a counter-will and must be subjugated to the Divine will. Only by returning to the eternal will that was before personal willing are human beings able to live in the Divine will.[22] For the spiritual practitioners of the Perfection of Wisdom discipline there is simply a desisting from grasping on to a concept of Buddhahood as if it were an object of knowledge; the goal is the release from a personal identification with one's socio-physical-personality-desires. There is no expectation of another universal will or divine force taking over. There is not even the engagement with unconscious numinous totality that is the non-ego, and which is a creative force for the development of the personality, as E. Neumann understood the numinous forces in mystical awareness.

The other side of the paradox in mysticism is that there is already an identity or union with the ultimate ineffable reality. In the mystical awareness one realizes one's own true nature, or the 'thusness' of life. Rufus Jones has pointed out that the essence of mysticism is the soul's communion with God. He explains that in the mystical experience 'one finds himself in direct relationship with the Over-World of reality of the same nature as his own inmost self and with which he feels akin'.[23] Similarly, Evelyn Underhill in discussing the characteristics of mysticism makes the following summary statement:

> Mysticism, in its pure form, is the science of ultimates, the science of union with the Absolute, and nothing else, and ... the mystic is the person who attains to this union, not the person who talks about it. Not to *know about*, but to *Be*, is the mark of the real initiate.[24]

The unification or the union of the individual with ultimate reality is especially important in our discussion because it highlights the mystics' common claim that the mystic awareness transcends conventional knowing in which the distinction between subject and object is of considerable importance. The knowledge of God (Brahman, Thusness) in the mystical insight is not simply subjective or objective since to know in the ultimate context is to 'become' or 'be' in an extraordinary way. M. Smith expresses this character of mystical awareness when she writes:

> The final stage of the Way is the Unitive Life, in which the soul passes from Becoming to Being, man beholds God face to face, and is joined to Him in a progressive union, a union which is a fact of experience consciously realized.[25]

Rudolf Otto, in his comparative study of Meister Eckhart and Shankara, quotes Eckhart and affirms that Shankara could also have agreed to this formulation:

> For in ... breaking through [all limitations] I perceive what God and I are *in common*. There I am what I was. There I neither increase nor decrease. For there I am the immovable (*achala*), which moves all things. Here man has won again what he *is* eternally (what he is *in principio, agre*) and ever shall be. Here God is received into the soul.[26]

Because there is a sense that the mystic's life is transformed in the mystical awareness by perceiving what one has been, is, and will be, such an awareness is regarded by the mystics as self-authenticating. There is no appeal to a further authority: logical, aesthetic, or empirical. On the one hand it is a profoundly personal, subjective perception, but since its character is said to participate in the very nature of 'thusness' the mystic cannot regard it as a private or merely subjective experience. W. T. Stace has seen this in his discussion of the question of 'objective reference' in mystical awareness.[27] Mystical experience, he says, is not objective in any simple sense, but it is trans-subjective. Whether he has proved this on the basis of his concern with orderly and disorderly experience is not an issue that can be considered here; below we will attempt to deal with the problem of the interaction of the subjective and objective aspects of different kinds of mystical awareness. It will be an alternative effort to deal with this question by focusing on the mental contribution to the formation of the 'objective' world.

*Descriptive and Transformative Functions
of Language in Mystical Awareness*

The philosophical and psychological discussions of the relation of
subjectivity and objectivity in mystical awareness as described
above have an assumption about the use of symbols; this is that the
function of symbols and concepts is descriptive. They assume that
the purpose for saying something is to describe either a subjective
state or an objective event. Thus, the reality of the mystical awareness is seen to be located in either or both of the (assumed) subjective
or objective realms of experience. This, I believe, gives a different
focus to the claims of some of the mystics themselves that the
perceptions, the will, and the thoughts have to be 'pure'; and that
such purity *transforms* the personality to its farthest reaches – to the
point that it perceives itself as new (reborn). The assertions of these
mystics are not focused on the locality of the mystic reality, but on
which conditions or practices allow a person's perceptions, will,
and thought to be pure; the concern is to free one from the limitations and deceptions imposed on the discriminating and binding
mechanisms of conventional reflections on one's ultimate nature.
The key function of such claims is to release the individual from
attachment to the assumption that words have a one-to-one correlation with separate entities in either ideal or physical experience.

The proposal here is that there is not only one function within
mystical claims, but a sliding scale of functions moving between
two interrelated poles: the descriptive function and the transformative function. The descriptive function applies predominantly
either to the conventional logical analyses and empirical percepts of
common experience or, at the other extreme, to the intuition of the
'wholly other'. The transformative function is found predominantly
in a person's perceptions, actions, and evaluations which are extended most comprehensively towards a totality. Where the transformative function is emphasized, claims derived from mystical
awareness are not completely without descriptive value; however,
the function of these assertions is not primarily descriptive. It is
evocative; the claims serve as a catalyst for release. Thus, the descriptive and transformative functions are not mutually exclusive;
both can be found to some degree in the same expression. The
labelling of a mystical expression as having either predominantly a
descriptive or transformative function indicates a relative, not an
exclusive, characteristic.

If one assumes that mystical claims are basically descriptive, one
tends to locate the assumed reality referred to by the mystics in one

of two places, the subject or object – as we saw before. This has led to a logical paradox of the sort arrived at by W. T. Stace in *Mysticism and Philosophy*. By examining his statement in relation to the understanding of a spiritual adherent in the *bodhisattva* path who tries to avoid 'abiding in' either objectivity or subjectivity, we will hopefully show how allowing for a transforming function of language in some mystics' claims both extends the conception of the possible content of mystical awareness, and provides an alternative understanding of the nature of these mystical claims.

In Chapter 6 of *Mysticism and Philosophy*[28] Stace describes the most prominent theories of mystical language. Among others he mentions two types of theories that regard mystical language as symbolical. One of these is the 'Dionysian theory'. Here language expresses attributes of the manifestation of God; these attributes are predicates that apply to the finite world which is God's manifestation. They do not apply to God directly because of God's absolute ineffability.[29] Thus, the function of words is to describe what can be known of God, but as a matter of fact they can only refer to the result of God's causal power. This theory of symbolic theory is criticized by Stace, however, because a person would not have even been aware that one was limited in thought without already having gone beyond that limit in order to make the judgement. Stace concludes:

> If the mystical consciousness were absolutely ineffable, then we would not say so because we should be unconscious of such an experience; or in other words, we should never have had such an experience.[30]

In this analysis we see that the only expectation regarding the function of language is to describe either God, which according to this theory it cannot do, or describe a transcendent experience – which, says Stace, it fails to do.

The second symbolic theory which Stace discusses is the 'metaphorical theory' – which has much the same understanding of symbol that Christian philosophically-oriented theologians have called *analogia entis*. Here the relation of the symbol to God is one of resemblance, not cause. The religious person can perceive a resemblance between God and some non-divine form, event, or relation in the world. This is the theory that R. Otto used to explain the relation of human thought to the *mysterium tremendum* in *The Idea of the Holy*.[31] This theory, too, is not a solution – claims Stace – because, while it claims to express the ineffable mystical experience through a concept that resembles it, the predication of the ineffable experience with a concept is to give a conceptualization of what cannot, by definition, be conceptualized. Secondly, something expressed in a metaphor must in principle also be indicated in a literal sense. Stace explains:

> The user of the metaphor, or whoever is to understand it, must already know what it is meant to symbolize. The metaphor can only operate to bring before his mind what he already knows or has experienced. It cannot produce a knowledge or experience which he did not have before.[32]

Here again we see that the assumed function of religious language is to describe either 'the unconceptualizable essence of God' or 'the mystical experience'.

Stace proposes a way of understanding the function of language that describes the mystical experience by distinguishing between what is conceptualized during the mystical experience and the remembered experience. We must keep in mind also that the content of the mystical experience is a trans-subjective Universal Self. He says:

> Mystical experience, *during* the experience, is wholly unconceptualizable and therefore wholly unspeakable. This *must* be so. You cannot have a concept of anything *within* the undifferentiated unity because there are no separate items to be conceptualized. Concepts are only possible where there is a multiplicity or at least a duality. . . . But afterwards when the experience is remembered the matter is quite different. For we are then in our ordinary sensory-intellectual consciousness. . . . Since we now have concepts, we can use words. We can *speak* of an experience as 'undifferentiated', as 'unity', as 'mystical', as 'empty', as 'void', and so on.[33]

If the mystical language is only the remembered mystical experience, and if all language of an ineffable experience refers to a unitary consciousness that can be described literally, then mystical language must be common language that classifies mental experience into 'sensuous and nonsensuous and assigns mystical experience to the latter class'.[34] The common mystical concepts of 'darkness' and 'silence', or the notion 'undifferentiated unity' then are not metaphors for something else. They are 'literal descriptions'. Stace argues as follows:

One empties the mind of all sensations, images, and thoughts – of all particular empirical contents. What is left is an emptiness. It is true that according to the mystics this emptiness, which is darkness, is also the shining forth of a great light. It is not merely the vacuum; it is the vacuum-plenum. But the undifferentiated unity is a description of the negative side, the vacuum. Since the multiplicity of particulars has been obliterated, it is a unity. And since there are no distinctions of one particular from another, it is undifferentiated. Plainly this is a literally correct description – if of course one believes that such a state of mind is ever reached, which is not now the question at issue.[35]

Here we see that for W. T. Stace the function of the language of mystics is to describe their mystical experience literally. This leads, however, to the difficulty that if this is a description of a mystic's mental state or of several mystics' extraordinary experiences there is no warrant for him to conclude that there is a universal cosmic self, as he asserted earlier in the book[36] unless he has personally experienced self-transcendence. By assuming the distinction between subjectivity and objectivity and trying to locate the mystical reality in one or the other realm on the basis of a descriptive function of mystical language, Stace has undercut his analysis of the trans-subjective reality affirmed by many mystics.

An alternative way to understand the function of language, when mystics make claims about the world or their experience, is to analyse their effort either to reinforce or to avoid the attachment to terms, common assumptions about the descriptive function of concepts, or habitual expectations regarding the attributes of a class of things. We will try to verify the hypothesis that the function of some mystical expressions is to evoke the knowledge of *how* to live freely rather than simply to give descriptive knowledge *that* the world is such and so. In the context of language usage, the central concern is to become aware that conceptual formation has uncon-scious control of one's perceptions of reality until the forces of concept-formation are brought to consciousness and then placed in the perspective of their usefulness to achieve spiritual freedom. If we accept the mystics' claim that the ultimate reality known in mystical awareness applies to both what is experienced in conven-tional life as 'subjective' and 'objective' reality, we must conclude that a major goal is not to describe literally some event or form assumed to be either in the mind or external to the mind; rather it is to indicate that the mystical language functions to recondition the expectations about the subjective factors in one's experience. While both functions are often evident in the same mystic or the same body of literature, we will contrast the expressions of these two functions to highlight the differences.

The remainder of this section will be an examination of some passages from the Indian Mahāyāna Buddhist literature, in particular a few from *The Perfection of Wisdom in Eight Thousand Lines* (*Aṣṭasāhasrikā Prajñāpāramitā*), abbreviated as *Ashta*. The analysis intends to show that the use of such apparently descriptive terms as 'Buddhahood', 'Tathagata' (the one who has 'thus-gone', attained enlightenment, a Buddha), 'Emptiness', and 'all-knowledge' do not primarily function to describe an assumed subjective state or objective entity; rather these terms are often used to evoke insight into the conditions of experience which (when combined with meditation and moral action) will free a person from attachments to conventional fears and false expectations. As we pointed out before in the *Ashta*'s claim that conventional thought is inadequate to comprehend 'all-knowledge', words and concepts are often misleading when one wants to communicate ultimate truth. However, words are regarded as useful to effect a spiritual change as long as they and the unconsciousness mechanisms of concept-formation do not themselves bind a person to fears and false expectations.

In the *Ashta* the state of all-knowledge is said to be unthinkable (*acintya*).[37] This, however, does not mean that all words are equally false, or that words, in principle or because of some essential inherent quality, are evil. Words, we read, can be useful to guide a person in the 'perfection of wisdom'. One *bodhisattva* should help another. He would 'explain this perfection of wisdom to him . . . make him rejoice in it, would, by his words, lead him to it, educate him in it, illuminate its benefits to him, cleanse his thought and remove his doubt'.[38] In this passage we note three functions of words: (i) to explain, (ii) to evoke a feeling of joy, and (iii) cleanse thought. Explanation is a very important part of the exposition in the *Ashta* itself and includes literal description even of aspects of the state of all-knowledge, for example when Subhuti – a disciple and spokesman for true understanding of perfection of wisdom – says:

A Bodhisattva who courses in perfect wisdom and develops it, should not stand in form, etc. Because, when he stands in form, etc., he courses in its formative influence, and not in perfect wisdom. For, while he courses in formative influence, he cannot gain perfect wisdom, nor exert himself upon it, nor fulfil it. When he does not fulfil perfect wisdom, he cannot go forth to all-knowledge, so long as he remains one who tries to appropriate the essentially elusive. For in perfect wisdom form is not appropriated. But the non-appropriation of form, etc., is not form, etc. And perfect wisdom also cannot be appropriated . . . The state of all-knowledge itself cannot be taken hold of, because it cannot be seized through a sign.[39]

When Subhuti claims that a *bodhisattva* who 'courses in formative influence . . . cannot gain perfect wisdom', I understand that to be a literal statement. The author of the *Ashta* wishes to give the reader (and probably listener originally) a piece of direct information. Likewise a phrase like 'perfect wisdom also cannot be appropriated' or 'the state of all-knowledge itself cannot be taken hold of' are literal statements that indicate that 'perfect wisdom' and 'all-knowledge' are terms which are misunderstood if they are perceived as indicators of objects of conventional perception or one of a series of mental classes. The passage describes a process of thought and a type of mental comprehension that a religious adept should avoid.

The second function of evoking an act of rejoicing becomes important for the process of attaining full enlightenment when it is seen in relation to the act of rejoicing not only in one's own perfection of wisdom but in the attainment of enlightenment by others. Chapter 6 of the *Ashta* explains that rejoicing in the merit of others is itself an unequalled meritorious act. Again, Subhuti explains:

[In his meditation the Bodhisattva] piles up the roots of good of all those, all that quantity of merit without exception or remainder, rolls it into one lump, weighs it, and rejoices over it with the most excellent and sublime jubilation, the highest and utmost jubilation, with none above it, unequalled, equalling the unequalled. Having thus rejoiced, he utters the remark: 'I turn over into full enlightenment the meritorious work founded on jubilation. May it feed the full enlightenment [of myself and of beings]!'[40]

We might ask here whether or not this apparent description of the relation between meritorious work, jubilation, and full enlightenment can be taken literally. According to Subhuti in subsequent paragraphs, it cannot. To do so would be to treat these terms as 'objective supports', as 'signs' of some essential qualities or entities. He warns:

> The thought by which one has rejoiced and turned over, or dedicated that [wholesome root connected with jubilation] – that thought of [rejoicing] is [at the time of turning over] extinct, stopped, departed, reversed. Therefore, what is that thought by which one turns over to full enlightenment? Or what is that thought which turns over into full enlightenment the meritorious work founded on jubilation? . . . Nor is it possible to turn over [or to overturn, to transform] that thought as far as its own being is concerned.[41]

This negation of the previous description of the function of jubilation in the attainment of full enlightenment indicates, I think, that the earlier description cannot be taken as a literal description. Rather the process of the dialogue is important as a way to shift the expectations of the reader. The rejoicing itself, like the description, cannot be taken to refer to feelings or to perceptions as such. The feelings and descriptions must be purified. This is the third function that words can have according to the earlier quote from the *Ashta*. Words can easily bring about perverted views. This is such a common affirmation in the Buddhist tradition that some Buddhist interpreters have suggested that all words, or all form, should be eliminated in full enlightenment.[42] This is also a common understanding among interpreters of mystical experience, who emphasize a non-cognitive intuition which rejects all form as the ultimate mystic awareness. In the *Ashta*, however, is the view that the highest awareness cannot be identified with either a dependence on words to describe reality accurately as if there were a one-to-one relation between them, or a total rejection of all form. Regarding the first alternative, the celestial *bodhisattva* Maitreya explains how to avoid perverted views that assume a one-to-one correlation between thoughts and referential entities that have preserved self-existent qualities or existence independent of the thoughts:

> The Bodhisattva must not, as a result of the thought by which he turns that [meritorious work] over, become one who perceives a thought. It is thus that the meritorious work founded on jubilation becomes something which is turned over into full enlightenment. If he does not perceive that thought [identifying it] as 'this is that thought', then a Bodhisattva has no perverted perception, thought or view. But if he perceives the thought by which he

turns that over, [identifying it] as 'this is that thought', then he becomes one who perceives thought. As a result he has a perverted perception, thought and view.[43]

Likewise, the opposite interpretation of eliminating all perception, and thought, i.e. all form, is also rejected. The Buddha is recorded as saying:

In the future there will be some monks whose bodies are undeveloped, whose moral conduct, thought and wisdom are undeveloped, who are stupid, dumb like sheep, without wisdom. Then they announce that they will expound the perfection of wisdom, they will actually expound its counterfeit. They will expound the counterfeit perfection of wisdom by teaching that the impermanence of form, etc., is to be interpreted as the destruction of form, etc. To strive for that insight, that, according to them, will be the coursing in the perfection of wisdom. But on the contrary, one should not view the impermanence of form, etc., as the destruction of form, etc.[44]

One important function of words, then, is to purify the use of language. Such a goal is important for the attainment of enlightenment according to the *Ashta*. One result of avoiding a simple correlation between words and enlightenment is that the only function cannot be regarded as a description of something either in the mind or in an objective ultimate reality that is known through a special faculty which eliminates all form. In the next section we will examine other aspects of the purification function of language in the *Ashta*.

Language and the Knowability of Ultimate Reality

One of the dominant characteristics of mystical awareness is the claim that the mystic knows ultimate reality or 'the way things are'. How are we to understand the spiritual knowledge as itself a conditioning process? Is this knowledge related to conventional knowledge, or is it completely different? The concern of this section is to indicate how the models of human experience, and especially the assumptions about language, contribute to the nature of ultimate reality communicated by different mystics. The discussion recognizes from the beginning that many mystics regard all verbal expression to be unsatisfactory for either accurate description of the reality or for the only form of cultivation of the mystical insight within a person. Nevertheless, all people who communicate something about mystical awareness use words – along with other expressions, such as a Zen master's shout or blow with a stick – and that different mystics and philosophers of mysticism evaluate the usefulness of language differently because they expect different things from it.

Where the highest mystical awareness is seen as a retreat into an undifferentiated Being – as described above by Underhill, Otto, Smith, and Stace – there is an emphasis on the non-cognitive intuition. The reality of the mystical awareness, then, is seen to reside in a wholly transcendent reality or in an undifferentiated intuition that is radically different from other ways of knowing. Underhill summarizes the nature of the 'true mysticism' in the following words:

> Its aims are wholly transcendental and spiritual. It is in no way concerned with adding to, exploring, re-arranging, or improving anything in the visible universe. The mystic brushes aside that universe, even in its supernormal manifestation . . .
> [Mysticism] is the name of that organic process which involves the perfect consummation of the Love of God: the achievement here and now of the immortal heritage of man. Or, if you like it better – for this means exactly the same thing – it is the art of establishing his conscious relation with the Absolute.[45]

The nature of ultimate reality is 'wholly transcendental', being available to the mystic in the 'unitive state'. The assumption about the nature of reality is that it is an ineffable reality that is eternal and unknowable with the mind. Underhill notes the necessity as well as the inability of the human mind to formulate descriptions through symbols:

> The mind must employ some device . . . if its transcendental perceptions – wholly unrelated as they are to the phenomena with which intellect is able to deal – are ever to be grasped by the surface consciousness.[46]

Similarly, Rudolf Otto describes the nature of Being as expressed in both Eckhart and Shankara; because God's being is totally different from being-in-the-world, human conceptions are inadequate to specify what God is:

> As pure Being (*esse*) God is completely 'fashionless', without 'How' or mode of being, neither this nor that, neither thus nor otherwise, just as Brahman is pure Being, is 'nirgunam' and 'neti,

neti', absolutely 'One'. Therefore it is already as *esse purum* and *simplex* above all conceptions and conceptual differentiations, and so beyond all comprehending and apprehending (*akaran-agocharam, avāgmanogocharam*). For our comprehension is bound up with distinctions, with *genus* and *differentia specifica*.[47]

Godhead can only be known without thought, because all human thought is classified as the sort of thing that by definition cannot perceive pure Being. In both Otto and Underhill – as also we saw before in Stace – is the basic assumption that mystical awareness is a knowledge *that* something is or is not the case. At the same time these scholars recognize that there is something radically different in the mystical awareness by comparison to conventional knowing. That difference is accounted for by Underhill and Otto by identifying the object of the knowledge as something radically different from the objects of distinctions in conventional awareness; and in order to know such a reality (God, pure Being) requires a different sort of awareness. This sort of awareness must be of a different class of knowledge by comparison to conventional knowledge because the different order of being that is assumed requires it. Stace, on the other hand, accounted for the difference by claiming that the mental experience of the mystic is radically different from conventional states of mind.

Where the knowability of ultimate reality is seen to reside predominantly in a non-cognitive mode of apprehension, which then by definition either is totally beyond any conceptualization or is a description only of a personal experience, the effort to relate the supernatural intuition (or extraordinary experience) to common experience is perceived to be part of a class of mental activities called 'common experience'. The attempt to conceptualize and articulate the mystical awareness results in paradoxes because two irreconcilable notions are juxtaposed: an undifferentiated whole and differentiated concepts and images interrelated through classificatory schemes and a principle of non-contradiction. It is important to note that the procedure for understanding the relation between the two classes of knowing (i.e. of pure Being and of conventional discrimination) where non-cognitive intuition is seen as the only process for knowing the pure Being requires two logical steps. One is the principle of non-contradiction. The knowledge of pure Being is different from the kind of knowledge used in conventional discrimination; this means that an expression of knowledge cannot at the same time in comparable conditions be both knowledge of pure Being and conventional knowledge. The second step is the assumption of the principle of the excluded middle, which applied here would mean a necessary choice of either the knowledge of pure Being or conventional knowledge as a mechanism for knowing. It entails the necessary affirmation of a double negation, such that the negation of non-conventional knowledge implies the knowledge of pure Being – and vice versa. Thus if the knowledge of pure Being is knowledge of any sort it must be knowledge that is wholly non-conventional.

As we have suggested before in looking at some of the material from the *Ashta*, not all mystical language functions predominantly to describe something which is either a subjective or objective reality. The attainment of all-knowledge is not participation in pure Being nor simply an experience of an undifferentiated whole. There is a different assumption about the role of language which I think can be correlated with the Buddhist ontological notion of 'dependent co-origination'. It expresses the Buddhist claim that the world we live in arises from temporary conditions and causes which people experience as 'subjective' and 'objective'. The world is neither the created realm of God, nor the composite emanation of a primordial, universal First Cause. All sentient beings (also in non-material realms of existence) help to cause the arising of the world as we know it. All particular forms in our world, whether physical, psychological, or mental, arise because of both objective conditions and subjective conditioning. Our knowledge of the world itself conditions the arising of the world as we experience it.[48]

The significance of this view of the ever-arising-and-dissipating world for our discussion is that it would give a theoretical basis for the claim made in the last section that the primary function of even the statements that describe what is happening in the world is to recondition the thinking–feeling mechanism of the readers of the *Ashta*, that is to purify their thinking. In contrast to the types of mysticism that espouse an extraordinary intuition of an undifferentiated whole or of an interpretation of the function of mystical language that sees it as primarily descriptive of either a subjective or objective reality, the use of mystical language in the *Ashta* suggests that words can function either to bind a person to, or release a person from, the world that one is helping to construct. While all-knowledge is depicted in the *Ashta* as 'unthinkable' this is because 'all-knowledge' is not something-in-itself; in the words of the *Ashta*: 'the very all-knowledge does not possess the own-being of all-knowledge'.[49]

Rather than 'pure Being', the true nature of things according to the mystical insight advocated in the *Ashta* is 'emptiness' or 'suchness'. Chapter 26 of the *Ashta* expresses the suchness of the Tathagata as follows:

> Born after the image of that Suchness is Subhuti the Elder; hence born after the image of the Tathagata. But that Suchness is also no Suchness, and after the image of that Suchness has he been born . . . And just as the Suchness of the Tathagata, which is immutable and undifferentiated, is nowhere obstructed, so also the Suchness of all dharmas, which is also immutable and undifferentiated. For the Suchness of the Tathagata, and the Suchness of all dharmas, they are both one single Suchness, not two, not divided. A non-dual Suchness, however, is nowhere, is from nowhere, belongs to nowhere. It is because it is a Suchness which belongs nowhere that it is non-dual.[50]

The suchness of oneself and all life is known through being non-attached to form without seeking the elimination of all form. The *bodhisattva* path – the spiritual process portrayed in the *Ashta* – requires the spiritual adept to perfect wisdom while also using skill in means to avoid the destruction of all forms. One must participate in forms, in signs, without being caught in them. The concern to attain 'full knowledge' without either destroying or being attached to forms is exposed by the celestial *bodhisattva* Maitreya when he says:

> [A bodhisattva] does not bring to mind nor turn over [that wholesome root] to full enlightenment if he brings about a sign by reflecting that what is past is extinct, stopped, departed, reversed; that what is future has not yet arrived; and that of the present no stability is got at, and that that which is not got at has no sign or range. On the other hand he also does not turn over to full enlightenment if he fails to bring about a sign or to bring to mind as a result of sheer inattentiveness, if he fails to attend as a result of lack of mindfulness, or of lack of understanding. But that wholesome root becomes something which has been turned over into full enlightenment on condition that he brings to mind that sign, but does not treat it as a sign. It is thus that the Bodhisattva should train himself therein. This should be known as his skill in means. When, through that skill in means, he turns over a wholesome root, then he is near to all-knowledge.[51]

The insight into all things is a knowledge of things as they are, not as they are artifically produced in illusion and attachment. To know things as they are is not to know an undifferentiated ground or source of all things as set over against particular forms. Rather it is to be freed from 'clinging'. Both 'the state of all-knowledge' (or Tathagatahood, Buddhahood) and the constituents or properties of experienced things (*dharmas*, *skandhas*) are without self-existent 'being' and thus incomparable, immeasurable, and unthinkable.[52] To be free one must not 'settle down' in form by grasping it; one must not even try to 'grasp' or settle down in all-knowledge by discriminating between form and a form-less reality.

Different Mystical Epistemologies and their Soteriological Expectations

In light of the foregoing analysis it is evident that there are various assumptions by mystics and philosophers of mysticism regarding the nature of the reality perceived in mystical awareness, and that these differences relate to differences in judgement about the role and functions of particular form – language, words, and perceptions. In this section we want to examine the relation between a mystical epistemology and its soteriological expectation. Where the mystical epistemology assumes an undifferentiated absolute as the ultimate reality and where words function primarily as descriptions of something radically (if not totally) different from that found in common experience, the soteriological expectation is that all particular forms lose their significance in a sea of undifferentiated bliss. The mystical epistemology will be different where a mystic assumes a transcendent awareness in which the reality is not undifferentiated being-itself but a dynamic process of neither being nor nonbeing. In this context words do not function primarily as descriptions of something, but as a catalyst to free the mystic from a mental–emotional attachment to either being or non-being. The soteriological significance will be to cultivate an awareness of the emptiness of both form and non-form in which one is neither attached to, nor fearful of, either. Both of these soteriological expectations are significant variations of the general mystical goal which is to transform a person's consciousness so that one may perceive fully the reality that is the basis for all existence. Such a transformation is regarded as a self-evident value that brings with it joy, peace, and harmony with all existence.

The deepest significance of the mystical transformation is that it is not only a psychological or epistemological shift, but an ontological shift. When one is united with the very Being of life, or when one attains the suchness of all things, a person purifies one's perception, will, and intention to the point that the religious community recognizes a new person. However, a person is not just a different expression of the many conventional ego-bound individuals when the insight into the truth of life dawns; one is now integrated with the ultimate reality in such a way that the ego-oriented will is dissolved; the result has been called 'submitting to God's will', or it is recognized in human actions that are effortless and spontaneous. The limits of the old personality, but more particularly the old approach to identifying and expressing oneself, are transcended. The former centre of experience and evaluation in one's personality has been enlarged. The way in which this process is understood, however, can be quite different in various mystic paths. Nevertheless, in none of these is transformation seen as just one interpretation of life among others. It is seen as non-limiting and self-authenticating. One reason why it is perceived in this way is that it is characterized by the experience of extraordinary power, a concentration of spiritual (psychic) energy, that gives one access to uncommon effort and awareness. It is in this context of such a comprehensive transformation in how one knows the nature of one's being that we will discuss the different functions of language in mystic epistemologies.

How does one know the totality of everything, that 'suchness' which is not bound by conceptual formation? The answers to this depend in part on an assumption about human participation in the creation or formation of existence. One must ask what is assumed about a person's contribution to the problematic character of life as it is commonly experienced. If the basic problematic is the separation of the self from God, of ego-centred satisfaction in distinction to the divine will, then the dissolution of personal wishes is important for life in God. Likewise, if the knowledge of God is by definition opposite to that which is personally or culturally formulated by human beings, then any cultural formulation must be eliminated for a different order of knowledge. This order of knowledge, as we indicated in the third section of the paper, will still emphasize the descriptive function of words based on the assumption that there is an eternal objective referent to words which, indeed, cannot adequately communicate the ineffable subjective experience or express Being itself. If, on the other hand, the basic problematic is the insensitivity to the reality ('suchness') of existence – an insensitivity due to illusory fabrication of expectations and perceptions – then the ego-centred satisfactions and limited perceptions are so many faulty analogies of something other than concrete forms, but faulty mechanisms of consciousness which keep one bound to the illusory fabrications. The knowledge of suchness is a transformation of the use of both form and the formless, not the elimination of the form for an absorption into the formless. The knowledge of 'non-duality' as expressed in the *Ashta*, for example, is not a knowledge of 'non-duality' as distinct from 'duality', but a release from the attachment to such a distinction. It is a knowledge that is a nondualistically-oriented analytical knowledge into the empty nature of things whether perceived, felt, or imagined.

The self-authenticating awareness is a de-conditioning or a reconditioning of a person's consciousness about oneself and the world. Processes of conceptualization contribute to one's perception of life.[53] Where a shift in consciousness opens access to the expression of the nature of existence, there the shift has ontological importance for the mystic. Either through union or identity with reality, the mystic's insight is not only a new perception of truth, but a self-purification that exposes the ultimate reality more perfectly. In the negation of the forms in the mystic intuition of Eckhart and Shankara as described by Otto, the intuition is ultimately an expression of Being-itself in which any differentiation is an expression of non-being. No designation of being or non-being is appropriate to Being-itself, but the *via negativa* is itself predicated on the reality of Being-itself. The nature of the mystic transformation is that the participant sees the particular entities of conventional consciousness as having more than relative value because their true nature is an unchanging universal whole. Concepts and analytic mental activity are then to be discarded for a different and more perfect mode of knowledge: intuition. In the *Ashta*, also, the ultimate reality is not to be identified with conventional construction of experience. However, the denial of the conventional constructions as expressive of self-existent reality does not require the affirmation of a self-existent reality in the ultimate reality (suchness). In contrast to the logical assumption of noncognitive intuition of the wholly other, the law of the excluded middle is not combined with the principle of non-contradiction. One is not required to affirm an absolute independent reality in the formless aspect of existence just because it is negated in the formed aspect. The dialectic awareness espoused in the *Ashta* is the continuing process of unattached 'emptying' of the content of every absolute term: existence or non-existence, being or non-being. In actualizing the infinite dynamic of 'Emptiness' the *bodhisattva* embodies the truth.[54] Concepts and analysis of thought can, in this context, be either binding or freeing depending on the structure of apprehension that is used.

The soteriological significance of language, then, is related to the function of language in communicating the nature of reality that is assumed in the mystical awareness. Where language is seen to refer to some indeterminate Being-itself, some subjective transcendent intuition, or both, it will have primarily a negative descriptive role. It may serve a descriptive function as providing an analogy of a radically different 'Other'; however, if the 'otherness' is stressed, its primary role is to indicate the uselessness of language. It may also have an evocative function as far as the consciousness is concerned in that the perception of knowledge will be extended beyond conceptual and empirical knowledge. While another mode of knowledge arising from an emanation of Being-itself, or revelation from God, is seen to be a necessary aspect of this mystical awareness, the use of language as a limited analogous description and a purgative can play a preliminary role in the mystical awareness.

On the other hand, in a type of mystical awareness that rejects a religious apprehension that requires an eternal transcendent reality in itself, but affirms an unattached, spontaneous awareness of the present in particular forms as an attitude of highest freedom, language serves centrally to evoke a sense of non-attachment to the very forms that give expression to freedom. Here, too, there is a negation of conceptual predicates where they are assumed to expose a self-existent entity. However, because language is not assumed to be primarily descriptive of something more real, the function of language is primarily to act as a catalyst to avoid 'establishing' (hypostatizing) or 'giving a basis for' any conception, perception, or feeling. In the context of the *Ashta*, as we pointed out before, 'all-knowledge' is not the elimination of all form, though it is the negation of conventional, attached ('impure') thought. It is a 'pure' (non-dualistic) cognitive state which does not treat concepts (predicates, 'signs') in the manner in which they are conventionally treated when most people speak of ultimate reality, i.e. as if they referred to things-in-themselves. Their primary religious function is not to refer to something – though at a conventional level of awareness they do that. Their primary religious function is to help people avoid the mistakes they made as a result of mental–emotional habits and the discriminating mechanism usually accompanying the use of words. While the means of knowledge in this mystical awareness also includes trance or contemplative mental quietness, and is recognized to be a 'purified' form of cognition, it is one that through purification of thought uses thought. The goal is not to know something else, even something else 'wholly other', but to be free.

In summary, then, we find that mystical awareness involves a recognition that this awareness is radically different from conventional knowledge though even conventional knowledge rightly understood exists as a result of the ultimate reality known in the mystical experience. The attempt to analyse the nature of mystical awareness (along with the reality of what it is aware) in terms of the descriptive function of language (concepts) has led to the attempts to locate the basic perceived reality either in a personal subjective experience or in a transcendent reality. Because this goes contrary to the claim of the unitive character of the mystical awareness between the experiencer and what is experienced, philosophers of mysticism are pressed to find a more adequate solution. Part of the problem in the location of the reality of mystical awareness in either the subject or in objective reality, we suggest, has come from the emphasis on the descriptive function of the concepts and symbols used in communicating the mystical awareness. Another function of language found in mystical language is just as important. It is to evoke a change in the attitudes and mechanisms of apprehension within the mystic adept, as exemplified in some of the mystical expression of Indian Mahāyāna Buddhist literature. By comparing the assumptions about the dominant function of language in two different structures of mystical apprehension we can see how the assumptions correlate with different views of the relation between ultimate reality and conventional existence. The ontological differences expressed in different mystical awareness become significant in light of the differences in the soteriological expectations that are described or evoked through the assumptions about the use of language. While all mystical expression seeks to get beyond the conventional use of concepts or everyday perceptions, the language used to express this itself has assumptions about its capacity to partially describe and to evoke a trans-conceptual awareness. Where there is an emphasis on the descriptive function and the wholly-other character of the reality, there language will have little positive value and must have a special intuition substituted for it. Where there is an emphasis on the transformative function and where the ultimate reality is assumed to be at least minimally in all particular forms there language is regarded as either useful or not useful for knowing ultimate truth depending on the 'purity' or unattached character of consciousness with which the language is used.

NOTES

1 N. Smart, 'History of Mysticism', found in P. Edwards, ed., *Encyclopedia of Philosophy* (London and New York, Macmillan, 1967), vol. 5, p. 420. For a brief structural analysis of the difference between the religious experiences of a 'personal apprehension of a holy presence' and 'mystic insight through spiritual discipline', see F. J. Streng, *Understanding Religious Life*, 2nd edn (Encino, Calif., Dickenson Publishing Co., 1976), chs. 5 and 8.

2 Tr. B. L. Bracey and R. C. Payne (New York, Meridian Books, 1959), ch. iv 'The Two Ways: The Mysticism of Introspection and the Mysticism of Unifying Vision'.

3 See, for example, E. Underhill, *Mysticism* (London, Methuen and New York, E. P. Dutton & Co., 1961); first published 1911; or M. Smith, *An Introduction to Mysticism* (London, Sheldon Press, 1977), first published 1930.

4 E. Neumann, 'Mystical Man', from *The Mystical Vision*: Papers from the Eranos Yearbooks, tr. R. Manheim, Bollengen Series XXX.6 (Princeton, Princeton University Press, 1968) or W. James, *Varieties of Religious Experience* (New York, Random House, 1902 and London, Fontana, 1971), pp. 370–420.

5 R. Hepburn, 'Nature and Assessment of Mysticism', found in P. Edwards, ed. *Encyclopedia of Philosophy* (London and New York, Macmillan, 1967), vol. 5, p. 433. R. Otto, *Mysticism East and West*, tr. B. L. Bracey and R. C. Payne (New York, Meridian Books, 1957), pp. 43–6.

6 (New Haven, Yale University Press, 1923), ch. vii, 'Intuition', pp. 93 ff.

7 Ibid., pp. 97–8.

8 Ibid., pp. 100–2.

9 See also the psychological shift from the 'normal' daily routine perception to both ecstatic rapture and Yogic *samōdki* as explained in A. M. Greeley, *Ecstasy: A Way of Knowing* (Englewood Cliffs, Prentice-Hall, 1974), pp. 38–48.

10 (London, Macmillan 1961 and New York, J. B. Lippincott Co., 1960), p. 144.

11 'Mystical Man', op. cit., pp. 380, 395, 398.

12 Bennett, op. cit., p. 102.

13 *Mysticism in Religion* (Chicago, University of Chicago Press, 1948), p. 154. Similarly, Ben-ami Scharfstein, in *Mystical Experience* (Oxford,

168 *Mysticism and Philosophical Analysis*

Basil Blackwell, 1973), p. 36, argues against the mystics' claim to an exclusive 'third eye' of wisdom. An advocate for the position of a special mystical intuition is M. Smith in her book *Introduction to Mysticism* (London, Sheldon Press), 1977), pp. 4–5. First published 1930.

14 *Mysticism in Religion*, p. 22; see also p. 135. For a similar expression see J. de Marquette, *Introduction to Comparative Mysticism* (New York, Philosophical Library, 1949), pp. 21–5.

15 *Mysticism in Religion*, p. 152.

16 Ibid., p. 161.

17 *Mysticism: Christian and Buddhist* (London, Allen and Unwin, 1973 and New York, Collier Books, 1962); first published 1957, pp. 18–20.

18 Ibid., p. 25. D. T. Suzuki stresses the discontinuity of mystical knowledge and common knowledge in both Christianity and Buddhism. However, for Eckhart – he says – Godhead 'is the unmoved', and as long as there is a trace of movement or activity God is still a something (p. 19). For a Zen advocate, however, the Absolute Emptiness is a reality seen in a kind of self-identity which 'identifies itself by going out of itself. Self-identity thus involves a movement . . . Self-identity is the logic of pure experience or of Emptiness.' (p. 30)

19 *Dialogues on the Supersensual Life*, Wm. Law and others, ed. B. Holland (New York, Frederick Ungar Publication Co., n.d.), p. 14.

20 *The Perfection of Wisdom in Eight Thousand Lines, and Its Verse Summary*, tr. Edward Conze (London, Buddhist Society, 1968 and Bolinas, Calif., Four Seasons Foundation, 1973), p. 180; abbreviated as *Ashta*.

21 *The Mystic Will – Based on a Study of the Philosophy of Jacob Boehme* (New York, Macmillan Co., 1930), pp. 11–12.

22 See also E. Underhill, op. cit., pp. 71–2 and 84–90 for an analysis of the necessity to surrender individual will to the ultimate object of love in order for any person to transcend his or her individual standpoint.

23 R. M. Jones, *The Testimony of the Soul* (New York, Macmillan Co., 1936), p. 202.

24 Op. cit., p. 72.

25 *Introduction to Mysticism* (London, Sheldon Press, 1977), p. 8. First published 1930.

26 Op. cit., p. 15.

27 Op. cit., ch. 3.

28 Ibid., pp. 277–306.

29 Ibid., p. 290.

30 Ibid., p. 291.

31 Tr. J. W. Harvey (Aberdeen, H. W. Turner, 1974 and New York, Oxford University Press, 1958), pp. 1, 2, 26.

32 Op. cit., p. 293

33 Ibid., p. 297.

34 Ibid., p. 299.

35 Ibid., p. 300.

36 Ibid., pp. 146–54, and 194–206.

37 Op. cit., p. 180.

38 Ibid., p. 121.

39 Ibid., p. 85.

40 Ibid., p. 126.

41 Ibid., p. 127.

42 For an example, see D. S. Ruegg, 'On the Knowability and Expressibility of Absolute Reality in Buddhism', *Indogaku Bukkyogaku Kenkyu*, vol. 20 (1971), pp. 495–589.

43 *Ashta*, p. 127.

44 Ibid., p. 122.

45 Op. cit., p. 81.

46 Ibid., p. 78.

47 *Mysticism East and West*, p. 6.

48 See my article 'Reflections on the Attention given to Mental Construction in the Indian Buddhist Analysis of Causality', *Philosophy East & West*, vol. 25, no. 1 (January 1975), pp. 71–80, for a brief analysis of the conditioning force of knowledge according to the Perfection of Wisdom Literature.

49 Op. cit., p. 86.

50 Ibid., p. 193.

51 Ibid., pp. 128–9.

52 Ibid., pp. 180–1.

53 For an analysis of three structures of religious apprehension in Indian religious life see my *Emptiness – A Study of Religious Meaning* (New York, Abingdon, 1967), chs. 7–9.

54 For a general exploration of the Buddhist use of negation in distinction to western philosophical analysis of being and non-being see Masao Abe, 'Non-being and *Mu*: the Metaphysical Nature of Negativity in the East and the West', *Religious Studies*, vol. 11, no. 2 (June 1975), pp. 181–92.

FREDERICK J. STRENG, M.A., B.D., Ph.D. (Chicago). Professor Streng is the author of *Emptiness – A Study in Religious Meaning* (1967); *Understanding Religious Man* (1969) revised and enlarged as *Understanding Religious Life* (1976); *Ways of Being Religious* (1973). He is the General Editor of the Religious Life of Man Series and was President of the Society for Asian and Comparative Philosophy 1970–2.

Mysticism and Meditation

ROBERT M. GIMELLO

> Begreifst du aber
> Wieviel andächtig schwärmen leichter als
> Gut handeln ist? Wie gern der schlaffste Mensch
> Andächtig schwärmt, um nur – ist er zu Zeiten
> Sich schon der Absicht deutlich nicht bewußt –
> Um nur gut handeln nicht zu müssen?
>
> Gotthold Ephraim Lessing,
> *Nathan der Weise*

> If you want to obtain a certain thing, you must
> first be a certain man, obtaining that certain
> thing won't be a concern of yours any more.
>
> Dōgen

In much of what has recently been written about mysticism – by philosophers, historians of religion, psychologists, and others – there is the assumption, usually implicit but sometimes explicit, that mysticism and meditation are very much of a piece. One common version of this assumption has it that meditation is a species of mysticism, a form of mystical experience. Thus, those who look for evidence of mysticism in traditions which stress meditation often look to the meditation literature of those traditions for such evidence and are wont to count therein all things meditative as mystical. Another and more sensible version of the assumption depicts meditation simply as a means to the end of having mystical experiences, as though it were just a practical instrument used by mystics. I shall argue in what follows that, at least in the case of Buddhism but perhaps also in other cases, it is both philosophically expedient and historically warranted to fashion a distinction between meditation and mysticism which is stricter than those that seem to be conventional. The historical warrant for such a distinction lies in the sort of critical and cautionary comment found in Buddhist meditation literature concerning those kinds of experience which correspond best to currently prevalent descriptions of mystical experiences. Such comment and such descriptions when taken together suggest that Buddhist meditation is at most a discipline which makes judicious, even wary, use of mystical experience, but which is by no means simply coextensive with mystical experience nor only a device for precipitating mystical experience. One might even say that the very particularity of Buddhism among religious traditions is to be seen especially in the distinctive way in which mystical experience is *employed* in the practice of Buddhist meditation. To readers of this volume, however, it is the possible philosophical utility of a Buddhist distinction between mysticism and meditation which is likely to be of foremost interest. And this, I believe, lies in the light which such a distinction can shed on several of the problems which seem most to preoccupy philosophical investigations of mysticism. Notable among these are:

1. The problem of how to distinguish between the mystical experience and the interpretation of it offered by the mystic himself, by others in the tradition with which the mystic is affiliated, or by still others whose vantage points are extrinsic to the mystic's tradition.
2. The problem of whether or not, or to what extent, mystical experience can be invoked to justify the truth-claims of certain propositions of religious or metaphysical belief.
3. The manifold problem of defining relationships between mystical experience and other areas of human concern such as morality, aesthetics, mental health, etc.

The distinction here to be proposed will not, of course, solve these problems, but it may well facilitate their solution. Finally, it will be argued that this distinction is more useful than its obvious alternative, which would be simply to argue that Buddhist meditation is a special variety of mysticism or a method in the service thereof.

The assignment of Buddhism and Buddhist meditation to the general category of mysticism, when done with care and appropriate qualification, can serve good purpose in the study of religions. Professor Ninian Smart, for example, has argued to the considerable avail of philosophers and historians of religion that certain strains of Buddhism (along with some varieties of Taoism, Hinduism, etc.) differ markedly from such prophetic religions as Judaism and Islam, and from religions related to the prophetic like Christianity, in that the religious experience most characteristic of the former is 'mystical', whereas that most characteristic of the latter is 'numinous'.[1] Of these two terms it is the latter which Smart seems, understandably, to have the easier time explaining. A numinous experience, he suggests following Otto, is one of an encounter with a being wholly other than oneself and altogether different from anything else. Such an encounter is usually said to be gratuitous, in the sense that those subject to it are not themselves responsible for its occurrence, and it is typically described as both overwhelming and self-authenticating. The mystical experience, by contrast, is not so much an encounter with a 'sacred other' as it is the interior attainment of a certain supernal state of mind. Such an attainment is usually held, except by mystics in traditions strongly committed to the numinous, to be the result of the subject's own efforts in following a certain contemplative discipline or method. Among the qualities typically ascribed to mystical attainments are bliss, ineffability, absence of a distinction between subject and object, timelessness, etc. The precise nature of the mystical goal in any particular case, Smart cogently argues, is defined by the rules enjoined for its attainment and by the presuppositions implicit in those rules. Smart further holds that neither one of these two primary forms of religious experience, the numinous or the mystical, is reducible to the other and that each generates a distinctive mode of religious discourse. The philosophical analysis of religious beliefs and their use is said to depend upon an appreciation of the differences between these modes of discourse and of the tensions between them in those traditions in which they are combined.

Smart's contrast between the numinous and the mystical strikes me as a breakthrough in the study of religions. It provides criteria for a far more discriminating investigation of the relationship between religious experience and doctrine. In respect of it, those who would assess such things as religious belief, religious speech, or religious knowledge must first identify the practical contexts of such activities. In so doing, for example, one will have to be alert to the likelihood that 'knowledge' in a religious tradition, the major activity of which is worship, may mean something quite different from 'knowledge' in a tradition in which meditation or mysticism is the regnant practice. Only after the varieties of knowledge thus revealed are marshalled can one hope adequately to distinguish between religious knowledge and the kinds of knowledge available through science or common sense. Apropos of mysticism in particular, Smart has been able to employ the distinction between the numinous and mystical to demonstrate that certain of the better-known difficulties surrounding the theological interpretation of mystical experience are the result of inherent tensions, if not incompatibilities, between the two; as in the case of a mystic whose theistic tradition variously imposes upon him the requirement of formulating expressions of his experience in the language of the numinous. Not the least of the uses to which Smart's categories may be put is that of accentuating the particularity of specific religious traditions, thereby to impede the tendency to homogenize religious experience and discourse and to conflate religious traditions. Had the appropriateness of these categories been appreciated sooner, far less ink would have been uselessly spilt over the question of the fundamental unity of religions; not to mention such specific issues as whether or not Buddhism is covertly theistic, whether or not Buddhists really do deny the soul (*ātman*), and so forth. We might also have been sooner rid of the compulsion to define religion substantively as something having invariably to do with 'the sacred' or 'the transcendent'. It is therefore useful to label Buddhism 'mystical' – if for no other reason, then at least to segregate it and the manner of its discourse from such fundamentally dissimilar traditions as Christianity and Vedānta.

Nevertheless, without wishing to subvert the intentions of a distinction like Smart's, indeed in the hope of furthering them, I think it must be recognized that there is a modicum of imprecision in the labelling of the most characteristically Buddhist experience and discourse mystical. It is certainly true that the numinous is a category hardly apposite to the mainstream of Buddhist thought and practice.[2] It is also true that experience of the sort conventionally described as mystical has a significant role to play in nearly all forms of Buddhism. However, not all that is not numinous need be classified as mystical, and it will be shown that there are important features of Buddhism, especially of its meditation disciplines, which seem not to fall neatly under the mystical rubric. Moreover, the normative traditions of Buddhist meditation harbour a deep-seated ambivalence towards those components of the discipline which are most evidently in accord with common cross-cultural and phenomenological descriptions of mystical experience. So much is this the case, I would suggest, that it is difficult to apply any of the widely accepted definitions or descriptions of mysticism to Buddhist praxis without the most serious reservations. There seems always to be some crucial element of the definition, some essential part of the description which just does not fit the Buddhist case. It will, of course, be anticipated that these disparities are not so much between mystical experience and the Buddhist meditative experience as between mystical experience and Buddhism's doctrinaire interpretation thereof. But I wish to argue that it is in the practice and experience of meditation itself that the distinction between mystical and meditative experience is evident, not simply in the post- or extra-experiential interpretations which Buddhists place upon their meditations. If, then, we are to persist in calling Buddhism and its meditation practice mystical – perhaps for the very good reasons outlined above – care must be exercised in specifying the precise manner of Buddhism's qualification as a mystical religion. What, then, is mystical experience, and what is Buddhist meditation?

It would surely not do to contrive an answer to the first of these questions especially tailored to support one's view of Buddhist meditation. But then neither is such an illegitimate though attractive ruse necessary. The ready-made article will suffice. One need only sample the standard and recent literature on the subject. Description, not to mention definition, of mystical experience – especially in view of the near-universal claim that it is ineffable – is a notoriously difficult undertaking. Given this difficulty, many of the available attempts are quite creditable. There is even something of a consensus among those who have offered such descriptions, despite the wide divergence among their interpretations and assessments of what they describe. The following are typical, if not exhaustive.[3]

W. T. Stace, whose book *Mysticism and Philosophy* has figured often in the philosophical discussion of mysticism since its publication fifteen years ago,[4] provides a convenient starting-point. He argues that mysticism is a distinguishable genus of human experience which, apart from some few distinctions which may be made between the two major species of the genus, is everywhere and always marked by a minimal set of common characteristics. These, taken together, constitute the 'common core' of mysticism. Stace argues, unconvincingly, that the characteristics he has culled empirically from allegedly typical accounts of mystical experience are 'psychological', by which he seems to mean that, even if they are not literally descriptive and pre-interpretive, then at least they embody interpretation of only a 'low-level'. It has already been pointed out that Stace's sampling of accounts of mysticism may not be broad enough to support his claim to have identified the common core of *all* mysticism and that his criteria for distinguishing between report and interpretation are simplistic.[5] Nevertheless, these flaws would seem to be of more serious consequence for his philosophical assessment of mysticism than for his depiction of its general features, for although others would perhaps add to his list of basic characteristics, few have challenged the broad relevance of those characteristics which he has selected. For Stace, mystical experience is invariably such as to provoke ascription of the following characteristics: ineffability, paradoxicality, a feeling of the holy, blessedness or peace, a sense of objectivity or reality, and a quality of oneness. The last characteristic admits of some variation depending on the species of mysticism in question. In what is called 'extrovertive' mysticism, the oneness is a *unifying* vision by which all things are seen as one and as possessed of the same indwelling vitality. For the 'introvertive' mystic, the oneness is a *unitary* or pure consciousness which is felt to be itself the whole of reality and which is averred to be insusceptible to distinctions of space and time. In whichever form, it is this oneness which Stace holds to be the key or 'nuclear' characteristic of all mystical experience. He does, however, give pride of place to the introvertive version on the grounds that it is historically the more important and because it seems to him to be the more consistent and fully realized embodiment of the idea of oneness.[6]

Clearly, those who accept Smart's contrast between the numinous and the mystical would have to remove from the list the characteristic of a sense of the holy. The ascription of this feature, where it is made, is likely to be the result of the numinous auto-interpretation of mystical experience. One might also cavil at the inclusion of blessedness or peace, citing claims by some who are called mystics for a mystical experience of high-pitched intensity or perfervid excitement. But the remaining four qualities do seem generally and cross-culturally appropriate. In fact all of them seem to appear, in one guise or another, in nearly every modern description of mystical experience. In the case of the quality of oneness, there is (appropriately enough) virtual unanimity among those who hazard descriptions of mystical experience[7] that oneness, in some sense, is always of the essence of such experience. Some would prefer to distinguish between varieties of oneness, e.g. between union or integration, which seems to presuppose a multiplicity to be unified, and sameness or an experience of the One as all, which seems to deny multiplicity outright. But those who would argue that there are qualitative distinctions to be made among the kinds of oneness achieved by mystics must ask themselves whether they might not be dealing with differences in doctrinal interpretation rather than with genuinely experiential differences. This, in turn, would require fully appreciating that interpretation can be actually ingredient in experience and need not be only something added to experience by the reflective intellect. It may well be, in other words, that the Christian or Jewish mystic who describes his experience as a communion with God rather than as a realization that God and he are one does so because the former are the categories that come immediately to mind, not only after the experience in moments of judicious reflection, but even in the midst of it. In other words, such categories may well be the very means by which the intellect participates in and thereby informs the experience. Admittedly, if we are to credit the accounts of their experiences given by most mystics, the manner of the intellect's participation in mysticism is decidedly unusual. Mystical experience is commonly alleged to be non-discursive, intuitive rather than cogitative, non-conceptual, etc. Some commentators go so far as to infer from such reports – illegitimately, I think – that mystical experience is therefore irrational or that it entails an abandonment of intellect. However, it is difficult to imagine that the intellect is entirely absent from the mystic's transport, particularly when one considers the way in which mystical experience, validly or not, serves regularly to reinforce commitment to certain beliefs. The mystical experience is not mindless, and in it the intellect clearly has some role to play. The only problem is that of specifying which role, and it seems reasonable to suggest that what has often been called interpretation, and held under that label to be extrinsic to the pure experience, is actually an essential part of the experience.

If all of this be the case, i.e. if oneness of some sort be characteristic of all mystical experience and if it be fruitless to attempt to distinguish between varieties of oneness because experience and interpretation are constitutive of each other and therefore not clearly separable, then it would seem sensible to be content, for general descriptive purposes at least, with relatively vague characterizations. This I take to be a major thrust of another recent attempt, Agehananda Bharati's, to isolate mystical experience from all other kinds of religious and non-religious experience: 'It is the person's intuition of numerical oneness with the cosmic absolute, with the universal matrix, or with any essence stipulated by the various theological and speculative systems of the world.'[8] Again, the quality of oneness is held to be central to the mystical experience, but no effort is made to explain the nature of that oneness by the use of terms with doctrinal ramification. A similar intention is manifest in Ben-Ami Scharfstein's identification of 'sameness' as the first of his 'eleven quintessences of the mystic state'.[9] By 'sameness' he means the mystic's conviction that the apparent differences among things are illusory. But what *that* in turn may mean depends upon the intellectual *problematik* of particular mystics. For a Proclus, it may mean that the real is utterly single; for a Shankara, it may imply superimposition (*adhyāsa*); for a Nāgārjuna, it may mean that all things are devoid of own-being (*svabhāva-śūnyatā*). Yet, whatever the meaning may be in any given case, the experiential event in which the meaning is seen to inhere is still characterizable as an experience of oneness. It cannot be accidental that nearly every mystic, however much he may disagree with others on the true significance of his or their experiences, resorts to terminology which may reasonably be organized by an impartial observer under the general heading of oneness. There must be some common factor in all of these experiences, however different they may otherwise be, for there to be such similarity of expression. This is not to say that the experiences are identical, for such a claim rests on the naive separation of experience and interpretation criticized above. It is merely to say that they must have something in common. And it is this common element that has led not only Stace, Bharati, and Scharfstein but also (though from quite different perspectives) Maslow,[10] Danto,[11] Eliade,[12] Fingarette,[13] Happold,[14] Hepburn,[15] and others, to identify oneness as a defining feature of mystical experience. I think it advisable that we accept their conclusions on this matter. Those who have urged that we should not, e.g. R. C. Zaehner,[16] have done so out of a concern to establish that some forms of mysticism convey ultimate truth while others do not, or that some are 'supernatural' while others are merely 'natural'. But Smart has shown convincingly that the truth of an interpretation of a mystical experience, be that interpretation theistic or monistic or whatever, cannot be established on the basis of the mystical experience itself. The question of the truth of mysticism is altogether distinct from the question of mysticism's homogeneity or heterogeneity, and one should not let an interest in finding a certain answer to the former question determine one's approach to the latter. In any case, to accept a vaguely defined 'feeling of oneness' as a distinguishing element common to all mystical experience hardly entails the judgement that all mystical experiences are the same. It still allows for the possibility of arguing, although on criteria other than those which seem implicit in Zaehner's works, that some mystical experiences are more true or more genuinely informative than others.

For the same reasons adduced in the case of the quality of oneness, I would suggest that other of the characteristics conventionally attributed to mystical experience also be accepted with as little punctiliousness as possible. Investigation of the philosophically most interesting aspects of mysticism need not wait upon the construction of an absolutely inerrant and universally adequate description of the essential features of mystical experience, even if such a thing were ever to prove possible. Let us then assume, without scruple over this or that particular case of mysticism, that mystical experience is roughly the sort of thing Smart, Stace, Bharati, Scharfstein, *et al.*, indicate it to be in their working definitions and lists of characteristics. For those not so easily shriven of their scruples, let us maintain the proviso that particular items may be dropped from these characterizations should the specific need arise and that others may be added if the evidence so indicate. Let it also be borne in mind that these characterizations comprise only a phenomenology of mystical experience and as such do not imply either the truth or the falsity of mystical reports, nor even any particular interpretations thereof.

For our purposes then, a mystical experience is a state of mind, achieved commonly through some sort of self-cultivation, of which the following are usually or often the salient, but not necessarily the only, features:

A feeling of oneness or unity, variously defined.

A strong confidence in the 'reality' or 'objectivity' of the experience, i.e. a conviction that it is somehow revelatory of 'the truth'.

A sense of the final inapplicability to the experience of conventional language, i.e. a sense that the experience is ineffable.

A cessation of *normal* intellectual operations (e.g. deduction, discrimination, ratiocination, speculation, etc.) or the substitution for them of some 'higher' or qualitatively different mode of intellect (e.g. intuition).

A sense of the coincidence of opposites, of various kinds (paradoxicality).

An extraordinarily strong affective tone, again of various kinds (e.g. sublime joy, utter serenity, great fear, incomparable pleasure, etc. – often an unusual combination of such as these).

In nearly all particular cases of mystical experience, these and other characteristics assume a certain 'shape' of meaning, i.e. they occur in an auto-interpretive context the elements of which the mystic himself brings to the experience in the form of deep-seated expectations and presuppositions. These latter, in turn, are often acquired by the mystic from the tradition in which he has been nurtured, or they may be 'programmed' into the discipline which he follows.

If the above may be accepted as a fair, albeit crude and highly generalized, description of mystical experience, we may then proceed to consider what Buddhist meditation is, how it is to be distinguished from mystical experience, and what role if any mystical experience plays in Buddhist meditation. Answering such questions as these is a task hardly less daunting than that of describing mysticism. Meditation has been the normative religious practice in Buddhism since the tradition's inception. In the course of Buddhism's two and a half millennia of development and in the process of its dissemination and modification throughout Asia, there has accumulated an enormous Buddhist literature on the subject of meditation. Although many works have been published on meditation by western scholars and advocates of Buddhism, we still have, by comparison with the primary sources, a very meagre western-language literature on the subject. Moreover, much that has been written in the west about Buddhist meditation has been written on the very assumption which we wish to challenge, viz. that Buddhist meditation is a form of mysticism or a means by which to attain mystical experiences. There are, therefore, at least two major constraints upon the effort to clarify the relation between meditation and mysticism in Buddhism: insufficient familiarity with the breadth and variety of the Buddhist meditation tradition and the prevalent influence of a certain, I think distorting, assumption about the practice. In respect of these constraints one must make only the most critical use of the majority of the secondary sources, discriminating especially between the work of philologists who take pains simply to present the tradition as faithfully as possible and those who leap too soon to the interpretive and judgemental tasks. The latter are valid and desirable undertakings but, considering the infancy of western Buddhist studies and of the western study of Asian religions in general, those who would theoretically interpret or philosophically assess these subjects must quell their enthusiasm and confidence with regular doses of such scholarly suppressants as Indology, Buddhology, Sinology, etc. In compensation, however, they may expect much. Not only will they thereby increase their store of information, but they may also discover, embedded in the studied traditions themselves, new categories of interpretation, new criteria of judgement. These, in turn, may not only better suit their Asian subjects, but may also prove cross-culturally more useful than their counterparts of western origin. In the case of mysticism or the contemplative life this is particularly to be anticipated. Mysticism and the arts of the spiritually contemplative life have always been comparatively marginal activities in the western traditions, being usually subordinate to prayer, ritual, the sacramental life, worship, moral endeavour, study of the Law, etc. In Buddhism, by contrast, meditation has always been one, if not *the*, central form of praxis. One should not be surprised, then, if it were found that Buddhism offers a more sophisticated set of analytical instruments with which to examine such phenomena as obtain in disciplines of mental cultivation. The Asian traditions have simply given more concerted attention to such matters than have, for example, Judaism or Christianity. Buddhism especially has nurtured a decidedly reflective and self-conscious attitude towards the contemplative life, urging not only that it be lived but also that it be examined with meticulous, even scholastic, precision.

It is from this array of traditional Buddhist categories for the classification and examination of the contemplative life that I shall draw the several fundamental concepts in terms of which I shall attempt briefly to characterize Buddhist meditation and to differentiate it from mystical experience. It will remain thereafter to be seen whether or not these specifically Buddhist concepts can serve the general philosophical consideration of mysticism.

The first of these Buddhist categories to be considered are two which form a pair used throughout Buddhism to classify the major components of meditation. They are 'calming' (Sanskrit: *śamatha*; Pāli: *samatha*; Chinese: *chih*;[17] Japanese: *shi*) and 'discernment' (Sanskrit: *vipaśyanā*; Pali: *vipassanā*; Chinese: *kuan*;[18] Japanese: *kan*). For purposes of expediency, we may avail ourselves of one of the typical scholastic definitions of this pair. It is late (*c.* fourth century AD) but reflective of the mainstream of the tradition:

What is calming? It is the interior collection of the mind, its establishment, its stabilization, its stilling, its maintenance, its controlled and utter tranquillization, its one-pointedness, its equanimity and composedness.

What is discernment? It is the examination, utmost scrutiny, complete deliberation, and judicious investigation of *dharma*[19]

done with the intention to counteract gross bondage, to overcome perverse thoughts, and to bring about the dispassionate
abiding of an unperverted mind.[20]

All elements of Buddhist meditation find their place under one or
the other of these two general rubrics. The Buddhist meditator, in
other words, is invariably engaged in calming, in discernment, or in
some combination of the two, although the former is usually held
to be preparatory to the latter. In less technical language, Buddhist
meditation is a discipline which one begins by first stilling or calming the mind and body. The degree of stillness recommended varies
from technique to technique but, once an adequate stillness is
achieved, one then proceeds analytically to review the meaning of the
fundamental teachings of Buddhism as they apply to whatever may
be the particular focus of the meditative exercise. Discernment is
the latter and most characteristically Buddhist part of the discipline. The following is an early and classical canonical example of
the relationship between the two:

> With his mind thus concentrated, purified, cleansed, spotless,
> with the defilements gone, supple, ready to act, firm, and impas-
> sable [all as a result of *samatha*], he [the meditator] directs his
> mind to the knowledge of insight.[21] He thus understands: 'This is
> my body; having shape, composed of the four elements,
> produced by a mother and father, a collection of nutriments,
> subject to change, pounding, breaking, and dissolution; this con-
> sciousness of mine is resting on this body, to this it is
> bound . . .'[22]

In this example we see that concentration and tranquillization,
which are often wrongly assumed to be the whole of Buddhist
meditation or its culmination, are really only the necessary prelude
to an analytic discernment of the 'truths' of dependent origination
(*pratītyasamutpāda*) and impermanence (*anītya*) as they apply to
the psychosomatic 'self'. It is this sort of analysis which is the true
culmination of the exercise.

Among the particular procedures which contribute to 'calming'
are such familiar devices as the postures (*āsana*) of meditation (e.g.
the cross-legged 'lotus posture'), restriction of the senses (*indriyeṣu
guptadvarata*), regulation of breathing, fixing of sensory and mental
attention on particular concrete or conceptual objects of meditation
like the ten 'devices' (Sanskrit: *kṛtsnāyatana*; Pāli: *kasiṇāyatana*),[23]
or counteraction of specific defilements by intensification of par-

ticular virtuous attitudes.[24] Especially important as methods of calming are the stages of 'absorption' or 'trance' (Sanskrit: *dhyāna*; Pāli: *jhāna*), which are classically described as follows:[25]

1. Entrance into the first absorption (*dhyāna*) in which the meditator is dissociated from sense-desires and unwholesome *dharmas*, and during which the following five factors (*aṅga*) arise in him:

    (a) Application of thought (*vitarka*), a result of the conquest of torpor and sloth.
    (b) Discursive thought (*vicāra*), a result of the conquest of perplexity.
    (c) Zest (*prīti*), a result of the conquest of ill-will.
    (d) Happiness (*sukha*), a result of the conquest of distraction and regret.
    (e) One-pointedness of mind (*ekāgratacitta*), a result of the conquest of sensuous desires.

2. Entrance into the second absorption in which application of thought and discursive thought are dispensed with; while zest, happiness, and one-pointedness of mind – all born of concentration (*samādhi*) – are retained. The meditator experiences an interior serenity (*adhyātmasamprasāda*) and supreme exaltation (*ekotibhāva*).

3. The third absorption in which zest is dispensed with while happiness and one-pointedness of mind remain. The meditator abides in equanimity (*upekṣā*), mindfulness (*smṛti*), and clear comprehension (*samprajanya*).

4. The fourth absorption in which happiness is dispensed with and only one-pointedness of mind persists. The meditator is purified in equanimity and mindfulness (*upekṣāsmṛtipariśuddha*) and attains mental liberation (*cetovimukti*).

5. The fifth absorption or first formless attainment (*arūpyasamāpatti*) in which the meditator passes beyond the notion of material-form (*rūpasaṁjñā*), suppresses all notions of resistance (*pratighasaṁjñā*) and multiplicity (*nānātvasaṁjñā*), contemplates the infinity of space, and resides in the sphere of the infinity of space (*ākāsānantyāyatana*).

6. The sixth absorption or second formless attainment in which the meditator passes beyond the sphere of the infinity of space, con-

templates the infinity of consciousness, and resides in the sphere thereof (*vijñānānatyāyatana*).

7. The seventh absorption or third formless attainment in which the meditator passes beyond the realm of the infinity of consciousness, contemplates that nothing exists, and dwells in the realm in which nothing exists (*ākiṁcanyāyatana*).

8. The eighth absorption or fourth formless attainment in which the meditator passes beyond the realm in which nothing exists and enters the realm of neither consciousness nor non-consciousness (*naivasaṁjñānāsaṁjñāyatana*).[26]

These eight levels of absorption fall also under another, perhaps better known, meditative rubric – that of 'concentration' or collectedness' (*samādhi*), which term is in many circumstances synonymous with *śamatha*.

As one might gather from even these few examples, described as sketchily as we have described them, the arts of *śamatha* and *samādhi* afford their practitioners a variety of extraordinary experiences. Many of these are of the sort commonly labelled ecstatic or, with greater precision, 'enstatic'.[27] Normal modes of perception of the external world, and even of introspection or self-consciousness, are suspended. Psychic and intellectual activity is reduced to the barest minimum. The turbulent and teeming flow of thoughts and emotions which constitutes normal consciousness is drastically simplified and its velocity slowed to near stasis. Such curious terms as 'infinity of consciousness', 'realm in which nothing exists', 'realm of neither consciousness nor non-consciousness' are meant not to label other worlds actually reached by the meditator but only to intimate the quality of experience under such abnormal, retrenched conditions. Moreover, these states of mind are held to be powerful, to confer on those who have them preternatural powers (*abhijñā*, lit. 'super-knowledges') of magical creation, transformation, clairaudience, clairvoyance, retrocognition, etc. The following is a typical celebration of these:

> The meditator thus gradually contemplates until he gains mastery over the manifold transformations. Being one, he becomes many. Being many, he becomes one. He appears [and disappears]. He passes through walls, barriers, and mountains. His body moves without impediment, as though through space. He sinks into the earth and re-emerges from it, as though it were water. He walks on water as though it were land, and moves

through the air like a bird in flight. He fondles the sun and the moon with his hands. Such are his supernormal powers, so great is his might, that he ascends even to the Brahma world.[28]

Whether or not these claims are taken literally within the tradition,[29] they clearly indicate that experiences of concentration and absorption at least *appear* to those who have them as though they were of another, higher order of reality. And we shall see that, as such, they are taken seriously enough to be held potentially dangerous.

Nevertheless, the Buddhist meditation tradition is virtually unanimous in holding that calm and concentration, even in the most sublime degree, are not themselves the goal of meditation. And the supernormal powers engendered in such states are viewed as little more than by-products of meditation, frequently quite useful in the hands of the enlightened but potentially seductive for all others. The real purpose of these disciplines is simply to prepare the meditator for the more crucial exercise of discernment (*vipaśyanā*). The analysis of Buddhist doctrine and the application of it to the data of experience cannot be carried on by those whose minds and bodies are constantly beset by agitation from within and distraction from without, and who are thereby numbed to the actual subtleties of experience. The transports of *śamatha*, *dhyāna*, and *samādhi* serve primarily the purposes of immunizing the meditator against such disturbance and of honing his faculties of attention. Apart from these functions, however, the extraordinary experiences of calming, absorption, and concentration are themselves only further data to be offered by the meditator to the scrutiny of his discernment. Discernment, in turn, will show these data to be 'dependently originated', 'impermanent', 'devoid of self-hood', 'illusory', etc. It is especially to be emphasized that *samādhi* and its associated experiences are not themselves revelatory of the truth of things, nor are they sufficient unto liberation from suffering. These paramount tasks are accomplished by discernment or insight, for which calming and concentration only establish the suitable mental conditions. Thus:

> The yogin, fixing his mind on the physical form of the Tathāgata (i.e. the Buddha visualized in meditation) as it might appear to his senses, practises calming. He attends continually to the form of the Tathāgata, brilliant as refined gold, adorned with the major and minor marks [of a superior person], situated in the midst of an assembly, working the weal of sentient beings with a

multiplicity of expedient means. Attracted by these qualities, the yogin quells all distraction and agitation and remains absorbed for as long as they appear to him distinctly, as if they were actually present.

Then the yogin practises discernment by scrutinizing the coming and going of these reflections of the Tathāgata's form. He considers thus: Just as these reflections of the form of the Tathāgata neither come from anywhere nor go anywhere, are empty of own-being and devoid of self and its properties, so are all *dharmas* empty of own-being, without coming or going like a reflection, and lacking the features of an existent thing.[30]

Here we have an example of an exercise in absorption which, notwithstanding its vividness and splendour, has been deliberately contrived to exemplify certain Buddhist doctrines. This intense and sustained meditative visualization of the Buddha, rather than foster and strengthen religious or metaphysical belief in the existence of such beings as buddhas, serves actually to instantiate the doctrine that buddhas and all other things are empty of independent substantial existence, that they are all like reflections in a mirror. The deliberate judgement that they are so, the 'seeing' of them as such, is discernment, and it is this which liberates. Specifically, according to Buddhism, it liberates from false views about the nature of beings and things.

In all versions of the story of the Buddha's life and in all systematic curricula of meditation, it is discernment, or its perfection as insight (*prajñā*),[31] which is the proximate cause of enlightenment, not *śamatha* or *samādhi*.[32] While it is true that discernment is not to be attained without some degree of calming as precondition, it is no less true that calming itself, without discernment, is of no soteric avail whatsoever. The differences among the various regimens of Buddhist meditation do not put this in question. Such differences have only to do with the relative proportions of the two ingredients, some requiring long and luxurious cultivation of calm while others require that only the minimum of calming be practised before plunging directly into discernment.[33]

As though to confirm the subordination of calming to discernment in Buddhist meditation, the later scholastic (*abhidharma*) traditions of Buddhism develop a distinction between the mundane (*laukika*) and the supramundane (*lokottara*) cultivations (*bhāvanā*).[34]

The mundane cultivation is the practice of the eight absorptions

and attainments listed above. One ascends through them by nurtur-
ing at any one point on the path an aversion for the lower stage,
once it has been reached, and by conceiving an aspiration for the
next higher stage. For example, having attained the first absorption
and having realized its benefits, one notes that there are certain
faults or dangers in it. Two of its five factors – application of
thought (*vitarka*) and sustained thought (*vicāra*) – are susceptible to
the distractions of discursiveness. Therefore one aspires for the next
level of absorption which, since these two factors are absent from
it, affords an even greater degree of tranquillity and concentration.
The language used in describing this procedure suggests that practitioners ascend from a realm of experience governed by sensuality
(*kamadhātu*) to a realm of the apprehension of pure material-form
dissociated from sensuality (*rūpadhātu*), to an immaterial and
purely noetic realm (*arūpadhātu*). Some texts speak of a still more
refined anoetic transic state (*saṁjñāvedita-nirodha*, the extinction of
concept and feeling) which is virtually an utter lack of consciousness and which approaches death. The dynamics of progress
on this path are still the dynamics of desire but, since the governing
object of the meditator's aspiration is the greatest possible tranquillity, advancement is marked by the progressive elimination of the
grosser sorts of desire until only a modicum of the most refined
desire, that for the ultimate in stillness, remains. However, the prac-
titioner is still left with a residue of passionate desire and, more
serious yet, is still hampered by misconceptions and ignorance concerning the 'four noble truths' and their corollaries. The latter im-
pediments re-emerge in the mind of the mediator when he emerges
from his admittedly temporary absorptions, and it is they which
obstruct his final liberation.

The supramundane cultivation consists in the review of the
'truths' of Buddhism – suffering, impermanence, insubstantiality –
by applying these concepts both to conventional experience and to
the rarefied experiences of absorption. Even the *dhyānas* themselves
must be seen to be species of pain (*duḥkha*), dependently originated,
ephemeral, etc. Although a certain measure of concentration is
necessary for these 'truths' to be seen in their clarity, the eradication of false views does not itself require entrance into the higher
absorptions. And it is the eradication of false views, of attachment
to ascriptive theories or ideas about reality, which is deemed the
most crucial requirement for final liberation.

Clearly the relation between the mundane and the supramundane
cultivations is analogous to the relation between calming and

discernment. And as with the latter pair, so in the case of the former, the ideal is a combination of the two members, a judicious balance of quiescence and insight. The exact proportion depends largely on the temperament or aptitude of the individual meditator. Nevertheless, there is wide agreement in the systematic treatments of meditation that pride of place belongs to doctrinal analysis as practised in the supramundane path. In fact, this is a point often made to distinguish Buddhism from other meditative traditions. It is acknowledged that even the highest absorptive attainments are available in the practice of heterodox paths (e.g. those taught by some of the Buddha's own pre-enlightenment teachers), but the qualification is always made that without insight into the 'truths' formulated by the Buddha these infidel yogis are still confined to *saṁsāra*.

One last set of traditional categories may be employed to clarify the content of the Buddhist meditative path. In the same contexts in which Buddhists distinguish between calming and discernment or the mundane and supramundane paths they also often distinguish between two kinds of obstacles to liberation: the affective obstacles (*kleśāvaraṇa*) and intellectual obstacles (*jñeyāvaraṇa*). The former are passionate defilements like lust, anger, hatred; the latter are of a conceptual order and consist of such misconceptions as a belief in selfhood or the permanence and substantiality of existent things. In meditation, it is calming, concentration, and absorption which conduce to the near-extinction of the affective obstacles, but it is discernment or doctrinal analysis supported by concentration which completely extinguishes them and which extinguishes also the intellectual barriers. *Nirvāṇa* is attained only when both kinds of obstacle are removed. This distinction again highlights the superior importance of discernment over calming.

On the basis of these three distinctions we have now drawn – between calming and discernment, mundane and supramundane cultivation, and the affective and intellectual obstacles to liberation – let us summarize our characterization of Buddhist meditation. It is in general a twofold discipline. On the one hand, there is what might be called a psychosomatic and affective component. This consists in arts of calming and concentrating the mind–body complex of the meditator, usually by the deliberate inducement of certain rarefied states of mind. These states are characterized by such qualities as ecstasy, joy, tranquillity, rest, equanimity, and one-pointedness of mind. These, in turn, precipitate or accompany extraordinary experiences in which the normal conditions of material, spatial, temporal, and mental existence seem suspended. Multiplicity, material resistance, distinction between subject and object, and the like – all vanish. The meditator feels himself to be endowed with an array of preternatural powers correlative to these experiences. The purpose allegedly served by these practices is that of quelling, if not extirpating, desire, attachment, and other elements of the affective life. On the other hand, there is an intellectual or analytic component of meditation. This consists in the meditatively intensified reflection upon the basic categories of Buddhist doctrine and in the application of them to the data of meditative experience. It is a form of discrimination, critical and sceptical in tone, which serves invariably to inhibit speculation or the formulation of views about the nature of reality. It does employ concepts – ideas like suffering, impermanence, emptiness, interdependence, etc. – but these it employs homoeopathically, as conceptual devices to counteract the mind's tendency to attach itself to concepts.[35] The final key to liberation for the Buddhist lies with this analytic destruction of false views. These two major components of Buddhist meditation are related to each other basically in two ways. Calming and concentration are to some degree practically necessary for the exercise of discernment: they establish the mental conditions for it. However, discernment itself is critical of the calming and concentration that make it possible and requires an intelligent, self-conscious 'distance' from them.

The point to which all of the above has been leading – both the derivative characterization of mystical experience and the general description of Buddhist meditation – is by now perhaps obvious. It is simply this: Mystical experience as it is conventionally understood corresponds closely to only one of the two major components of Buddhist meditation. It resembles the sort of experience which in Buddhism falls under the general heading of calming and the particular headings of absorption or concentration. It is in the practices of calming that one will find experiences like 'a feeling of unity or oneness', a 'cessation of *normal* intellectual operations', 'paradox', 'strong affective tone', and a compelling vividness that might well instil 'strong confidence in the "reality" or "objectivity" of the experience' if it is not scrutinized properly. Conversely, it is among experiences conventionally identified as mystical that one will find non-Buddhist analogues to such experiences as 'zest', 'interior serenity', 'supreme exaltation', 'absence of all notions of resistance and multiplicity', and entrance into 'the realm in which nothing exists'. I would suggest, therefore, that if the words 'mysticism' and 'mystical' are to be used of Buddhism and Buddhist meditation, their use should be restricted to the characterization only of *śamatha, samādhi*, and their sub-species. What then of discernment? This, it seems to me, is something quite different from what is normally meant by 'mystical experience'. It is rather an intellectual operation which, though it may be abetted by mystical experiences, is also *performed upon them*. It is a form of meditative analysis, employing the concepts and propositions of Buddhist doctrine, for which mystical experience is both enabling condition and subject-matter, especially the latter. However, despite the interdependence of discernment and mystical experience in Buddhist meditation, the two are categorially different. Indeed, the above descriptions suggest that discernment may be a category of religious experience or religious act as distinguishable from mystical experience as are the categories of prophetic revelation, prayer, worship, and ritual. The nature of the distinction in the Buddhist case is apparent in the assignment of discernment to a governing role over the other elements of meditation. Discernment is the meditative procedure by which Buddhists critically evaluate their mystical experiences, disenchant themselves of them, and use them as experiential correlatives of particular doctrines. Specifically, discernment combats the tendency, manifest in other 'mystical' traditions, to ontologize the content of mystical experience. As Bharati has observed, Buddhists seem long to have realized what 'very few mystics through the ages knew', viz. that the mystical experience 'cannot confer existential status on its content'.[36] What Bharati seems not fully to appreciate, however, is the mechanism by which Buddhists inhibit that quite natural tendency. That mechanism is discernment.

Those who have followed recent philosophical debates over mysticism might argue that the distinction I have laboured to establish is simply a variation of the distinction between mystical experience and its interpretation. I would not find this suggestion objectionable, provided it be also recognized that interpretation need not be only a rationalization contrived after the fact of mystical experience but may be actually coincident with and determinative of the experience. In fact, I would hold that the Buddhist subordination of the *śamatha* to the *vipaśyanā* component of meditation is an example of just that. Furthermore, although it has been observed that experience and interpretation are often difficult to discriminate, Buddhism, with its division of meditation into quiescence and analysis, provides us with at least one example in which clear criteria of discrimination are available.

Another possible objection must also be anticipated. Buddhism acknowledges that both of the components of meditation which we have discussed belong to the 'path' (*mārga*) to enlightenment or liberation. Could it not then be that the true 'mystical experience' in Buddhism is neither calming nor discernment but rather enlightenment (*bodhi*) itself, the goal of the path? This objection, admittedly, is not so easily dealt with as the first – at least not without the sort of historical distinctions among kinds of Buddhism that we have hitherto carefully avoided. My hypothesis is that liberation (*vimokṣa, nirvāṇa, bodhi,* etc.) throughout Buddhism is not the sort of thing that is usually denoted by the term 'mystical experience'. In the case of Theravāda or '*hīnayāna*' Buddhism, however, such a hypothesis is difficult to prove. The difficulty has to do no doubt with Theravāda Buddhism's refusal or inability to define *nirvāṇa*. This, of course, is a claim for ineffability, a common characteristic of mystical experience. But by itself this proves nothing. Whereof we cannot speak, thereof we may not even say 'mystical'. All silence need not betoken the same thing.[37] In the case of Mahāyāna Buddhism, however, my hypothesis is more easily substantiated. The key to its substantiation lies in the universal Mahāyāna claim that its soteric goal (usually *bodhi* rather than *nirvāṇa*) is not an 'experience' at all. How then could it be a 'mystical experience'? Rather, Mahāyāna enlightenment is said to be a way of life, a pattern of conduct, a manner of acting. The human ideal of Mahāyāna, the *bodhisattva*, is precisely the being who does not abide in or succumb to his own salvific experiences, but rather turns them compassionately to account in his work among and for all sentient beings. It is he who deliberately, with great effort of will and intellect, refrains from *nirvāṇa* so that he may remain in *saṃsāra*, 'the limit of one being the limit of the other'.[38] By contrast, it is the '*hīnayāna*' Buddhist (the *śrāvaka* or *arhant*) who, as the foil of Mahāyāna polemic, becomes 'intoxicated on the liquor of *samādhi*'[39] and in his mystical stupor mistakes (mystakes?) his mindless, trance-like self-absorption for a distinguishable *nirvāṇa*. The only *nirvāṇa* worthy of the *bodhisattva* is *apratiṣṭhita-nirvāṇa* the 'nirvana of no fixed abode', which does not impede a life of this-worldly compassionate activity but actually is that very life. Even the wisdom gained by the *bodhisattva* in his pursuit of so active an enlightenment does not qualify as a mystical attainment. The *bodhisattva* must achieve 'non-discriminating wisdom' (*nirvikalpajñāna*), wherein distinctions are not possible and 'sameness' (*samatā*) prevails, so that he may liberate himself from the bonds of passion and misconception. Nevertheless, he must not abide in this. He must rather overcome it by the cultivation of 'subsequently attained wisdom' (*tatpṛṣṭhalabdajñāna*), which is defined as his mastery of compassion (*karuṇā*) and skill-in-means (*upāya-kauśalya*) to be used upon his 'return' to *saṃsāra* and its 'non-sameness' (*asamatā*).[40] To effect this return, he adds a further dimension to the classical distinction between calming and discernment. Thus:

> When the *bodhisattva* is without false discrimination of *dharma*, this is known as calming. But when he combines true knowledge of *dharma* according to ultimate truth with the worldly wisdom of universal expedience, this is called discernment.[41]

Here we see the full impact of the Buddhists' subordination of mystical transport to analytical discernment. The meditative path itself, not only its goal, becomes a way of action rather than simply a contemplative withdrawal. Witness Vimalakīrti on the topic of meditative absorption (*pratisaṃlayana*):

> O Śariputra (a *śrāvaka*), you need not sit in this way to practise still-sitting (quiescent meditation). As for still-sitting: not to manifest the body or mind in any of the three realms (the sensual realm, the realm of form, the formless realm) this is to practise still-sitting. To display all manner of dignified comportment without arising from the attainment of cessation, this is to practise still-sitting. To display worldly characteristics without abandoning religious qualities, this is to practise still-sitting. The mind dwelling neither within nor without, this is to practise still-sitting. To exercise the thirty-seven aids to enlightenment without fleeing the various views, this is to practise still-sitting. To enter *nirvāṇa* without extinguishing the defilements, this is to practise still-sitting. He who sits in this manner wins the Buddha's seal of approval.[42]

Vimalakīrti, the lay *bodhisattva*, speaks for all of Mahāyāna in his denial of the assumption that meditation is merely the pursuit of supernormal experiences. He even says that the *bodhissattva* ought not to extinguish the passionate defilements (*kleśa*), which as we saw are precisely the obstacles destroyed by the quiescent or 'mystical' practices of meditation.[43]

It is this sort of Mahāyāna comment on meditation and on the sort of experience one might call mystical, which lies behind the characteristic Zen claim that Zen is just 'carrying water and chopping wood', that 'the Zen mind is the everyday mind', or that 'practice itself is enlightenment'. Note that in the famous 'Ten Oxherding Pictures' used in Zen to symbolize the meditator's progress towards enlightenment, the stage that we might identify as a mystical attainment is symbolized by a blank circle – an apt symbol for 'oneness' and the like. But the penultimate and ultimate stages are symbolized in paintings rich in detail and action, and the last is entitled 'Return to the Marketplace with Gift-Giving Hands'.[44]

The further examples we might adduce are innumerable, but even the few we have given should make it clear that especially in Mahāyāna Buddhism neither meditation nor its goal of enlightenment is merely a matter of having mystical experiences; this even though it is also clear that mystical experience has a significant role to play in the discipline. In other words, in the words of the tradition itself, the goal of Mahāyāna practice is a truly quotidian enlightenment – a continuing personal transformation manifest not in the attainment of particular experiences, however rare and wonderful, but in a sustained attitude toward life articulated in each and every daily activity of life. Nor is this quality of life simply the consequence of an enlightenment experience; it is averred to be enlightenment itself. Thus:

So Dōgen said, 'We should attain enlightenment before we attain enlightenment.' It is not after attaining enlightenment that we find its true meaning; the trying to do something in itself is enlightenment.[45]

Assuming that one may accept, or at least entertain, the key distinctions drawn above – between calming and discernment, and between mystical experience and Buddhist meditation – of what use, if any, might such distinctions be to those engaged in the philosophical investigation of mysticism? At the outset of this essay it was suggested that they might have some pertinence to three clusters of philosophical problems concerning mysticism. Let us conclude by briefly addressing each one of them, not in the expectation that they may be fully dealt with, but only with a view towards suggesting what light the proper understanding of the Buddhist example may shed on them.

Apropos of the problem of distinguishing between mystical experience and its interpretation, Buddhist meditation serves as an example of a contemplative discipline in which the auto-interpretation of mystical experience is systematically and self-consciously applied to this experience itself. This application is made as the experience is occurring or while the imagery of the experience is still directly present to the meditator's attention, rather than after the experience in a 'cool moment' of tendentious reflection. Moreover, the discipline of meditation is designed to induce just those mystical experiences which will, when properly analysed, best exemplify basic Buddhist doctrines. Thus, rather than speak of Buddhist doctrines as interpretations of Buddhist mystical experiences, one might better speak of Buddhist mystical experiences as deliberately contrived exemplifications of Buddhist doctrine. In view of this possibility, it seems worth considering whether mystical experiences in other traditions are not also, though less deliberately, induced; and whether doctrine is not elsewhere similarly determinative of religious experience, rather than determined by it.[46]

Regarding the problem of whether or how mystical experiences may be cited in support of the truth-claims of certain propositions of belief, Buddhist meditation displays an attitude of wariness and of concern over the powerful delusive potential of mystical experience. In prescribing such practices as trance, absorption, and concentration Buddhists explicitly recognize that they are dealing in potentially hazardous remedies, the misuse of which can be more serious than the diseases they are intended to cure. They are especially concerned so to control such experiences, by the force of disciplined and doctrinally formed intellect, that they may not be occasions for the formulation of beliefs about the nature of reality, much less for the commitment to such beliefs or the strengthening of them. In fact, discernment is held to be destructive of all views, even and especially such as mystical experience might inspire. Mystical experiences are used in Buddhism in much the same way that doctrines are used, as expedient devices rather than as objects of faith. The only view confirmed by the Buddhist use of mystical experience is a reflexively negative one, namely the view that no views capture the nature of reality. And this itself is not a 'view about reality' but only a 'view about views'. Likewise it is certain that Buddhists do not ontologize the contents of their mystical experiences, nor people the cosmos with mystical entities, since their very purpose in having them is to 'discern' their illusoriness. All of this may suggest to the philosophical investigator of mysticism that there is a legitimacy to the suspicion cultivated by some philosophers about the use of mystical experience to 'prove' the truth of theism, monism, pantheism, panentheism, or whatever.

At least in the case of Buddhism we have one reflective mystical tradition which denies the validity of such use.

Regarding finally the problem of the relationship between mystical experience and other human concerns, Buddhist meditation, especially as it is defined in Mahāyāna, suggests that there may be connections between them deeper than normally supposed. The point of Buddhist meditation, including the mystical experiences it allows, is, as Dōgen has said, 'not to obtain a certain thing' but to 'become a certain man'. Mystical experience thus has no sovereign autonomy in Buddhism. Rather it is seen to have important consequences for all areas of human life – not the least of which is morality – and to be judged according to those consequences. The mystical experience affects the moral life, Buddhists believe, and they therefore take the greatest pains in their meditative disciplines to see to it that its effect is the proper, just, and compassionate one. In so doing, they may offer instruction to those who examine mystical claims for antinomianism or the transcendence of good and evil, and may offer caution to those who would hold that mysticism can be a refuge from a life of moral responsibility.

The above are really only possibilities offered for further consideration, but perhaps even they are sufficient to indicate that the philosophical analysis of mystical experience may profit by careful attention to the Buddhist 'meditative analysis' of the same.

NOTES

1 Ninian Smart, *Reasons and Faiths: An Investigation of Religious Discourse, Christian and Non-Christian* (London, Routledge and Kegan Paul, 1958). This is Smart's earliest and most extensive statement of the distinction, but it also appears in several of his later writings.

2 There are, of course, important exceptions, as in the cases of tantric Buddhism (Vajrayāna) with its dazzling array of hieratic imagery, Pure Land Buddhism (Chinese: *Ching-t'u*, Japanese: *Jōdo*) with its *bhakti*-like piety, and the Mahāyāna scriptural tradition with its pantheon of celestial buddhas and bodhisattvas. As might be expected, however, the interpretive problems that arise in these cases are mirror images of the problems that beset the interpretation of mystical experience in theistic traditions. The appearance in Mahāyāna of literary and ritual symbolism redolent of the numinous may not be taken as evidence for the claim that Mahāyāna is a departure from the sobriety and austere 'agnosticism' of early Buddhism. For every fabulous 'buddha realm' of Mahāyāna scripture there is a Zen master urging, 'If you meet a buddha, kill him.'

3 Examples are taken only from works which approach mysticism from a philosophical and/or cross-cultural point of view. Thus classics like Evelyn Underhill's *Mysticism* and Gershom Scholem's *Major Trends in Jewish Mysticism*, which deal with mysticism in only one tradition, will not be considered. However, it must be noted that the influence of such works, especially of the former, is considerable, even upon the writings of philosophers who are not concerned with only the western traditions. For a useful survey of the contemporary discussion of mysticism, see P. G. Moore, 'Recent Studies of Mysticism', *Religion: Journal of Religion and Religions* 3 (1973), 146–56. Since the compilation of Moore's review several major studies have appeared, e.g. Agehananda Bharati, *The Light at the Center: Context and Pretext of Modern Mysticism* (Santa Barbara, Ross-Erikson, 1976); Arthur C. Danto, *Mysticism and Morality* (New York, Basic Books, 1972); Ben-Ami Scharfstein, *Mystical Experience* (Oxford, Blackwell, 1973 and New York, Bobbs-Merrill, 1973); Frits Staal, *Exploring Mysticism* (Berkeley, Univ. of California Press, 1975).

4 W. T. Stace, *Mysticism and Philosophy* (London, Macmillan, 1961). The influence of Stace's work has been more often to stimulate criticism than to elicit agreement. Ch. 2 (pp. 41–133) is the one most relevant to the present discussion.

5 See Moore, 'Recent Studies', p. 149, and N. Smart, 'Mystical Experience', *Sophia* 1 (1962), 19–26.

6 One suspects special pleading here, for much of Stace's latter argument for the objectivity and paradoxicality of mysticism will depend on this subordination of multiplicity to unqualified unity.

7 Not all who discuss mysticism do describe it. Smart, for example, says little more than that mystical experience is the attainment of a special state of mind, usually as a result of having followed some spiritual discipline, which state of mind cannot be accounted for in terms of such numinous categories as 'prophetism', 'devotionalism', etc. This reluctance to amplify a characterization of mysticism may seem curious in view of Smart's statement that 'phenomenologically, mysticism is everywhere the same' (see N. Smart, 'Interpretation and Mystical Experience', *Religious Studies* 1 (1965), p. 87), but there is good reason for it. Although it is certainly desirable to have as wide as possible an acquaintance with mysticism, thereby to avoid too parochial an impression of the subject, it is precisely such breadth which would make the task of comprehensive description virtually impossible and which would then impede other sorts of consideration of the phenomenon. Staal too refrains explicitly (p. 9) from definition or general description, claiming to have only some 'intuitive notions' which never become explicit. This, of course, is not to suggest that either scholar avoids description of particular instances of mystical experience.

8   Bharati, p. 25. The use of the qualifier 'numerical' in this definition may be a needless over-specification of mystical oneness.

9   Scharfstein, pp. 142–6. The other ten quintessences are separation, uniqueness, inclusion, familiar strangeness, depletion, aggression, conscience, mirror-reversal, humour, and reality.

10   Abraham H. Maslow, *Religions, Values and Peak Experiences* (New York, Viking, 1970), pp. 59–60.

11   Danto, pp. 56–8.

12   Mircea Eliade, *Yoga: Immortality and Freedom* (London, Routledge and New York, Pantheon, 1958), p. 5 *et passim*.

13   Herbert Fingarette, *The Self in Transformation* (New York, Harper & Row, 1965), pp. 290–305.

14   F. C. Happold, *Mysticism* (London, Penguin, 1970), pp. 46–7.

15   Ronald W. Hepburn, 'Mysticism, Nature and Assessment of', *The Encyclopaedia of Philosophy* (London and New York, Macmillan, 1967), p. 429.

16   Zaehner's concern to establish, not only differences among various mysticisms, but also a hierarchy of mysticisms is developed in both his early writings (e.g. the well-known *Mysticism: Sacred and Profane* (Oxford: Clarendon Press, 1957) and his later works (e.g. *Concordant Discord* (Oxford: Clarendon Press, 1970)) and *Zen, Drugs and Mysticism* (New York, Pantheon, 1973).

17   For the Chinese graph, see *Mathew's Chinese–English Dictionary*, revised American edition (Cambridge, Mass., Harvard Univ. Press, 1943), no. 939.

18   *Mathew's* no. 3575.

19   The Buddhist term *dharma* is notorious for the multiplicity of its meanings. Here it may mean either 'items of doctrine' (e.g. the 'four noble truths') or 'constituent elements of reality'. It may well be that both are intended, but traditionally the former is emphasized in connection with *vipaśyanā*.

20   Asaṅga, *Abhidharmasamuccaya*, the Chinese translation of Hsüan-tsang (T1605:31.685b5-10). Note that quotations from the Chinese Buddhist canon are from its Taishō shinshū daizōkyō ed. (abbreviated 'T'), cited by serial no., vol., page, column, and lines.

21   *Jñāna-darśana*, more literally 'knowing as seeing', roughly a synonym for *vipaśyanā*.

22   *Majjhima Nikāya*, ii.17.

23   Literal translations of this term, e.g. 'entirety-field', are of little help. The ten are: earth, water, fire, air, blue, yellow, red, white, light, and space. An example of their use may clarify the meaning. In the case of the earth device, the meditator focuses his visual attention on a disc of light-reddish earth situated a few feet in front of him, letting that

stand for the 'whole' or 'entirety' of the element earth. He proceeds first to note all of its features, then to fashion an internal and subtle eidetic image of it, then to transform that image into a kind of abstract concept or symbol of 'earth-ness'. The theory is that, as the device is being transformed into an eidetic image and then conceptualized, the mind–body complex of the meditator is also undergoing an analogous refinement. For a fuller account of the complexities of this process see Buddhaghosa's *Visuddhimagga* (*Path of Purification*), tr. Bhikkhu Ñyāṇamoli (Colombo, Gunasena, 1964), pp. 122–84.

24 For example, the four 'divine abodes' (*brahma-vihāra*) or 'immeasurables' (*apramāna*) – compassion (*karuṇā*), benevolence (*maitrī*), sympathetic joy (*muditā*), and equanimity (*upekṣā*) – which are thought to be antidotes to particular spiritual maladies like hatred, anger, selfishness, distraction, etc. Again, see *Visuddhimagga*, pp. 321–53.

25 This outline is abstracted from the *Sāmaññaphala* and *Poṭṭhapāda Suttas* of the Pāli *Dīgha Nikāya*.

26 For an expert discussion of these factors as they are presented in the Theravāda Buddhist canon, see L. S. Cousins, 'Buddhist *Jhāna*: Its Nature and Attainment according to the Pāli Sources', *Religion: Journal of Religion and Religions* 3 (1973), 115–31.

27 See Eliade, *Yoga*, pp. 79–84, and *passim*.

28 Upatissa, *Vimuttimagga* (*Path of Liberation*), in the Chinese translation of Sanghapāla (T1648:32.442a23–28).

29 On this point, there is an interesting passage in the same text. The question is there raised of whether a meditator who unexpectedly emerges from his absorption in the midst of a meditative 'flight' will then plummet to earth. The answer is that he will not. He will simply see himself once more sitting in his original position (T1648:32.442a20–23). The question of literalness, however, is not so simple. A careful answer to it requires determining also what counts as 'literal' in the Buddhist world view. Illusions are perhaps not so unreal in a world held to be itself 'like an illusion'.

30 Kamalaśīla, *Uttarabhāvanākrama*, trans. from Giuseppe Tucci's edn. of the Sanskrit, *Minor Buddhist Texts*, Pt. III (Rome, Istituto Italiano per Il Medio ed Estremo Oriente, 1971), pp. 4–5. The references to 'coming and going' mean that the imagery of the meditation – in this case the eidetic image of a Buddha – are intrinsic to the meditation and have no independent existence apart from it.

31 '*Vipaśyanā* is the name given to the investigation and examination of *dharma*. When *vipaśyanā* is thoroughly penetrating it is called *prajñā*' – Ching-ying Hui-yüan, *Ta-ch'eng i-chang* (T1851:44.665c4–6). Another common translation of *prajñā* is 'wisdom'.

32 See, for example, the *Sāmaññaphala Sutta* (*Dīgha Nikāya*, ii) according to which the various absorptions and 'attainments' (*samāpatti*) are

only preliminary to a series of 'fruits' (*phala*) of meditation, the first of
which is 'knowledge and vision'. Also, in the *Visuddhimagga*, the last
three and highest of the seven stages of purification are three species of
'purity of knowledge and vision'. In this regard the *Visuddhimagga*'s
most important scriptural source is the *Rathavinīta Sutta* (*Majjhima
Nikāya*, i. 24). See I. B. Horner, tr., *The Middle Length Sayings*, Vol. I
(London, Pali Text Society, 1954), pp. 187–94.

33   The classic discussion of these two approaches to release is Louis de
La Vallée Poussin, 'Musīla et Nārada: le chemin du Nirvāṇa',
Mélanges chinois et bouddhiques, 5 (1937), 189–222. The issue there is
whether or not certain entirely anoetic meditative experiences, like
saṃjñāvedita-nirodha (extinction of notion and feeling) or *nirodha-
samāpatti* (attainment of extinction) are truly tantamount to *nirvāṇa*
and, if so, is it therefore possible to dispense with *prajñā* and intellect
and to rely entirely on *samādhi* or *dhyāna* in one's pursuit of enlightenment. This question has been the focus of considerable scholastic
argument (see *Abhidharmakośa* II. 43) but something approaching a
consensus is to be found in the Mahāyāna conviction that such attainments discourage compassion (see, for example, Kamalaśīla's *First
Bhāvanākrama*, G. Tucci, *Minor Buddhist Texts*, II, Rome, ISMEO,
1958, pp. 120, 169–70, 211–14), and in the Theravāda view that even
this highest form of *samādhi* is but a temporary taste of *nirvāṇa*
secured only through prior perfection of insight (see P. Vajirañāṇa,
Buddhist Meditation in Theory and Practice, Colombo, Gunasena,
1962, p. 454). The most thorough study of the dialectic between intellectual insight and mental quiescence in Buddhist practice is Guy
Bugault, *La notion de 'prajñā' ou de sapience selon les perspectives du
Mahāyāna*, Publications de l'Institut de Civilisation Indienne, 32
(Paris, Éditions É. de Boccard, 1968). It has recently been suggested
by Stephan Beyer that the tension between these two emphases is a
result of early Buddhism's having created its own forms of meditation
by combining pre-existent disciplines that may have been separately
cultivated in pre- or non-Buddhist traditions. See Charles Prebish, ed.
Buddhism: A Modern Perspective (University Park, Pennsylvania, The
Pennsylvania State University Press, 1975), p. 137.

34   My summary account of these two cultivations is drawn largely from
Vasubandhu's *Abhidharmakośa* (in Hsüan-tsang's Chinese translation,
T1558:29.123c–134b. See also Louis de la Vallée Poussin's French
translation (Paris, Geuthner, 1925), vol. 4, pp. 119–303), but the distinction is widely employed throughout Buddhist literature.

35   This is the subject of another essay, but I would be prepared to argue
that the doctrinal concepts or theories of Buddhism, e.g. dependent
origination, are not so much theories or concepts about the world as
they are theories and concepts about 'theories and concepts about the
world'. Their proper use is to disabuse the meditator of his attachment

to any and all concepts. In the end, they themselves must be dispensed with. To use a famous Buddhist simile, like a raft which has served its purpose of ferrying one across the river, they must be left behind.

36 Bharati, pp. 45 and 82.

37 There is perhaps one strategy for bearing out my hypothesis in the case of Theravāda. That would be to argue, as I think is possible, that there is greater continuity between Theravāda and Mahāyāna than either is wont to admit. If that is true, and if, as I am about to argue, the hypothesis is probable in the case of Mahāyāna, then one may infer that it would hold for Theravāda as well. But the implementation of such a strategy is well beyond the scope of the present essay. For more on this see the fundamental observations of S. Katz in his paper published in this volume.

38 Nāgārjuna, *Mūlamadhyamikakārikā*, XXV:30 (Kumārajīva's Chinese trans., T1564: 30.36a10).

39 *Laṅkāvatārasūtra*, Śikṣānanda's Chinese trans. (T672:16.607b10).

40 See, for example, Asaṅga's *Mahāyānasamgraha*, Hsüan-tsang's Chinese trans. (T1594:31.147b19–148c11) on the two *jñāna*. On 'non-sameness', see, for example, the *Gaṇḍavyūha-sūtra*, Suzuki's revised ed. of the Sanskrit (Kyoto, 1949), p. 523.

41 Asaṅga, *Mahāyānasamgraha*, Hsüan-tsang's Chinese tr. (T1594: 31.539c24–26).

42 *Vimalakīrtinirdeśa*, Kumārajīva's Chinese trans. (T475:14.539c19–26).

43 See, for example, Hsüan-tsang's *Vijñaptimātratāsiddhi* (T1585:31.2a9–24, 23c19–29).

44 A reproduction of two versions of this sequence of Zen paintings may be found in D. T. Suzuki, *Manual of Zen Buddhism* (London, Rider, 1974 and New York, Grove Press, 1960) between pp. 128 and 129 and on pp. 135–44. On the differences between versions, see Suzuki's introductory comments.

45 Shunryū Suzuki, *Zen Mind, Beginner's Mind* (New York and Tokyo, Weatherhill, 1970), p. 118. I have not been able to trace Suzuki Rōshi's quotation from Dōgen.

46 For a fully developed philosophical discussion of this issue see S. Katz's paper in this volume. See also the remarks by C. Keller in his paper published herein.

ROBERT M. GIMELLO: Ph.D. (Columbia University). Dr Gimello has taught at Columbia University and at Dartmouth College, and is now an Assistant Professor in the Department of Religious Studies of the University of California at Santa Barbara. He has published articles on Chinese and Buddhist thought in *Philosophy East and West*, and has several articles forthcoming.

Intuition and the Inexpressible

RENFORD BAMBROUGH

T. S. Eliot speaks in *Four Quartets* of the poet's intolerable wrestle with words and meanings, a struggle in which

> each venture
> Is a new beginning, a raid on the inarticulate
> With shabby equipment always deteriorating
> In the general mess of imprecision of feeling,
> Undisciplined squads of emotion.

Earlier in the same work there is a cry of anguish from the same battlefield:

> Words strain,
> Crack and sometimes break, under the burden,
> Under the tension, slip, slide, perish,
> Decay with imprecision, will not stay in place,
> Will not stay still.

In an essay on Literature and Philosophy I quoted these two passages and made this comment:

There is the risk here and in other passages of pining for what will have the stillness of the Chinese jar and still have the power of the slipping, sliding, perishing words to live and move and have a being that consists in and makes possible their expressing and communicating the shifting surfaces that are the depths and dimensions of the Word. Like Rudolf Otto on the inexpressible, Eliot seems at times to be aspiring after impossible modes of communication that would capture the truth on a blank canvas or a silent gramophone record. Kant once and for all rebuked such aspirations: 'The light dove, cleaving the air in her free flight, and feeling its resistance, might imagine that its flight would be still easier in empty space.' The stresses and strains and resistances are as indispensable to thought and understanding as they are to the Chrysler building or the Sydney Harbour Bridge. Eddington's table stands firm only while the bees buzz.[1]

I quote that paragraph because it is a promissory note that is now due for payment. It makes a statement and hints that good reasons could be given for the statement, but it offers less than a hint of what the reasons are.

Like many other poets, philosophers and theologians, Eliot and Otto were concerned both with the limits of thought and with the limits of language. Though we speak separately of thought and language, of reason and communication, we need still to be conscious of the unity of thought and the modes of its expression that is marked in Greek by using the one word *logos* for both speech and reason. The problem of the limits of reason and the problem of the limits of language are two connected problems, and if a proposed solution to either of them is to have any plausibility it must have something to offer towards the solution of the other. Since they are both philosophical problems, a contribution to their solution is already made by any thinker who states the problems clearly. When the poets and the theologians describe what they take to be the limits of thought and the limits of language they are contributing to our understanding of thought and of language by indirect means, by means analogous to those through which any persuasive sceptic, when arguing that such and such a kind of knowledge does not deserve the name of knowledge, contributes to the understanding of the knowledge whose credentials he is attempting to impugn. What they succeed in doing is to make clear the differences between the modes of reason or of expression that they are demeaning and some other mode or modes of expression or of reason that they take as paradigmatic, or the requirements of some model or picture or definition of knowledge or communication that does not even fit the paradigms that are offered in its name. Reason and language have many mansions, and we can do justice to the varieties that Otto and Eliot are describing without being driven to represent them as above and beyond thought and language, or below and beneath thought and language.

Intuition

'Intuition an unnecessary shuffle.'[2] This phrase is a marginal aside in Wittgenstein's discussion of 'following a rule'. It is surrounded by double brackets, and is not provided with a verb. But into this nutshell is packed much of what needs to be said about intuition in ethics, aesthetics, and religion as well as in logic and mathematics. The words 'by intuition' are offered as an answer to the explicit or implicit question 'How do we *know* that this is valid, or good, or beautiful?' Sometimes we may claim to know the truth of a logical or mathematical proposition and to be able to establish the truth of the proposition by a proof. But when we take somebody over the steps of the proof, we expect him to understand the steps of the proof, one by one, without asking for a *proof* that each step is valid. If he does challenge a particular step, and we are able to offer some further explanation or demonstration of the soundness of the step, the procedure must nevertheless come to an end at some point at which he either recognizes that there is a valid step or cannot follow the proof. At the point at which the procedures of proof and explanation come to an end we are still disposed to ask 'How do we know this? How do we know that there is a valid step when there is no proof that the step is valid?' It is then natural to answer that it is by *intuition* that we know this. From Wittgenstein's nutshell we can unpack the suggestion that this answer has nothing but its outward form to distinguish it from saying that it is not by any *procedure* that we know that the step is sound. We know this, but there is no procedure by which we can be said to know it. To say that we just know it, without its being necessary or possible to give any reason for it, sounds dogmatic. To say that there is a faculty by which we acquire the knowledge that we do not acquire by any procedure may sound less dogmatic, but it is no more than a disguised way of making the same point again: that here is something that we know without the application of any procedure or the invocation of any faculty. Only the form is changed, and the content, dogmatic or not, remains the same. If it is dogmatic, the dogma is inescapable.

The things that we may or must know without applying any procedures are of many kinds, and they include all the things that deserve to be called the foundations or ultimate grounds of all the rest of our knowledge.

At the present time I know that my feet are firmly on the floor of this room. I know that my right foot is to the right of my left foot – that I am not standing with my feet crossed. This is something that I could know by observation. I can now look down and assure myself that I was telling you the truth. But I did already know this when I first announced it to you a moment ago, and I did not then know it by observation or by any other procedure, just as I now know without looking down that since I first spoke of the position of my feet I have moved my left leg so that it is now crossed over my right foot.

When I look at a British pillar-box I know without the use of any procedure that the pillar-box is red. I could know this as the result of carrying out a procedure. I could measure the wavelength of the light reflected by the surface of the pillar-box, and could then determine its colour by making use of the known correlations between the wavelengths of light reflected from the surfaces of objects and the perceived colours of the objects. But I ordinarily know that a pillar-box is red without the use of such a procedure. What is more, I can only use that or any other procedure for establishing that the pillar-box is red if, and because, I can know the same thing without the use of any procedure, just as I can know by means of a thermometer that one thing is hotter than another only if I can know without the use of a thermometer that one thing is hotter than another; since unless we are capable of discriminating hotter things from colder things without the use of instruments we cannot design and calibrate a thermometer.

Wherever there are procedures there are things that can be known without procedures, and whose knowledge is necessary for the devising and validation of the procedures. The examples that I have given so far are all from the sphere of sensation and perception: I *feel* that this is hotter than that; I *see* that the pillar-box is red; and my knowledge that my feet are on the floor, though it is neither sensory nor perceptual, and raises interesting issues of its own, is sufficiently close to the other examples to join them in the contrast that must be made between them and the important group of cases in which we speak or can be persuaded to speak of *intuition*.

Intuition is spoken of in cases where there is knowledge that is acquired without procedures and which is not sensory or perceptual knowledge. Because of the important analogy between those cases and the cases of perceptual knowledge, intuition is commonly conceived as a kind of metaphorical perception. The application of this metaphor is least controversial when it expresses the idea of logical insight: I *see* that the individual step in the proof is valid; I see with the same eye of the mind that $2 \times 2 = 4$, and that every proposition is either true or false and not both, and in general it is the source of my knowledge of all that I need to know in advance of devising or employing *procedures* of proof or argument or calculation. Philosophers become more quarrelsome when some of their number suggest that in morals and criticism, as well as in mathematics and logic, there are some things that can be known without proof and can serve as the basis of proof and argument. There are many contexts in which almost any of the issues mentioned in this paragraph would need to be pursued in great detail if referred to at all. Here I can be spared most of that labour because I introduce the notion of intuition for the sake of a contribution that it can make, even if not pursued much further than this, to the resolution of my disagreement with Otto and Eliot about the inexpressible; as usual, to face a problem about reason or speech is to face a problem about speech and reason. When we recognize the nature and extent of the unconscious and unreflective understanding that is the background of all our understanding we shall be on the way to grasping the relation between what we can formally articulate and what is expressible, if at all, by informal and indirect modes of utterance.

There is no definite limit to the extent of this unreflective understanding, acquired without conscious attention to reasons, argument, or evidence, and we are constantly extending its range. When we are doing philosophy we tend to remember the more formal and dramatic means whereby we add to our knowledge: proof, experiment, testimony, conscious observation. We are liable to forget how effortlessly it is possible to come to know more than we knew at first about a strange place, or a new acquaintance, or an unfamiliar play or novel, or a new subject of study – genetics, or pottery, or the history of a particular place or period. And even when the play or the person, the place or the subject, has become more familiar, we may and ordinarily do continue to increase our familiarity by these undramatic, imperceptible means.

The same applies to learning about life in general, to the gathering of experience, both in childhood and when life, too, has become more familiar. Sometimes we know that in the light of what has happened today things will always look different. We know that something has been discovered or revealed, noticed or experienced. But these are not the only times when we are acquiring experience and knowledge in whose light things will later look different. Often we become aware of such a change only when we see how different something looks.

At the cinema, in the days of 'continuous performance', there was a common experience that illustrates this possibility without giving more than a hint of its wide scope. If you went in a few minutes before the end of the film you would see a more or less unintelligible ending. By the time you had seen the whole of the rest of the film and then saw the ending again it looked altogether different while still looking exactly the same. Nothing was changed except the light in which you were now seeing what you had already seen. We do not always need new information, new data, in order to learn something new, and even when, as in this case, the learning includes the addition of new data, its significance is not usually exhausted by the acquisition of the new material. It will often need to be set in its relation to much that is already known to us, and the setting is a process which may continue long after the new data have been added to the stock.

A recognition of the nature and scope of these methods of acquiring and extending knowledge would weaken the impulse, present in all of us and strong in many, to try to settle bounds and limits to what can be understood and to what can be expressed. If the impulse is indulged it expresses itself in forms that are dangerous to the human understanding and disrespectful to its powers: in crude distinctions between feeling and reason, emotion and understanding, which threaten the dignity of thought by threatening its unity, whether their authors insist that what is outside the scope of reason is too high for reason or too low.

The same lesson is taught by Wittgenstein's observation, made in many parts of the philosophical forest, that we are liable to confuse the possession of a skill with knowledge of the truth of propositions. Because a skill can be partly expressed or displayed as knowledge of the truth of propositions, we are inclined to identify with this theoretical knowledge what should be seen primarily as a practice. Wittgenstein himself develops this point most fully in the case of the use of language. To know how to use a word is to know how to *do* something, even though this skill may be manifested at least partly by a description of the skill, by an articulation of the implicit structure of the practice. The philosopher's predilection for explicitness leads him either to identify the skill with its articulation or to see it as not wholly rational because it is not wholly theoretical.

The exploration of a space is also a skill, whether the space is physical or logical. 'A philosophical problem has the form: "I don't know my way about."' [3] When I know my way about in Cambridge or Melbourne my knowledge includes knowledge of the truth of indefinitely many propositions about the spatial relations between churches and parks, shops and suburbs. But my knowing my way about has a unity and an inexhaustibility that cannot be matched by any list of propositions. It involves knowing propositions but does not consist in knowing them. It is a skill in the practice of travel and exploration. The same is true of most of our knowledge, even of most of our theoretical knowledge. We know how to manoeuvre and meander in logical space, how to move from question to question, from proposition to proposition, and on favoured occasions – which are not so rare as the philosophers think – from question to answer.

The Inexpressible

Rudolf Otto advertises in the sub-title of his book the terms in which he will think and speak of thought and speech. His work is called *The Idea of the Holy: An inquiry into the non-rational factor in the idea of the divine and its relation to the rational.*[4] In his chapter on the scope and limits of expression, under the title 'Means of Expression of the Numinous', he is as modest and hesitant about our powers of communication as he is in the sub-title about our power of understanding. The paradox is that he makes effective use of the powers whose feebleness he labours to expose. It is a familiar paradox. It has been said of Carlyle that he believed that silence was golden and proved the fact in fifty octavo volumes. Plato wrote what is now printed as five volumes of closely argued Greek in the Oxford Classical Texts series, including his conclusion that the most important thoughts are inexpressible in writing. Spinoza celebrated the importance of writing in the hearts of men and not in books, but it is by his books that he wrote in men's hearts. It is only to be expected that it is in a book that Otto tells us not to put our trust in books but in the *viva vox*. The paradox is like that of the sceptic who tries to reason us into a mistrust of reason. In this case, as in that, it pays us to ask what lies behind the bold front of the contradiction.

We talk about the limits of reason and the limits of language when we are conscious that we have reached the limits, at least for the present, of our own powers of thought and expression. But it is just at that point, where the bewailing of our limitations is most natural, that it is also most dangerous. The lesson of our limitations, and of our sensing them as limitations, is that there are unrealized potentialities for transcending the particular limits by which we may be bound. If contingent limitations are represented as *a priori* barriers we shall be discouraged from just the effort that needs to be made if we are to pass beyond the ridge or river that we have reached.

T. E. Hulme said of one of his opponents in controversy, 'Haldane prefers a guide-book to an actual visit.' Otto speaks in a similar tone of the difference between listening to music and hearing tell of a musical performance. We sometimes need these reminders of the order of priority between experience and report, art and criticism, life and literature; but there is a danger of an exaggeration on the other side. The music is more than the description, but the description may help us to understand the music. To say that guide-books are no substitute for travel need not be to say that guide-books are of no value to the traveller – before, during, and after his journey. The sceptics about speech, like the sceptics about reason, have a point, but one that must be answered by a counter-point.

They have another point. A man may use what we can see to be all the right words, the words that do succeed in expressing as well as words could the mood or matter, upshot or downfall, that we know he is trying to convey, and yet still himself fall short of understanding what he is saying. It will help us here to think of an experience we have all had, of confronting for the first time something long familiar: the Alps or the Mona Lisa, the Acropolis or Sydney Harbour.

We have all seen pictures of the Acropolis – engravings, drawings, still and moving-photographs. We have looked at models, read and heard descriptions. Hardly any of us, when presented with the physical reality of the Parthenon for the first time, could be surprised at its general shape and appearance, and if we notice any physical detail that we have not noticed before, it is likely to be one that we might well have noticed in one or more of the pictures or descriptions if we had paid them closer attention. It would certainly be possible for an architect or archaeologist to know the building so well before he saw it that he would not be surprised by any detail of its structure or appearance. But that does not mean that it would not be worth while for such a man to go to Athens to see the Parthenon; and when he does see it he will understand the temple, and recognize the force of the claims that it makes upon our attention, in a way that he did not when he was simply looking at pictures and models.

The example may stand for others more important than itself, for other cases where we have to learn the meaning of an experience we thought we already understood. If you have carefully read a novel or carefully watched a play about the death of a child, or even if you have been close to somebody who has lost a child, and could yourself give an account of the experience in the same words that would be used by those who have suffered it, you will still have something to learn of the same experience if and when you lose a child of your own. You may have no new words to offer, but you will see more meaning in the old words than you had seen before.

These points deserve the emphasis that is given to them by the critics of our powers of expression, and we need to see the wide range of their application: we may think that we know, and yet still be able to learn, the meaning of poverty or treachery or hard work or despair or shipwreck. The mistake that the critics make is to think that these points mark limitations in our powers of understanding and expression, whereas they can also and more justly be construed as themselves illustrating, in a manner wholly typical of the operation of sceptical criticism, the powers of human beings to understand and to express their understanding. Philosophers use and recognize too narrow a range of the resources of the understanding and its modes of expression. Eliot in *Four Quartets*, Joyce in *Ulysses,* are still expressing the expressible. If we find the works difficult, the difficulty is that of understanding the understandable. Beyond the limit of our understanding there cannot be a total blank, but only something further to be understood.[5]

The same and similar examples serve also to expose the mistake that we make if we speak depreciatively of 'mere words', forgetting that even when we speak in words we can call on means of expression that go beyond the choosing of the words themselves. We have all the resources of context, of pointing and gesturing, the conveying of different meanings by different tones. Above all (and this is where what I have to say about the 'inexpressible' is most in debt to what I have said about intuition), there is the power of invoking, in our efforts to explain ourselves and our world to ourselves and each other, the things about the world and ourselves that we already know, and of which we share the understanding.

This power of context is most clearly displayed in conversation about specialized topics. It takes a physicist to talk about physics to another physicist. If one of us who knows no physics spends an hour with a physicist, it is likely that he will be able to tell us things that we did not know, but even if we could be said to be learning physics – and that is very doubtful – we could hardly be said to be talking about physics. But when a physicist speaks to a physicist he can speak to him of physics; they can talk about their subject because each can rely on, even when he does not explicitly invoke, the knowledge that they share.

The same power is harnessed in every conversation, even when it is not a conversation between physicists or historians or any other specialists. Every conversation is a conversation between human beings, and human beings as such, before all specialisms, share a vast fund of knowledge that need not be explicitly drawn on in order to be among the means whereby they now try to convey, one to another, what they have done or seen or suffered. It may operate silently and unobtrusively, but it is part of the machinery by which they compose and print their thoughts for communication.

There are intermediate cases that point the same moral; intermediate, that is, between the highly specialized talk of physicist to physicist and the universal case of man or woman talking to woman or to man. If you both know Greek tragedy, or the Old and New Testaments, each of you has access to a shared understanding and to means of making that understanding speak. If and because we have shared experiences, whether as coal-miners, sailors or soldiers, or in everyday life outside all dramatic contexts, then we also have a body of understanding on which we can rely without consciously or explicitly appealing to it, and which is none the less central and indispensable for the understanding and description of what is *now* happening.

Otto himself helps us to remember that there are arts other than the art of speech through which we can express and communicate thoughts and feelings. He writes persuasively of architecture, of what is conveyed and recorded by Chinese temples, or the Pyramids of Egypt. He tells us of what is conveyed by sculpture, by statues of the Buddha and the Sphinx, that could not be conveyed by words. He overlooks the possibility that we might here speak of the *language* of the bronze or marble, and of the part played by convention and tradition in the representation of gods and men. But he rightly celebrates our capacity, both in religion and in the rest of life, to express ourselves through symbols and analogies, and not only in the arts that use words and literal metaphors.

He also writes affectionately of Chinese painting, and remarks upon its use of empty space, of uncoloured background, as part of its mode of expression. A similar point recurs in a passage about music, which I quote because it is integral to Otto's view of expression and to what I want to say about his view:

Not even music, which else can give manifold expression to all the feelings of the mind, has any positive way to express 'the holy'. Even the most consummate Mass-music can only give utterance to the holiest, most numinous moment in the Mass – the moment of transubstantiation – by sinking into stillness: no mere momentary pause, but an absolute cessation of sound long enough for us to 'hear the silence' itself; and no devotional moment in the whole Mass approximates in impressiveness to this 'keeping silence before the Lord'. It is instructive to submit

Bach's Mass in B minor to the test in this matter. Its most mystical portion is the 'Incarnatus' in the 'Credo', and there the effect is due to the faint, whispering, lingering sequence in the fugue structure, dying away *pianissimo*. The held breath and hushed sound of the passage, its weird cadences, sinking away in lessened thirds, its pauses and syncopations, and its rise and fall in astonishing semitones, which render so well the sense of awe-struck wonder – all this serves to express the *mysterium* by way of intimation, rather than in forthright utterance.[6]

The ambiguity of the last sentence is only one sign of a pervasive unclarity. Is Otto suggesting that the music achieves an utterance which is not forthright, or that this intimation, since it falls short of forthrightness, should not be called an utterance? The passage as a whole and the chapter as a whole give the impression that these examples illustrate something that is not a mode of utterance or of expression, in spite of the occurrence of those words in its description. There seems also to be the implication that silence and empty space can serve as vehicles of communication and expression.

There was once a radio play about a recording enthusiast who had an unparalleled collection of silences. It is to be hoped that he also collected the sounds that surrounded the silences, and gave to them their individualities, and such significance as they might achieve. Not even the most solemn intimations could be conveyed by an empty canvas or a silent record, unsupported by such surroundings of tone or colour. It is significant that Otto himself can describe this effective mode of communication in such intricate and indeed such technical language. What he describes is the sound and not the silence. He is using one elaborate method of communication in the presentation of the character of another. We are back with Kant's dove, cleaving the air and wishing for the vacuum in which, if it did but know, it would crash to the ground.

There is a parallel to be noticed now between the idea of communication without a medium and the idea of intuition as a faculty giving immediate awareness, a perceptiveness without any medium through which it perceives. Not even the most powerful or refined feminine intuition can operate through a brick wall. It may be that neither the possessor of the special gift nor anyone else can explain how the intuition works, but it is at least clear that it needs material to work on: tones of voice, facial expressions. Even when the perception and its mode of operation are unconscious, it still involves an unnecessary shuffle to represent it as operating without its medium and its material.

The empty spaces and the silences beloved of Otto belong to the tradition of the *via negativa*, the way of characterizing by negation, of which so much has been heard in theology. But characterization by negation is still characterization, and is still positive characterization: *omnis negatio est determinatio*. There is no irreducible difference between describing something by comparison and describing it by contrast. If you did succeed in saying only what was negative, you would not escape the fate that Berkeley ascribed to Locke: you would find yourself giving elaborate names to what others are content to call non-entity, to nothing at all. Nothing is conveyed if everything is denied.

But I deny what Otto says in order to underwrite what he means. Like other sceptics he expresses what is true by saying what is false. Both he and Eliot help us to remember that there can be understanding which is inarticulate. Philosophers are so devoted both to understanding and to articulateness that they may easily come to think that neither can be found without the other.

St Augustine said that, when nobody asked him what time was, he knew what it was; but when somebody asked him, then he did not know. He is here making a distinction between two things that may be meant by saying that I don't know something. Sometimes I say that I don't know when I mean that I cannot give you an account of the matter. That is what Augustine meant when he said that when asked what time was he did not know. (One way of saying that I don't know is to say 'I couldn't say'.) But when Augustine said that he did know what time was when he was not being asked what it was, he meant that he could operate accurately and effectively in his dealings with clocks and days and months and calendars, and that these dealings expressed and constituted the understanding of time that he could not otherwise articulate.

The same distinction helps us to understand and then to repudiate the assumption of Socrates that being able to *say* what justice or knowledge is, is a necessary means to or a necessary condition for understanding what we mean by knowledge or justice. There is indefinitely wide scope, and not only in philosophy, for the inarticulate understanding that the philosopher denies or demeans. And not only the philosopher.

When a politician dines at high table he may strike the historians and economists and political scientists as a person of sadly limited understanding. He seems not to know what he is doing at all.

Socrates spoke for these professors when he said that politicians must achieve whatever they achieved by a kind of divine dispensation – *theia moira* – since they clearly did not know what they were doing. But the politician or the businessman may know very well what he is doing, even if he does not know how to convey to others a theoretical articulation of his practical understanding. The dealer in antiques or pictures may know that this is a forgery and that is authentic without knowing how to describe the difference that makes the difference. Tea-tasting and wine-tasting are modes of discrimination whose exponents may or may not be able to articulate some of the grounds of their powers of discernment.

Levin, in *Anna Karenina*, struggles to understand life and death. His struggle to understand is at the same time a struggle to express his understanding. Yet it seems to him that Kitty and Dolly and the peasants on his estate do understand what life and death are, though they neither struggle for their understanding nor have words to express it.

To hold that there may be inarticulate understanding is not to hold that there may be any understanding that could not be articulated. Here again there is an instructive parallel between speech and reason: we may recognize that some questions are unanswered and some problems unsolved without concluding that some problems are insoluble and some questions unanswerable. Just as the location of what seems an insoluble problem is at the same time the adumbration of the approach to its solution, so is the identification of what cannot now or by any of us be expressed the signpost to the direction in which its expression may be looked for. A failure to express is a failure, and there is no failure where no success is thinkable. It is easy enough to set limits to our own powers of understanding and expression, but these are not to be confused with the limits of the expressible and the comprehensible.

It is not clear that there need be any limit to the extent to which our understanding and its expression may be increased, as individuals and as a species. We are rightly conscious of the limits of our powers and the feebleness of our efforts, and the consciousness may express itself in disappointment or even in despair. Yet in that despair, in the uncertainty and perplexity that Levin is tempted to yield to, there may lie the seeds of just that growth in understanding and articulation that he and we are looking for. To mark the limit of a power is to sketch a further potentiality. There are two sides to every frontier, wall, barrier, obstacle. Every limitation under which we labour is one that we may labour to transcend.

The shape of ignorance is the same as the shape of knowledge, just as the shape of the coastline of Australia is the same as the shape of the surrounding ocean.

The philosophers and poets who speak of the limits of thought and the limits of understanding represent as an impossibility what is only a difficulty, as a barrier what is only a boundary.[7]

NOTES

1 Bambrough (ed.), *Wisdom: Twelve Essays* (Basil Blackwell, 1974), pp. 286–7.

2 Wittgenstein, *Philosophical Investigations*, Part I, § 213.

3 Wittgenstein, *Philosophical Investigations*, Part I, § 123.

4 Tr. John W. Harvey (Pelican Books, 1959).

5 See my essay 'The Shape of Ignorance' in H. D. Lewis (ed.), *Contemporary British Philosophy* (Fourth Series) (Allen and Unwin, 1976).

6 Otto, op. cit., p. 85.

7 This essay is based on the Samuel Lovell Bequest Lecture 1975, delivered at Launceston on 25 July 1975 and at the University of Tasmania in Hobart on 28 July 1975, under the title 'Mysticism, Intuition and the Inexpressible'. The Samuel Lovell Bequest Lecture was instituted as a memorial to James Martineau. I am grateful to the University of Tasmania for inviting me to give the lecture, and to Professor W. D. Joske, Mr Frank White, and many others for their kindness and hospitality during my visit.

RENFORD BAMBROUGH, M.A. (Cambridge). Among Mr Bambrough's many publications the most important are: *Reason, Truth and God* (1969); *The Philosophy of Aristotle* (1963); *Conflict and the Scope of Reason* (1974); *New Essays on Plato and Aristotle* (1965); *Plato, Popper and Politics* (1967); and *John Wisdom: Twelve Essays* (1974). In addition he has contributed numerous articles to such journals as *Analysis*, *Philosophy*, and *The Proceedings of the Aristotelian Society*. He began his teaching career as University Lecturer in Classics in the University of Cambridge and is now University Lecturer in Philosophy at Cambridge and Fellow and Dean of St John's College, Cambridge. He has also been a visiting Professor at Cornell University, the University of California at Berkeley, the University of Oregon, and the University of Melbourne. He has given the *Stanton Lectures* in the University of Cambridge (1962–5); the *H. B. Acton Lecture* at the Royal Institute of Philosophy (1973), and the *Samuel Lovell Bequest Lecture* at the University of Tasmania, Australia (1975). Since 1972 he has been the Editor of *Philosophy*, the journal of the Royal Institute of Philosophy.

On Mystic Visions as Sources of Knowledge

NELSON PIKE

Theologians from within the Roman Catholic mystical tradition generally make a distinction between what is sometimes called a 'private revelation' and the 'public revelation',[1] i.e. between a message communicated to some specific individual by way of a mystic vision or locution, and the body of truth revealed to the entire Christian community by way of Scripture. The latter is interpreted and duly recorded in the doctrines and teachings of the Church. In some cases, a private revelation consists of a proposition already included in the public revelation. So, for example, in Chapter 18 (para. 23) of his celebrated treatise on mystical theology, the *Graces of Interior Prayer*, A. Poulain writes as follows concerning the vision of the Trinity that not uncommonly accompanies the state of mystic contemplation called 'rapture':[2]

> Even if we did not know by the Church's teaching how many persons there are in God, and how they proceed One from the Other, we should come to know it, and, by way of experience, through seeing it [in rapture].

In other cases, private revelations consist of propositions not included in the public revelation. As regards the latter, two types can be distinguished, viz. those in which items of a doctrine-like nature are revealed, and those in which information of a more mundane nature, having little or no specifically religious import, are imparted. In the *Interior Castle* (6th Mansion, ch. 4), Teresa of Avila remarks in a general way about some cases of the first sort. Here she says that in the state of rapture, the mystic learns 'certain mysteries', i.e. 'certain truths about the greatness of God' that were not known before. These, she says, are 'secret things' that an individual comes to know by way of mystic visions. She adds that in some cases, these 'secret things' are describable and in some cases not. Unfortunately, no example is given – not even one of the 'secret things' that is describable. With respect to instances of the second sort, in the *Summa Theologica*, II-II, Q. 174, a. 4, Thomas

Aquinas reminds us that Solomon received information via mystic visions concerning the nature of certain trees, beasts, and fishes indigenous to lands surrounding Israel. After defeating the English at the Battle of Orleans, Joan of Arc was awakened during the night by the 'voices' that attended her throughout her career. She was informed that the English were, at that moment, preparing a counter-attack on the city. This information was used as a basis for action. Joan marshalled the French forces and repelled the attack. These last two cases illustrate the sorts of private revelations sometimes contained in mystic visions and locutions that bear no recognizable similarity to articles included among the doctrines of the Church.

Return for a moment to the passage cited above from Poulain concerning the vision of the Trinity that usually accompanies the state of rapture. This vision is here being thought of as a source of information that is independent of Scripture and Church doctrine. Though the vision delivers information already contained in the latter, the fact that mystics have seen the Trinity seems clearly to be functioning as an independent reason for accepting the doctrine of the triune nature. It is functioning, in other words, as reconfirming support for a doctrine already included among the articles of faith. With respect to the claims made by St Teresa in the passages mentioned above, again, the point seems to be that mystic visions sometimes serve as sources of religious knowledge that are independent of the public revelation. Here the vision is regarded as a potential source of new information rather than as a source of reconfirming support for something already known. In this paper I shall attempt to formulate and clarify the position usually taken in Roman Catholic theological sources regarding the conditions under which a mystic vision or locution can function as a source of new or reconfirming information. In my presentation, I shall work closely with several classical mystical texts, but shall draw heavily as well on materials provided in Chapters 20–22 of Poulain's *The Graces of Interior Prayer*. During the course of the discussion, I shall also deal in some detail with an attack on the traditional position issued by Alisdair MacIntyre in an essay entitled 'Visions' that appeared some time ago as part of the collection *New Essays in Philosophical Theology*.[3] It is my hope that the interplay between these various sources will force to the surface some of the more subtle workings of the reasoning pattern traditionally used by christian mystical theologians when dealing with issues related to the epistemic value of mystic apprehensions.

I

I shall begin by sketching a theory which can be found in one version or another, though with varying degrees of explicitness, in most modern manuals of Catholic mystical theology. Advocates generally present it (or whichever of its elements they discuss) without supporting argument or clarificatory elaboration. Modern theologians who use it clearly think of it as traditional, i.e. as being an item of consensus among classical mystical authors such as St Teresa, St John of the Cross and St Thomas Aquinas. At the centre of this theory are the following two epistemic principles:[4]

Principle A:
   If a mystic apprehension containing a revelation is produced by God, then the apprehension in question is a reliable source of information: the revelation therein contained is true.

Principle B:
   If a mystic apprehension containing a revelation is not produced by God (i.e. is either not produced by an agent or is produced by some agent other than God, e.g. Satan), then the apprehension is not a reliable source of information: the revelation therein contained may or may not be true.

   Several phrases require clarification:
   The expression 'mystic apprehension' is here used to cover two classes of mystical phenomena, viz. mystic visions and mystic locutions. Mystic visions are visual or visual-like experiences. Mystic locutions are auditory or auditory-like experiences. Mystic apprehensions can be mixed, i.e. they may be experiences having both visual and auditory elements. I shall not here attempt to identify the various types of mystic visions and mystic locutions usually distinguished in classical mystical texts.[5] Also, I shall not here attempt to circumscribe the import of the qualifier 'mystic' as it occurs in the phrases 'mystic apprehension', 'mystic vision', and 'mystic locution'.
   A mystic apprehension (A) will be said to contain a revelation (R) just in case R can be properly described as 'the meaning' of what the mystic sees or hears when having the experience A.[6] In this paper, I shall not deal with any of the complex issues that arise in connection with the problem of determining whether a given apprehension contains a revelation or, given that it does, what the specific content of the revelation is.[7] With respect to all of the examples to be used, I shall simply assume that what is seen or

heard by the mystic has a meaning and that the meaning in question is well understood both by the mystic and by us.

A mystic apprehension contains a revelation if the meaning of what is seen or heard can be formulated in a proposition to which can be assigned a truth value. Commands, words of advice, words of encouragement and the like will not count as revelations. Apprehensions containing only commands, words of advice, etc., will thus not be of interest in the discussion. Revelations may be either true or false. In this context, the phrase 'false revelation' is in no way paradoxical or odd.[8]

An apprehension will be said to have been 'produced by God' (to have 'come from God' or to be 'divine') just in case the apprehension occurs as the result of some action on the part of God. Several kinds of cases can be distinguished. For example, if Christ were to (veridically) appear to a mystic, the resulting visual experience would count as having been produced by God. So, too, would a visual experience in which, for example, St Paul was (veridically) seen – assuming that St Paul had been sent by or commissioned by God so to appear to the apprehending mystic. In a case of this sort, St Paul would qualify as God's envoy: the experience could then be said to have resulted, ultimately, from some action on the part of God. Apprehensions that are produced by God need not be veridical sense perceptions. God (or one of God's envoys) might cause an individual to see an angel or hear the words 'Love thy neighbour' even though no angel was actually present or even though no one actually spoke the words 'Love thy neighbour'.[9] Perceptions caused by the hypnotist using post-hypnotic suggestion or perceptions caused by the psychobiologist via direct stimulation of the cortex can be used as models for these last-mentioned cases.

Principles A and B tell us (in effect) that a given mystic apprehension is a reliable source of information if and only if it results from some action on the part of God. Of course, revelations contained in reliable apprehensions are true. But it should be noted that revelations contained in unreliable apprehensions are not, for that reason, false. A revelation contained in an unreliable apprehension (e.g. one produced by Satan) might be true. Principles A and B specify conditions under which apprehensions are to be judged reliable or unreliable. Room must be left, however, for the case in which an unreliable source delivers a piece of correct information.[10]

Given a system of thought in which Principles A and B govern judgements concerning epistemic reliability, the problem of deter-

mining reliability in a given case reduces to the problem of determining whether the relevant apprehension was produced by God.
No such system would thus be of use unless it also included mention of the criteria to be used when estimating the origin of a given
apprehension. Though the list of such criteria (usually called 'signs')
differs depending on which specific mystical theologian one con-
sults, two are constant and appear to be of central importance. For
purposes of the present discussion, I shall restrict attention to just
these two. Subject to an amendment that I shall add in a postscript
at the very end of the paper, I shall assume throughout that a given
apprehension is to be included in the class of divine productions if,
and only if, it passes both the tests (possesses both of the 'signs')
that I shall now attempt to make clear.

Speaking of visions that are produced by God in Bk II, Chapter
24, sec. 6 of the *Ascent of Mount Carmel*, John of the Cross writes
as follows:[11]

> The effects these visions produce in the soul are: quietude, il-
> lumination, gladness resembling that of glory, delight, purity,
> love, humility, and an elevation and inclination toward God.
> Sometimes these effects are more intense, sometimes less. This
> diversity is due to the spirit that receives them and to God's
> wishes.

Visions produced by Satan can be used for clarifying contrast. In
the succeeding section of the same chapter, St John describes them
so:

> The devil's visions produce spiritual dryness in one's communica-
> tions with God and an inclination to self-esteem, to admitting
> them and to considering them important. In no way do they
> cause mildness of humility and love of God ... The memory
> of them is considerably arid and unproductive of the love and
> humility caused by the remembrance of good visions.

St Teresa says much the same thing in various passages that
besprinkle her writings. On her account, apprehensions from God
usually result in happiness, joy, and a sense of peace. Even if
fraught with pain and remorse, they result in a sense of humility, a
sense of one's own sinfulness, an inclination towards virtue and an
awareness of one's need for God. Teresa emphasizes, too, that
apprehensions from Satan have precisely the opposite effects. One
so afflicted is '. . . troubled, disturbed and restless; [one] loses that
devotion and joy [that one] previously had and cannot pray at

all'.[12] What I shall refer to in the sequel as the 'spiritual-effects test' (or the 'spiritual-effects sign') can be abstracted from these passages and many like them from the writings of other Christian mystics. I shall summarize it as follows:

> Apprehensions produced by God result in positive affective states as well as dispositions conducive to spiritual development (including dispositions toward virtue) on the part of the apprehending mystic.

The second test (or sign) that is to be used when attempting to determine whether a given apprehension is produced by God deals specifically with the propositional content of the revelation contained in the relevant apprehension. It is, in part, formulated by St Teresa in the following passage from Chapter 25, para. 17 of her *Life*:[13]

> For, so far as I can see and learn from experience, the soul must be convinced that a thing is from God only if it is in conformity with Holy Scripture; if it were to diverge from that in the least, I think I should be incomparably more firmly convinced that it came from the devil than I previously was that it came from God, however sure I might have felt of this. There is no need, in that case, to go in search of [other] signs, or to ask from what spirit it comes; for this is so clear a sign that it is of the devil that, if the whole world assured me it came from God, I should not believe it.

In the paragraph immediately preceding the one from which this last passage is taken, Teresa writes to the same effect with respect to cases in which the revelation contained in a given apprehension conflicts with some doctrine or teaching of the Church. In Chapter 22, para. 33 of the *Graces of Interior Prayer*, Poulain put this latter point curtly as follows:

> With regard to dogma, if one sure point is contradicted, as has happened many times in supernatural communications, it is sufficient to allow us to affirm that the speaker is not one of God's envoys.

In what is to follow, I shall refer to the criterion described in these passages as the 'Scripture-dogma test' (or the Scripture-dogma sign). In a sentence, it can be formulated so:

> The revelations contained in apprehensions produced by God do not conflict with propositions affirmed in Scripture or with

propositions included among the dogmas, doctrines, or teachings of the Church.

I mentioned earlier that for mystics and mystical theologians such as St Teresa and A. Poulain, the mystic apprehension is regarded as a potential source of religious knowledge that is independent of the public revelation. As such, it can provide data that reconfirm or supplement the various items communicated in this latter source. But if an apprehension can function as a source of knowledge that is independent of Scripture and Church doctrine, the question must surely arise as to what would happen if the content of a private revelation were to conflict with some proposition contained in the public revelation. Would there then be two independent knowledge-sources delivering two contrary propositions? How would one judge as to which of the propositions (if either) is true? Given the provision that has just been attached to the general theory, the answer to this question should be clear. By virtue of the Scripture-dogma test, under the conditions just imagined, the apprehension containing the conflicting private revelation would be excluded from the class of divine productions. Principle A would not apply: Principle B would govern procedure. The apprehension in which the private revelation was contained would be rejected as a source of reliable information. The upshot is this: Though the mystic apprehension is regarded as a source of knowledge that is independent of the public revelation, the epistemic apparatus consisting of Principles A and B, together with the various tests provided for determining whether a given apprehension is produced by God, guarantees that this source will provide no grounds for rejecting some item officially accepted in the wider non-mystical community. While the mystic apprehension continues to function as a source of knowledge that can reconfirm or supplement the articles included in Scripture-dogma, procedures are so arranged as to make it in principle impossible for it to serve as a basis upon which to reject, or even correct, some item included in the public revelation. I have taken the trouble to emphasize this feature of the procedural theory employed in traditional mystical theology because it seems to me to be an element that is likely to peak philosophical suspicion. I turn now to the critique of mystical theological procedure offered by Alisdair MacIntyre in his essay 'Visions'. That part of MacIntyre's paper in which I am principally interested seems clearly to be focused on this point.

II

I think I can best approach the critical line advanced in MacIntyre's article to which I want to draw special attention by first considering an argument which, though not clearly contained in the text, is at least suggested in a passage occurring early in para no. 3. The argument in question presupposes that we have in mind a case of the following sort: A visionary sees an angel and the angel speaks a sentence that entails 'God exists'. Perhaps the sentence is, simply, 'God exists', or, more realistically, perhaps it is something like 'God desires that you cease in your sinful ways.' In response to the apprehension, the visionary affirms that God exists and cites the experience as grounds for the truth of this theological claim. MacIntyre writes:

> We could never know from such experiences that they had the character of messages from the divine, unless we already possessed a prior knowledge of the divine and the way in which messages from it were to be identified. The decisive evidence for the divine would then be anterior to the experience and not derived from it, whereas what we are concerned with here is how far the experience itself can provide such evidence.

The interpretation of this passage that seems to me to provide the most penetrating critique of a reasoning pattern at least resembling one found in actual mystical literature is as follows: The revelation contained in the apprehension is that God (i.e. 'the divine') exists. But in order to establish that the revelation is true, the mystic must first establish that the experience can be trusted as a source of knowledge. This he attempts to do by assuming (or in some way determining) that the vision 'has the character of a message from the divine', i.e. that the angel was sent by God or that in some other way the experience resulted from some action on the part of God. Thus, in the process of arguing that the experience is a reliable source of information, the visionary assumes or, at least, draws on prior knowledge of God's existence. The upshot is that the vision has not been established as a ground for belief in the existence of God. It could serve in this capacity only had its reliability been successfully argued without presupposing the truth of the very proposition for which it is supposed to be supplying support. The principle of evidence underlying the reasoning seems to be this:

An apprehension (A) can serve as a source of evidence for 'God exists' only if (i) there is reason (R) to think that A is a reliable source of information and (ii) R does not entail 'God exists'.

No datum counts as support for 'God exists' if, in order to show that the datum has the status of evidence, one must presuppose the truth of 'God exists'. The mystic just considered has violated the second clause of this principle. He is thus guilty of what would appear to be a kind of circular reasoning.

Without commenting on the adequacy of this critique, I want now to present and clarify the passage in MacIntyre's text that is of special interest to me in the present discussion. I quote this time from para No. 5:

> What criteria does the believer invoke to distinguish true visions from false? The only criterion possible is presumably the congruence of the messages delivered in the vision with such theological doctrines as are already believed. If this be admitted, it might be argued that vision could never be the original ground of a belief yet might afford it confirmation. This will not do. Since we should only accept as genuine those experiences which did in fact afford confirmation to the belief, the statement that genuine religious experience affords confirmation of belief would be an empty tautology.

The point again seems to be that the visionary who attempts to support religious belief by reference to the content of a mystic apprehension is involved in a kind of circular reasoning. The thrust of this second argument thus seems to be in line with the first. However, the sort of reasoning that MacIntyre here seems to be criticizing is different from the reasoning criticized earlier. Three differences seem to me to be apparent.

First, the target of the attack has been broadened to include cases in which the visionary agrees that the vision cannot be used as the 'original ground' of a religious belief but attempts to use it as a source of further support for a proposition already accepted for other reasons. I am not sure how important this difference is. I imagine that the logical relation that a datum must bear to a hypothesis in order to count as evidence of any sort is the same whether the datum be entertained as the 'original ground' or as reconfirming support. I thus suspect that if one were to agree that a given datum is such that it could not, in principle, serve as the 'original ground' of a given hypothesis, one would be committed to agree that it could not function as reconfirming support for that hypothesis either. If this is right, then although the target has been widened, the issues remain the same. The thesis is, simply, that visionary experience cannot be used as support of any kind for the truth of a religious doctrine.

Secondly, the target of the attack has obviously been broadened in another way as well. The critique with which we started was aimed at the mystic who attempts to employ a mystic vision as a source of support for a very specific religious belief, viz. belief in the existence of God. Had it not been this specific belief that was involved, no circularity in the visionary's reasoning would have emerged. Presumably, the circularity in question stemmed from the fact that the existence of God was presupposed in the argument by which the mystic attempted to establish that the vision is reliable and thus can be taken as a source of support for belief in the existence of God. However, the criticism offered in the passage before us seems clearly to be that some kind of circularity is involved whether the case be one in which the visionary attempts to support belief in the existence of God or whether it be one in which he attempts to support some other religious belief such as, for example that God created and sustains the universe, that God is a Trinity, that Christ died for our sins or whatever. Of course, this second thesis is more directly in line with the conclusion MacIntyre draws in the end than is the thesis considered earlier. In the closing paragraph of the article, MacIntyre claims to have shown not just that belief in the existence of God cannot be supported by appeal to mystic apprehensions, but that religious belief in general cannot receive support from this sort of datum.

Thirdly, in the passage we are now considering, MacIntyre is dealing with a mystic who reasons very differently from the one criticized in the opening part of our discussion. In the earlier case the visionary was characterized as attempting to establish the reliability of the apprehension by appeal to its *origin*, i.e. by assuming or perhaps determining that the apprehension resulted from some action on the part of God. But in the case before us, the reasoning under attack is not of this sort. Here, MacIntyre is considering the visionary who attempts to establish the reliability of the apprehension not by reference to its origin but by calling attention to what MacIntyre describes as 'the congruence of the message delivered in the vision with such theological doctrines as are already believed'. Though the import of the term 'congruent' is not explicitly circumscribed in the text, context leaves little doubt as to its intended meaning. MacIntyre is here supposing the case in which the argument used to establish the reliability of the apprehension turns importantly on the claim that the revelation therein contained simply repeats, or, perhaps, is entailed by some item of doctrine accepted by the mystic prior to the experience. That the message, as MacIntyre says, 'confirms' some item of doctrine is the reason given by the mystic in support of the claim that the vision is 'genuine', i.e. that the vision can be trusted as a source of information. It is the point underpinning this third difference, I suspect, that explains why MacIntyre thinks he is entitled to conclude in the end that religious belief in general (and not just belief in the existence of God) are not susceptible to support by appeal to visionary experience. So long as the epistemic reliability of the apprehension is made to rest on the fact that the revelation therein contained is entailed by some doctrine, the claim that the apprehension provides support for that doctrine can be rejected no matter what the specific content of the doctrine might be. The trouble here, I think MacIntyre is saying, is that the argument for reliability makes use of the assumption that doctrine is true and thus that the revelation contained in the relevant apprehension – which is entailed by the very doctrine for which the apprehension is supposed to be supplying support – is true. The reasoning is thus subject to the same sort of criticism as was issued above where the content of the private revelation had only to do with the existence of God and where the visionary appealed to the origin of the apprehension when attempting to establish its epistemic reliability. In fact, the principle of evidence operative in this second criticism seems simply to be a generalized version of the one operative in the first:

> An apprehension (A) can serve as a source of evidence for a doctrine (D) only if: (i) there is reason (R) to think that A is a reliable source of information, and (ii) R does not entail D.

Again, it is violation of the second condition that constitutes deficiency – a kind of circularity – in the reasoning attributed to the mystic.

III

In the opening paragraph of his article, MacIntyre reminds us that there have been both Catholic and Protestant contemplatives who have attempted 'to found religious belief upon the evidence of religious experience'. Presumably, it is to the programme of such contemplatives that the challenge we have just reviewed is addressed. The implication seems to be that MacIntyre intends us to understand his critique as directed against mystics and mystical theologians such as St Teresa and A. Poulain, i.e. actual historical figures who have regarded mystic apprehension as possible sources of religious knowledge. In this connection it is of interest to note that, although MacIntyre proceeds without identifying a specific Catholic or Protestant mystic who has actually said that mystic apprehensions have positive epistemic value and without supplying textual evidence for his estimate of the way in which actual mystics and mystical theologians have reasoned when attempting to justify claims of epistemic reliability, the argument of his paper makes contact with at least two basic, traditional themes. On the interpretation I have given of the first passage quoted from his text, the import is clearly critical of a mystic reasoning in accordance with Principle A. The second passage quoted, is also aimed in a historically relevant direction. As we have seen, appeal to the content of Scripture-dogma is a vital part of traditional procedure when determining the reliability of a mystic apprehension. Further, it seems to me that there is something initially plausible about MacIntyre's argument when considered as a critique of the reasoning-pattern outlined in the first section of this paper. We noticed above that, although the epistemic apparatus employed in the mystical tradition permits apprehensions to serve as sources of information that can reconfirm our supplement accepted doctrine, the Scripture-dogma test of origin (and thus reliability) works in such a way as to assure that they will never serve as a basis for rejecting some proposition contained in the public revelation. The latter are obviously being assumed true at the outset. The consequence of conflict on the part of some private revelation is that the apprehension containing the private revelation is dismissed from the class of reliable information-bearers. MacIntyre's charge that the reasoning doubles back on itself rendering tautological and thus vacuous the claim that reliable apprehensions reconfirm doctrine, appears on the surface to be deftly placed. I turn now to a more careful examination of this idea. I shall begin by looking again at the two reasoning-patterns that were assigned to the mystic in the preceding section and which were argued to be deficient as ways of establishing epistemic reliability for mystic apprehensions.

Case I: The mystic sees the angel and the angel affirms a proposition that entails 'God exists'. The mystic believes that God exists and cites the apprehension as grounds for his conviction. When pressed concerning the reliability of the apprehension, the mystic claims that it resulted from some action on the part of God and thus can be trusted as a source of information.

This reasoning is circular in the way indicated above. The same could be said had the revelation contained in the apprehension been some proposition that is other than, but entailed by, 'God exists' and had the apprehension then been cited by the mystic as a source of support for this second proposition. For example, assume that the function 'If x is God then x is an omnipotent being' is analytic and that the revelation contained in the mystic apprehensions had been 'There exists an omnipotent being.' Given the pattern of reasoning employed in Case I, the argument for reliability would then presuppose the existence of an omnipotent being. The mystic would thus be subject to a charge of circularity had he attempted to employ the apprehension as support for belief in the existence of an omnipotent being.

Case II: The mystic sees an angel and the angel delivers a message other than 'God exists' or some proposition entailed by 'God exists': he says, for example, 'Christ died for our sins.' The mystic believes that Christ died for our sins and appeals to the content of the apprehension as support for this belief. As regards the reliability of the apprehension, the mystic maintains that the revelation therein contained is, to use MacIntyre's phrase 'congruent with' (i.e. entailed by) standard doctrine. Since standard doctrine is true, the revelation is true. The conclusion is that since its revelation is true, the apprehension is reliable. The apprehension is thus taken as reconfirming support for the doctrine of the atonement.

This is the line of reasoning that MacIntyre seems to be criticizing in the second passage cited from his text. It is, as he rightly says, circular in the way specified. However, this case is not of interest if our study be restricted to an examination of the reasoning-pattern used in actual mystical texts. The structure of the argument used to establish reliability departs what is found in the traditional mystical literature on at least two important counts: (1) For the mystic portrayed in Case II, the fact that the revelation contained in the apprehension is entailed by doctrine and is thus true serves as a sufficient basis for concluding that the apprehension is reliable. This is not in accord with traditional procedure. On the traditional view, while it follows that a private revelation is true if it is entailed by doctrine, the truth of its revelation is not sufficient to guarantee that a given apprehension is reliable. In traditional mystical theology, provision is explicitly made for the case of the true revelation that is contained in an *unreliable* apprehension. (2) In Case II, the argument used to establish reliability involves no reference to the origin of the relevant apprehension. It thus lacks what would appear to be the central premise of the corresponding argument used in actual mystical texts. In the latter it is assumed that an apprehension is reliable if and only if it is produced by God. Thus, for these two reasons, Case II must be modified and MacIntyre's criticism suitably adjusted if the exchange is to make contact with the classical mystical tradition.

Case III: This is a repeat of Case II except that, when the reliability of the apprehension is challenged, the mystic maintains that it was produced by God and thus can be trusted as a source of knowledge. Concerning the claim that the apprehension is of divine origin, the mystic argues that it passes both of the tests (bears both of the 'signs') mentioned earlier, i.e. (i) it had beneficial spiritual effects and (ii) the revelation contained in the apprehension is, in MacIntyre's sense 'congruent with' accepted doctrine. Since the apprehension meets both of the conditions required for inclusion in the class of divine productions, it can be taken as a source of reconfirming support for the doctrine formulated in the proposition 'Christ died for our sins.'

I suspect MacIntyre would respond as follows:

Focus on the second of the tests mentioned in the preceding argument. Again it is being assumed that standard doctrine is true and thus that the revelation contained in the apprehension is true. At bottom, what is serving as the second sign that the apprehension is from God is that the revelation therein contained is true. The consequence is that, while the truth of the revelation is no longer serving as a sufficient condition of apprehension-reliability (as it did in Case II), it is still retained as a necessary condition. Thus, 'Christ died for our sins' occurs as a premise (though not the only premise) in the argument used to establish the divine origin of the apprehension. It thus occurs as a premise in the argument offered to show that the apprehension is reliable and, as such, provides reconfirming support for the doctrine of the atonement. Hence, the reasoning is still circular. Case III differs from Case II only in that circularity is buried a little more deeply and is thus a bit more difficult to detect.

Consider again the passage cited earlier from the writings of St Teresa in which is formulated the Scripture-dogma test. In this passage, Teresa says that revelations contained in apprehensions from God will be in conformity with the propositions contained in Scripture and dogma. By itself, the phrase 'in conformity with' is as vague as MacIntyre's 'congruent with', but I think that the rest of what is said in this passage makes clear how it is to be understood. As articulated by Teresa, and as formulated in the passage quoted earlier from Poulain as well, the Scripture-dogma test does not require that the revelation contained in an apprehension from God be, in MacIntyre's sense, 'congruent with', i.e. entailed by, some article of the Faith. What is required is that the private revelation be *consistent with,* i.e. that it *not conflict with,* any such item. Put another way, what is required is that the *negation* of the private revelation *not* be entailed by some proposition included in Scripture-dogma. This difference seems to me to be of crucial importance. It accounts for what I judge to be the major error involved in MacIntyre's understanding of, and thus criticism of, the traditional mystical theological procedure. I will end these reflections with an attempt to make this last point clear.

Return for a moment to the case of the 'voices' that announced to Joan of Arc that the British were preparing a counter-attack on Orleans. Joan was apparently convinced that the apprehension was reliable and thus that its revelation was true. Let us construct an argument that would support this conviction using the argument-pattern with which we have been working. The argument would have two basic premises: viz. (i) Joan's auditory experience had beneficial spiritual effects and (ii) the revelation contained in apprehension is consistent with, i.e. does not conflict with anything included in, Scripture-dogma. We could then conclude that the apprehension was produced by God and the rest would follow by Principle A. Clearly, this argument would not make use of the claim that the revelation contained in the apprehension is, in MacIntyre's sense, congruent with, i.e. entailed by, Scripture-dogma. That the British were preparing a counter-attack at Orleans is surely not an article of the Faith. More generally, but I think not less clearly, the truth of the revelation contained in Joan's apprehension would not be presupposed in the argument for reliability. The relevant premise would be, only, that the negation of the revelation is not entailed by some proposition included in Scripture-dogma. That the private revelation is true is the conclusion of, but not a premise in, the argument based in part on this negative observation.

Now let's suppose that the proposition 'Christ died for our sins' is like 'The British are preparing a counter-attack at Orleans' in that it is not itself included among the articles of the Faith but is not inconsistent with anything therein contained. The case would then be methodologically indistinguishable from the one just considered. Reliability of the apprehension containing this revelation could then be argued via the traditional pattern without hint of circularity. This would be an instance of the sort discussed by St Teresa in the *Interior Castle*, i.e. one in which standard doctrine was supplemented by appeal to the content of a mystic apprehension.

But, of course, 'Christ died for our sins' is not like 'The British are preparing a counter-attack at Orleans.' It *is* part of standard doctrine. As such, its truth is accepted by the orthodox Christian quite independently of any considerations regarding the content of mystic apprehensions. And this, I think, is at the root of the trouble. What is needed here is a distinction between what the mystic *believes* given that he is an orthodox Christian and what the mystic *makes use of as a premise* when arguing the reliability of a mystic apprehension. As an orthodox Christian, the mystic believes that standard doctrines are true. Thus, in the case we have been considering, we can assume that the mystic enters the picture believing that the doctrine of the atonement is true. But the question of interest in the present discussion is not whether the mystic believes that 'Christ died for our sins' is true. It is, rather, whether the mystic is justified in claiming that the apprehension containing this (true) proposition as a revelation is reliable and, as such, can be taken as an independent source of support for the proposition already accepted. More specifically, the point at issue is whether the argument used by the mystic when urging an affirmative answer to this second question makes use of a premise in which is affirmed the truth of the proposition 'Christ died for our sins.' The answer is that it does not. What the argument includes, instead, is a premise to the effect that the revelation contained in the apprehension is consistent with the items of Scripture-dogma. What it includes, in other words, is a premise to the effect that the proposition 'Christ died for our sins' is consistent with itself and with every other article of the Faith. This premise, it is clear, entails nothing whatsoever as regards the actual truth-value of the proposition in question.

IV

Given the way in which mystics and mystical theologians have traditionally argued when attempting to establish the epistemic reliability of mystic apprehensions, and given that MacIntyre is right in supposing that an argument for the reliability of a given apprehension that presupposes the truth of the very doctrine for which the apprehension is supposed to supply support is circular and, for that reason, deficient, the proposition 'God exists' cannot be successfully supported by appeal to the content of mystic apprehensions. The same holds for propositions that are directly entailed by 'God exists'. This much seems to me correct. It is, I think, the only conclusion warranted by the preceding reflections that imposes anything in the way of a logical restriction on mystical theological procedure. I should add that I have yet to discover a mystic of consequence from within the Roman Catholic tradition who has claimed (or even suggested) that mystic apprehensions can serve as a source of support for belief in the existence of God. Though we have uncovered a genuine restriction, I suspect it is one that will not be felt as such by those engaged in the actual practice of mystical theology.

According to the theory outlined in the first section of this paper, mystic apprehensions have positive epistemic value only on condition that they are produced by God (Principles A and B). One assigns epistemic value to mystic apprehensions in accordance with this theory, only if one assumes at the outset that the basic, theistic world-picture is correct. Further, the traditional reasoning-pattern requires that apprehensions be excluded from the class of divine productions (and thus from the class of reliable information-bearers) if the revelations therein contained conflict with items of Scripture-dogma. Of course, this last requirement makes sense and is accepted as relevant and reasonable only because it is being assumed that the items included in Scripture-dogma are true. It is thus clear that the theory as a whole is designed to appeal only to those who are antecedently committed not only to the basic, theistic world-picture but to the more detailed articles of doctrine professed in the Roman Catholic community. However, the conclusion is not that the traditional reasoning-pattern is circular or in some other way logically deficient. As I have argued above, this conclusion is unwarranted even in the case where the theory is used to support the claim that a mystic apprehension provides reconfirming support for a proposition contained in Scripture-dogma. Still, the theory might be judged defective on quite another count. Its address is severely limited. It can be applied appropriately only where the context of discussion is one in which substantive matters of doctrine are not at issue. I suspect it is this, and not the detection of logical deficiency, that ultimately accounts for the dissatisfaction expressed by those (such as MacIntyre) who approach the mystical literature in a sceptical posture regarding the content of religious belief and who demand to find there a theory addressed to the secularly-minded, philosophical critic which justifies the claim that mystic apprehensions have positive epistemic value. But, then, how this circumstance is to be evaluated is yet another question. Perhaps in the end what needs to be revived is the arbitrary demand made by the secularly-minded philosophic critic as to what the mystical literature should contain.

POSTSCRIPT I

In the above discussion, I have worked with a version of traditional mystical thinking in accordance with which an apprehension is judged to be of divine origin (and thus reliable) if, and only if, it possesses the features described in the spiritual-effects test and the Scripture-dogma test. Such is the picture one gets in a good many primary mystical tests. However, modern theological treatments of this topic tend to be a bit more complex than this. While the spiritual-effects sign and the Scripture-dogma sign are invariably retained as necessary conditions for inclusion in the class of divine apprehensions, some theologians specify other conditions that must be met as well. Poulain, for example, mentions a number of others in Chapter 22 of the *Graces of Interior Prayer*, e.g. that revelations contained in divine apprehensions will not conflict with truths established by history or science,[14] and that apprehensions produced by God will involve no visual or auditory presentations that violate normal standards of decency, modesty, or morality.[15] Of course, the addition of such requirements makes it more difficult to judge in a given case that an apprehension is of divine origin. But, so far as I can see, these additional requirements introduce no issues of theological import. In the interest of simplicity, I thus put them aside above. I mention them here for purposes of completeness.

POSTSCRIPT II

Focus for a moment on Principle A: it is clearly the mainstay in the theory we have been examining. What reason could be given for supposing that apprehensions produced by God can be trusted as sources of correct information? The answer I suspect (though I have found it in explicit form only once in the mystical literature)[17] rests on an idea used by René Descartes in the third of his *Meditations on First Philosophy*, viz. that God is no deceiver. For Descartes, this latter was presumably grounded on an analysis of the moral qualities traditionally assigned to the Christian God. God, being perfectly good, would not so arrange things as to encourage one of his creatures to embrace false belief. However, it is not at all clear that from such considerations alone one can derive the conclusion that God would not, under any circumstances, produce an apprehension containing a revelation that is false. Sometimes it is better that one believe what is false. Who is to say that there might not be circumstances under which even an omnipotent and omniscient being would be fully justified (morally) in leading a visionary into false belief?

I offer this comment less in the spirit of refutation than in the hope of eliciting some clarification and defence of Principle A from the partisans of the mystical tradition. Though the aim of this paper has been to explicate rather than to evaluate the pattern of reasoning found in traditional mystical literature concerning the conditions under which a mystic apprehension can be accorded positive epistemic value, now that it is out in the open, this is the element of theory that seems to me to require most immediate critical attention.

NOTES

1 The specific phrases 'private revelation' and 'public revelation' are taken from R. Garrigou-Lagrange's *Christian Perfection and Contemplation* (St Louis, Herder, 1942), pt. VI, art. 5, p. 440.

2 Ch. 18, para. 23. Tr. L. L. Yorke Smith from the 6th French edn. (1910).

3 Ed. Flew and MacIntyre, London, Macmillan, 1955.

4 Though these principles obviously underpin the whole of the discussion in ch. 21 of Poulain's text (see especially para. 25), their most explicit formulation is given in para. 3. See also St John of the Cross's *Ascent of Mount Carmel*, Bk. II, ch. 19.

5 Poulain discusses this topic in ch. 20. See also St John of the Cross, *Ascent of Mount Carmel*, Bk. II.

6 In Bk. II, chs. 25 and 26 of the *Ascent of Mount Carmel*, St John of the Cross uses the term 'revelation' to designate a sub-category of mystic apprehensions – a sub-category on a par with, though distinct from mystic visions and locutions (see esp., ch. 25, sec. 3; see also ch. 23, sec.

1). From what he says in this part of the text, revelations appear to be apprehensions of the sort that would be classified by Poulain (ch. 21, para. 5) as intellectual locutions, i.e. they are thoughts that are communicated directly and without the medium of definite words or other sensible forms. However, in ch. 27 of the same text – speaking of revelations in which are disclosed what St John calls 'secrets and mysteries' (and these, he says, are more properly referred to as 'revelations' than are those discussed in chs. 25 and 26) – John says that revelations are 'truths' that are imparted by way of words or by way of other 'signs, figures, images, or likenesses' (secs. 1 and 3). On this second account, revelations cannot be apprehensions. Truths are propositions. Apprehensions are not propositions, they are experiences. A revelation is here portrayed as that which is communicated by way of an apprehension. Precisely this same dual use of the term 'revelation' can be found in Poulain's *Graces of Interior Prayer*. In the titles of all of the chapters making up Part IV of his text, Poulain juxtaposes the terms 'visions' and 'revelations' in such a way as would make sense only if they were being used to name distinct sub-classes of a single category – the category of mystic apprehensions. 'Revelation' here seems to be functioning as an alternative name for what was referred to in ch. 26 as a 'locution'. In para. 6 of ch. 22, Poulain explicitly says that a revelation is a mystic 'state', i.e. an apprehension or experience. However, in ch. 21, Poulain seems clearly to be using 'revelation' in the second senses distinguished above. The second section of this chapter is entitled 'Five Causes of Absolutely False Revelations'. Revelations are the sorts of things that can have truth values – they are sometimes false. They must then be propositions, not 'states' or apprehensions. Apprehensions do not have truth values: it makes no sense to describe an experience as being false. In para. 8 of ch. 21, this second sense of the term 'revelation' is determined a little more closely. Here Poulain discusses several cases in which visionaries failed to grasp the messages contained in a mystic vision. The message is referred to as the revelation. The revelation, Poulain says, is 'the meaning of the vision'. In this paper, I am restricting 'revelation' to this second sense.

7 In Bk. II, chs. 18–20 of the *Ascent of Mount Carmel*, St John of the Cross argues that, although the revelations contained in apprehensions produced by God are always true (Principle A), in no case can one be sure that one has grasped the revelations (meaning, message) therein contained. God communicates in a kind of code for which we do not possess the key. Thus while we can be sure that whatever it is that is being communicated is true, we can never be sure that we know what it is. The upshot is that for St John, mystic apprehensions do not have value as sources of knowledge (cf. Bk. II, ch. 21, sec. 4 and ch. 27, sec. 4). Though I shall not review or critique them here, the

arguments given by St John of this position seem to me to be weak. I suspect, however, that John's sceptical position concerning the possibility of uncovering something that can be legitimately referred to as '*the* meaning' of a mystic vision or locution could be reargued with considerable force.

8 As mentioned in footnote 6, sec. 2, ch. 21 of Poulain's text is entitled 'Five Causes of Absolutely False Revelations'. I should add here that although St John of the Cross speaks of revelations as 'truths' (*Ascent of Mount Carmel*, Bk. II, ch. 27, secs. 1 and 3), he clearly allows the possibility that a given revelation might be false. Revelations from Satan are a case in point.

9 Poulain identifies two sub-types of what are called corporeal visions in which the objects 'seen' are not physically present (cf. Poulain, ch. 20, paras. 42 and 43). In an article entitled 'Vision' in the *New Catholic Encyclopedia*, Lucian Roure refers to these as 'divine hallucinations'.

10 See Poulain, ch. 22, para. 33. See also St John of the Cross, *Ascent of Mount Carmel*, Bk. II, ch. 27, sec. 4.

11 Tr. K. Kavanaugh and O. Rodriguez, *The Collected Works of St John of the Cross* (New York, Doubleday, 1964).

12 See Teresa's *Life*, ch. 20, para. 31; ch. 21, para. 10; ch. 25, para. 5; ch. 28, para. 19. The last quoted passage is from *Life*, ch. 28, para. 15. See also Poulain, ch. 22, paras. 16, 49–50.

13 Tr. David Lewis (Westminster, Newman Press, 1962). See also Teresa's Revelation VII, paras. 15–18.

14 Teresa's texts are a case in point. There are places, in fact, in which Teresa at least suggests that the feature described in the spiritual-effects test is a sufficient and not just a necessary sign of divine apprehensions. Cf. e.g.

15 Para. 33.

16 Para. 34.

17 Albert Farges, *Mystical Phenomena*, Pt. II, ch. I, sec. 6, subsec. iv.

NELSON PIKE, M.A. (Michigan); Ph.D. (Harvard). Among Professor Pike's publications are *God and Evil* (1964); and *God and Timelessness* (1970). He has also published a considerable number of articles and reviews in a variety of philosophical journals. He has taught at U.C.L.A. and Cornell University and is now Professor of Philosophy at the University of California at Irvine.

Real v.
Deceptive Mystical Experiences

GEORGE MAVRODES

This is a paper on the epistemological significance of religious experience, on the way in which a religious experience might generate a piece of knowledge. I focus primarily on some classical mystical experiences, but (as I indicate towards the end) I believe that the argument of the paper is quite general. My exposition is divided into four parts. In the first section I make some preliminary distinctions and formulate the problem. The second section contains the bulk of the substantive argument. In the third section I discuss two somewhat peripheral suggestions. Finally, in the fourth section, I try to draw together the threads of the argument into what seems to me to be their fullest significance.

I

There are, no doubt, many different lines along which a person might try to assess the significance or importance of religious experiences. In this paper I will focus upon epistemological assessments, i.e. on the way in which such an experience might serve as a justification or reason for holding some belief. A person who had this interest in religious experience might direct his attention to his own putative experiences or to those of other people (as they are represented, I suppose, in testimony and description). In this paper I will focus on the case of the person who is assessing primarily his own experience.

We must make still a third preliminary distinction, and this one will take, perhaps, a little longer. A person might take religious experience to be a distinct and identifiable sort of phenomenon, and one which is known to be associated regularly, or even without exception, with some other sort of fact or situation, probably via some causal connection. When he notices such an experience occurring in himself he may then infer, either probabilistically or conclusively, to the presence or occurrence of the other sort of fact. Whatever may be its use in the religious case, this seems to be a rather standard way of dealing with some of our experience. A diabetic, for example, may learn that such experiences as a feeling of dizziness or a few seconds of blurred vision are caused (probably) by hypoglycaemia. When he notices such experiences occurring in himself he may then form the belief, presumably with some justification, that his body is in a hypoglycaemic condition, and he may go on to eat a doughnut to redress the proper balance of blood sugar. The analogous case would be that of a person who believed that a certain identifiable sort of experience, say that of intense euphoria, was caused, either probably or certainly, by the direct act of God upon a person. If he then noticed that he himself was in a state of intense euphoria (or that he had been) he would infer that God was (or had been) acting upon him directly.

Purely as a matter of terminology, I will say that a person who treats an experience in that way considers it to be a 'sign'. Some bits of experience, I think, are properly to be treated as signs. In any such project, however, one of the most important and interesting questions is that of how one acquires (in, it is to be hoped, some justified way) the 'connecting' proposition, the one which expresses the relation between the experience and the fact with which it is to be correlated. If we are to treat religious experience as a sign leading to any very interesting theological beliefs this sort of question will be especially troublesome. But in this paper I will not pursue this question, since my focus will not be on treating religious experience as a sign.

What is the alternative to treating an experience as a sign? Some experiences are, we might say, 'intentional'. They seem to contain within themselves, as an element of the experience itself, a reference to something which transcends the experience, to something which has its own life, its own character, its own existence beyond the experience. This is not a rare feature of exotic experiences. It is a commonplace in our ordinary sensory encounter with the world. When I look out of my window and see a tree, standing bare now in the snow, my experience, which is a part of my biography, presents itself as 'intending' a tree. It seems somehow to point to, or to claim to lay hold of, a tree – a tree which is not wholly a part of my biography, but which has its own career of facthood in the world. So strong, indeed, is this feature of much ordinary sense experience that we often name the experience by referring to what I have been calling its intentionality. If we then discover that the intentionality was not in fact satisfied we retract the name which we gave to our experience and describe it in some other way.[1]

Now, we very often form beliefs by relying on the intentionality of our experience. We take it that, in this case, what the experience points to is really there, that the experience really does lay hold of what it seems to lay hold of. We rely, in a word, on the *veridicality* of our experience. Some religious experiences have the feature which I have called intentionality, and some people who have such experiences may form some of their theological beliefs in reliance upon the veridicality of those experiences. And that is the 'use' of religious experience upon which I will focus here.

It may be worth emphasizing here that the notion of the veridicality of an experience seems to be firmly linked to the intentionality of experiences; it seems to have no application to experiences taken as signs. A diabetic who has been successful in adjusting his diet by taking his dizzy spells to be signs of hypoglycaemia will probably form the corresponding belief on the occasion of his next dizzy spell too. If that particular onset of dizziness happens to be caused not by hypoglycaemia but by a brain tumour the diabetic will be mistaken in his belief. But his dizziness will not on that account be a non-veridical experience. Nor will it be veridical. It will have a cause about which we can be correct or mistaken. But it does not present itself as referring to something beyond itself – it does not present itself, for example, as an apprehension of hypoglycaemia or of a brain tumour – and hence it is neither veridical nor non-veridical. 'Seeing' an oasis in the desert has the intentional character, however, and is a veridical experience if there really is the oasis there, non-veridical if there is not.

This last observation brings us to what is, perhaps, the most troublesome feature of experience as an epistemic mode, and that is the fact that an experience apparently can have intentionality without having veridicality. If we rely upon such an experience in forming or adopting a belief then we will be mistaken in that belief, or, at best, we will be correct in it merely by accident. Perhaps we will say that we have been 'deceived' by such an experience. But however we describe it, the danger (I would suppose) is commonplace enough and familiar to all of us.

In view of this epistemic danger associated with reliance upon the intentionality of experience it looks as though it would be desirable to have at hand a criterion for distinguishing those experiences which are veridical from those which are not. If such a criterion were to be epistemically useful, of course, it would have to be such that we could apply it prior to acquiring the information which is presented via the intentionality of the experiences which are in fact veridical (if any are). But if we did have a criterion of this kind, we could sort the veridical from the non-veridical, and then proceed with epistemic safety to rely upon the intentionality of those which we had certified as veridical. In this paper I want to explore the question of whether there is any criterion which can, in any radical way, serve this function.

Some Christian mystics apparently were troubled by a special form of the problem which interests us here. They had experiences which were often strange ones, and some of which apparently had the quality of intentionality. But these mystics were troubled by the possibility that these experiences might be non-veridical, and for a special reason. The experiences, they feared, might have been produced by the Devil. Most of my own discussion here will utilize this form of the problem. I believe, however, that the arguments and conclusions to be deduced will apply equally to every form in which this problem can be cast.

My intent is primarily theoretical and analytic, not historical or exegetical. No part of my argument depends in any important way on a proper understanding of what any particular mystic has claimed. Nevertheless, there is some interest in looking at a particular case. St Teresa of Avila,[2] a Spanish nun of the sixteenth century and one of the greatest of the Christian mystical writers, has left us an account of an extraordinary series of personal experiences, along with what might be called her 'theorizing' about such experiences, and (probably the main intent of her works) a great deal of advice and instruction on the conduct of one's 'spiritual life'. It seems clear that Teresa took many of her most striking experiences to have what I have been calling 'intentionality'. Consider, for example, this account:

I was at prayer on a festival of the glorious Saint Peter when I saw Christ at my side – or, to put it better, I was conscious of Him, for neither with the eyes of the body nor with those of the soul did I see anything. I thought He was quite close to me and I saw that it was He Who, as I thought, was speaking to me. Being completely ignorant that visions of this kind could occur, I was at first very much afraid, and did nothing but weep, though, as soon as He addressed a single word to me to reassure me, I became quiet again, as I had been before, and was quite happy and free from fear. All the time Jesus Christ seemed to be beside me, but as this was not an imaginary vision, I could not discern in what form: what I felt very clearly was that all the time He was at my right hand, and a witness of everything that I was doing, and that, whenever I became slightly recollected or was not greatly distracted, I could not but be aware of His nearness to me.[3]

It seems clear that, despite the fact that this vision has no sensory imagery associated with it, Teresa takes it to be the case that Christ was actually present in her room, and that her experience, the vision, constitutes an apprehension of that fact. A couple of paragraphs later, still discussing this vision, she says

It is not like another kind of consciousness of the presence of God which is often experienced, especially by those who have reached the Prayer of Union and the Prayer of Quiet. There we are on the point of beginning our prayer when we seem to find Him Whom we are about to address and we seem to know that He is hearing us by the spiritual feelings and effects of great love and faith of which we become conscious, and also by the fresh resolutions which we make with such deep emotion. This great favour comes from God: and he to whom it is granted should esteem it highly, for it is a very lofty form of prayer. But it is not a vision. The soul recognizes the presence of God by the effects which, as I say, He produces in the soul, for it is by that means that His Majesty is pleased to make His presence felt: but in a vision the soul distinctly sees that Jesus Christ, the Son of the Virgin, is present. In that other kind of prayer there come to it influences from the Godhead; but in this experience, besides receiving these, we find that the most sacred Humanity becomes our Companion and is also pleased to grant us favours.[4]

Here Teresa seems to make just the distinction which I have made in terms of experiences as signs versus experiences as intentions, and identifies this experience with the latter branch of this distinction.

Teresa apparently had no lack of associates to suggest to her that this and similar experiences might not be veridical. She tells us, for example,

Many are the affronts and trials that I have suffered through telling this and many are the fears and persecutions that it has brought me. So sure were those whom I told of it that I had a devil that some of them wanted to exorcize me. This troubled me very little, but I was sorry when I found that my confessors were afraid to hear my confessions or when I heard that people were saying things to them against me.[5]

On some occasions Teresa herself seems to have had suspicions of this sort. Earlier she had described a vision of Christ which she saw 'with the eyes of the soul', i.e. it was a vision which involved a sensory representation of Christ, though not one which depended upon the use of her physical eyes. The vision had a powerful immediate effect upon her, but apparently doubts soon arose. We read,

> It did me great harm not to know that it was possible to see anything otherwise than with the eyes of the body. It was the devil who encouraged me in this ignorance and made me think that anything else was impossible. He led me to believe that I had imagined it all, and that it might have been the work of the devil, and other things of that kind.[6]

Teresa, then, certainly seems to have the problem with which we are here concerned. The intentionality of her experiences seems to draw her powerfully, but influential and respected associates are rather insistent in drawing her attention to the possibility of non-veridicality – indeed, to that special version of non-veridicality which would be produced by demonic deception. And their suggestions do not fall upon entirely deaf ears.

Furthermore, Teresa cannot be satisfied, apparently, with simply 'playing it safe', and refusing to rely upon any such experiences because they might be delusive. For she recognizes that there is something to be lost by taking that course too. If she were to proceed in this way, then, in case some of the experiences were in fact veridical, she would be forfeiting the information she might have gained from them. And some of that information might be very important. In fact, as is clear from the passage last quoted, she realized that the Devil might deceive her not only by making her take a delusive experience for a veridical one, but also by making her take a veridical experience for a delusive one. She believed that he had actually carried out this very deception in connection with the vision of Christ which she described there, and that the result involved serious damage to her spiritual life. She cannot, therefore, simply withdraw from the contest with the Devil and thus secure herself from the danger of his deceptions. For the suggestion that she do that might itself be one of his deceptions.

II

So much, then, for the problem which Teresa faced. Did she also suggest any ways of coping with it? Yes. In this section I want to consider a group of such suggestions, and I will argue that these, and any other suggestions which are of the same general sort, are incapable of providing a radical and fundamental solution to her problem (though they might play a subsidiary role).

What are some of these suggestions? One of them occurs in the following passage:

> As far as I can see and learn by experience, the soul must be convinced that a thing comes from God only if it is in conformity with Holy Scripture; if it were to diverge from that in the very least, I think I should be incomparably more firmly convinced that it came from the devil than I previously was that it came from God, however sure I might have felt of this.[7]

This seems to be a purely negative proposal. Experiences whose content fails to conform to Scripture will be judged as coming from the Devil. There is no suggestion, however, that this will serve to identify all of the demonic experiences, nor that all those which pass this test will be divine or veridical. A criterion of even limited applicability, however, would be better than none. We might formulate the principle which seems to be operative in this one as follows:

> Since the content of Scripture is true, any experience whose content is incompatible with the content of Scripture is non-veridical and not to be relied upon.

However, this principle is by itself epistemically useless. In order actually to rule out any experience, E, one would have to have a further judgement to the effect that

> The content of E is incompatible with the content of Scripture.

The fact that a general principle of this sort will not do the work we need without the addition of a judgement of particular fact will be of importance in much of the remainder of our discussion. Before beginning on it, however, let me mention another criterion.

Teresa describes a type of experience which she calls a 'locution'. In this experience it seems to her as though someone is speaking to her. But, 'though perfectly formed, the words are not heard with the bodily ear; yet they are understood much more clearly than if they were so heard, and, however determined one's resistance, it is impossible to fail to hear them'.[8] Sometimes, apparently, an identification of the purported speaker is part of the experience, and she identifies some of her locutions as having been spoken to her by Christ.[9] But some locutions, she thinks, are spoken by the Devil, presumably under some false *persona*, passing himself off as Christ or some other holy personage. But, says Teresa,

> When a locution comes from the devil, it not only fails to leave behind good effects but leaves bad ones. This has happened to me, though only on two or three occasions, and each time I have immediately been warned by the Lord that the locution came from the devil. Besides being left in a state of great aridity, the soul suffers a disquiet . . .[10]

The suggestion that experiences which are of demonic origin have untoward spiritual effects, while those of divine origin are productive of genuine spiritual values, such as humility, love, faith, etc., is often repeated by Teresa. The principle of this criterion might be stated thus:

> Experiences of divine origin generate such effects as humility, love, peace, etc., while those of demonic origin produce aridity, discontent, pride, etc., in the soul of the recipient.

As before, this principle is by itself epistemically useless. It has no bearing at all on the origin or veridicality of any experience, E, unless it can be supplemented by some particular judgement, such as

> The result of my having had experience, E, is that I have become more humble, loving, fervent in faith, etc.

Teresa proposes a few more characteristics of genuine and delusive mystical experience. She says, for example, that if locutions were generated by ourselves, then we could hear them whenever we wished. But the divine locutions come upon us involuntarily.[11] And again, the Devil may give us an imaginary vision of Christ, 'but he cannot counterfeit the glory which the vision has when it comes from God'.[12] For our purposes, however, the criteria which I have summarized will be sufficient.

Let us think first about the criterion of compatibility with Scripture. Let us imagine that Teresa has an experience with the right sort of content to be compatible or incompatible with the

Scripture. Perhaps the ideal sort of experience for the application of this criterion would be one which either consisted of a locution or at least contained a locution, and in which the locution was a statement about some subject which we might expect to find treated in the Bible. Let us imagine it to be so. Well, Teresa has her principle. But we have already noted that the principle by itself is of no use. She must also have a judgement about the particular experience. Let us suppose that she has that, too. Imagine that she has made her own study of the Bible and of the commentaries, and that she has consulted her confessor, the bishop, and some devout scholars besides, and that all of these sources converge upon the judgement that the content of her experience is compatible with, perhaps even identical with, the doctrine of the Bible on this subject. Can Teresa now be confident that her experience has at least survived the negative criterion of scriptural conformity? So far as I remember, Teresa herself expresses no doubt about this. But it is not entirely easy to see how she can be justified in this confidence. Remember that she wants such a criterion in the first place because she worries over the possibility that the Devil might impersonate Jesus Christ himself, might put locutions into her head, and so on. But if this is a possibility worth worrying about should she not also worry about whether the Devil may not also have been at work on the preceding day and on the succeeding day, trying to forestall and vitiate her attempts to catch him out in his devilish deceptions?

There are two routes along which we might pursue this difficulty, and they correspond to the two elements which Teresa needs in order to use this criterion. In the first place, Teresa should concern herself, it would seem, with whether the Devil may not have deceived her about the principle itself. After all, the mere fact that something is presented as a principle does not at all guarantee that it is true. People make mistakes about principles all the time, with or without the assistance of the Devil, and this fact can hardly have escaped an astute observer like Teresa. And so, must she not have a doubt as to whether this principle itself is not one of his devilish deceptions, and thus be in need of a further criterion by which to judge whether this is indeed a true principle?

I believe that there are interesting and important questions about how we do, or should, adopt principles, especially basic principles. These questions apply to Teresa's principle here, but also to those other principles which many would find more basic and attractive, principles of logic, perhaps, or of rationality, and so on. In this paper I will not, however, pursue those questions, except incidentally. I propose to conduct my argument largely along the other route, that of the judgements about particulars which are also required by these criteria. But in any case the arguments which I would put forward about our commerce with principles are similar to those which I will advance about particulars, and those who are attracted by the latter arguments will perhaps be able to reconstruct the former for themselves.

Let us turn then to the second route. Teresa needs a judgement about the scriptural compatibility of the particular experience which she has had. She has asked the bishop, we suppose, and he has said yes, it is compatible. But if there is a danger that the Devil may impersonate Jesus Christ in a vision is there not a danger that he may impersonate the bishop in his study? If the Devil is really intent on deceiving Teresa may it not be his strategy to give her two delusive experiences instead of one, a lying vision of Christ when Christ is not present and a lying vision of the bishop when the bishop is not present? Must not Teresa have a criterion for determining whether her experience of the bishop is veridical, whether it is, as we might say, an 'episcopal' experience rather than a demonic one? It would seem so.

Maybe the Devil need not go so far as to impersonate the bishop. Suppose that the bishop is really present and that he answers Teresa straightforwardly. 'Teresa,' we may imagine him saying, 'the locution which came to you is definitely heretical, completely incompatible with the teaching of the Bible and of the Church.' But just at this point the Devil intervenes. He needs to cause only two errors in Teresa's hearing, making her hear the word 'orthodox' in place of 'heretical', and 'compatible' for 'incompatible'. If he should succeed in doing that without arousing her suspicions, then her reliance upon her principle and her visit to the bishop will have entangled her even more securely in the Devil's snare rather than having delivered her from it.

In a normal conversation such as we imagine here for Teresa and the bishop, of course, people quite naturally rely upon the intentionality of their auditory experience. Their hearing presents itself to them as a hearing of what other people are saying – what they really are saying – and by and large that is how they take it. Furthermore, people in such an ordinary conversation (in contrast, perhaps, with people seeing a vision or hearing a locution) do not normally think at all about the possibility that the Devil is deceiving them. But the fact that we do not think about the Devil seems unlikely to have much to contribute to our safety from the Devil.

Would not such a situation, indeed, be close to the ideal from the Devil's point of view? Where could he better practise his demonic wiles than in those contexts in which his victims are accustomed to give him no thought at all? Teresa may be confident when she reads the Bible in the library or talks to the bishop in his study, more confident than when she is seeing visions and hearing locutions in her cell. But how is that confidence to be justified?

At this point someone may object that I seem to be attributing to the Devil powers without limit. What reason, they may ask, do I have for thinking that the Devil can do things like this at all? And the answer to that is, no special reason. So far as I know, the Devil may be completely unable to impersonate a Spanish bishop, or to interfere in any way with what people hear in ordinary conversation. Could that help Teresa? Well, yes, in one way it can help her, but in another way not. If the Devil cannot impersonate a bishop then in fact Teresa is safe when she goes to consult him, and if she relies upon what she hears in his study she will not go astray. But if she does not already have a good reason for believing that the Devil is limited in this way then her confidence, though it will work out correctly, would seem to be no more than a matter of luck. Remember, it might have been the other way around. It might be that the Devil can easily impersonate a bishop, and cause us to mishear conversations, but that he cannot meddle at all with visions and locutions. And in that case Teresa would be better off to formulate a criterion which relied on visions to check on the veridicality of conversations with the bishop rather than vice versa. And if she has no good reason for supposing that the Devil is limited in one of these ways rather than the other it would seem that she is as much in need of a criterion for the one case as for the other.

Perhaps at this point it would be useful to turn to Teresa's other major criterion, for it provides a convenient focus for another sort of approach to these problems. That criterion, we remember, involves the different effects which Teresa believed would become manifest in her own spiritual state, depending upon whether a given experience had its origin in the Devil or in God. Again, Teresa needs two things – the general principle which associates such effects with divine and demonic agency, and particular judgements about the effects which have actually been produced by, or have at least followed upon, this or that experience. As in the previous case, it seems to me that Teresa should concern herself, if she is to use this criterion at all, with the question of whether the Devil may not have deceived her about the principle itself. And again, I propose to set aside this line of inquiry, turning rather to the particular judgements about the effects of her experiences.

Well, what happens here? Teresa, we imagine, has some mystical experience. After whatever is the appropriate time she turns to assess its spiritual effects in her own life. And she finds that she is indeed now more humble than she was before the experience, more fervent in prayer, more filled with a love for God and for her sisters, and so on. These effects have certainly followed the experience, and she judges that they are the results of that experience. And so she is inclined to judge the experience to be of divine origin, and therefore reliable and veridical. Now, it may seem to us that in this assessment the weakest link is the judgement that the desirable effects were caused by, or are in some way at least to be attributed to, the mystical experience. Maybe this is a weak link, but in this paper I intend to ignore it, in order to focus upon the problems raised by what seems to be the much stronger link, Teresa's judgement that she is in fact better off spiritually after the experience than she was before.

Teresa thinks that she is now more humble, etc., than she was before. Is it possible that this judgement is one foisted upon her by the Devil, as part of a complex plan whose first step is a demonic vision or locution and whose second step is this perversion of Teresa's attempt to check on that experience? If we can muster any sympathy at all for Teresa's worries about the Devil in the first place, then we can probably muster some sympathy for this worry too. (In fact, I think that many spiritual writers would think that a person is not bound to be correct in assessing his own spiritual state.) Of course, Teresa might seek the judgement of her sisters in the convent, of her confessor, and so on, on the question of whether she really has grown in the spiritual graces. But this would raise just the same problems as those canvassed in the preceding section. We need not cover them again. A somewhat different suggestion, however, is this. Perhaps there is some spiritual grace (or perhaps it is a spiritual defect; for this purpose it does not matter) such that it is not possible for the Devil to deceive a person about his possession of that property. And this impossibility would be generated not by some limitation on the powers of the Devil, for that again would raise problems which we have discussed above, but rather by some peculiarity in the property itself, a sort of logical peculiarity. The property would be such that, while a person could easily lack it, it would not be even logically possible that a person should simultaneously lack this property and believe that he possessed it. So

if the Devil could, no matter by what means, get Teresa to believe that she had this grace, then he would, one way or another,
guarantee that she in fact had the grace, and hence she would
not be deceived. If there were a property like that, we might
think, then Teresa could safely rely on her judgement that she
possessed that property, and she could use that judgement in the
evaluation of her mystical experiences. The Devil himself could not
penetrate her armour at this point, for it would be a logical armour.

If, *per impossibile*, nothing in the preceding discussion had
reminded us of Descartes, this suggestion should certainly do so.
For Descartes, who also concerned himself with the deceptions of
the Devil (although, I think, much more rhetorically and less
'existentially' than Teresa) was intrigued by propositions which
have just the features which I have been suggesting. 'I think' and 'I
exist' are not necessary truths – that is, there are logically possible
worlds in which they are not true. But it is a necessary truth that if I
believe them then they are true – the logically possible worlds in
which I believe those propositions form a sub-set of the possible
worlds in which they are true. Consequently, if the Devil gets me to
believe one of these propositions he does not thereby deceive me,
for if he gets me to believe it then it is true. This is, then, a point at
which the Devil's deceptive projects must fail. And so Descartes
believed that in such propositions he had found a demon-proof
starting-point for the development of his cognitive life.[13]

Are there any propositions of this sort which might serve
Teresa's purpose? I don't know. It is not obvious that claims like 'I
am now more humble than I was before', 'I now have more love
for God and for my sisters than I used to have,' and so on, are
bound to be true if I believe them. Possibly, however, there is some
property which will generate propositions of the required sort, and
which is such that it will connect with Teresa's principle about the
spiritual effects of divine and demonic visions, etc. I propose that
we simply assume for the present that there is such a property, and,
without prejudice, let us name it 'H'.

The propositions with which Descartes was intrigued bore a
special relation to him, and it was, I think, this relation which
intrigued him. I propose to say that these propositions were *cartesian-safe for him*. The notion can be defined in this way:

A proposition, P, is cartesian-safe for N if and only if P is contingent and it is necessarily true that if N believes that P then it is
true that P.

And part of what I have proposed that we assume about Teresa for the moment can now be put as follows:

(1) The proposition which Teresa could express by saying 'I have H' is cartesian-safe for Teresa.

The rest of what we are assuming is that the proposition referred to in (1) will connect with Teresa's principle so as to yield an evaluation of an experience. And it may now seem to us that we have found a way in which Teresa can secure heself from the deceptions of the Devil. But perhaps this is a mistake.

The following is, I should think, a necessary truth:

(2) If (1) is true and Teresa believes that she has H, then Teresa does have H.

From (1) and (2) we can deduce

(3) If Teresa believes that she has H, then she does have H.

and from (3) it follows that

(4) If Teresa believes that she has H, then she is not (in this belief) deceived by the Devil.

And does not that identify a place where she is safe from the Devil?

Well, maybe so. But we should at least notice that the general procedure we have followed does not depend upon anything special about H. For any belief whatever that Teresa may have, no matter what its subject may be, it is easy to find an assumption from which it will follow that Teresa is not (in that belief) deceived by the Devil. Let us assume, for example, that

(5) Jesus Christ really was present in Teresa's cell, close by her right hand, on the feast day of St Peter.

From (5) it follows that

(6) If Teresa believes that Jesus Christ really was present ... etc., then she is not (in this belief) deceived by the Devil.

In order for the Devil to deceive a person it is necessary for him to get the person to believe something false. If the Devil gets a person to believe some truth, then he does not deceive that person. And it does not matter in this connection whether the truth is contingent, necessary, cartesian-safe, or anything else. If Teresa really could make herself safe from the Devil with respect to a certain belief merely by assuming something from which it would follow that (in the belief in question) she was not being deceived, then her project would be simple indeed. She would need nothing as involved as any of the principles which we have been examining. She could simply assume, for any such belief, that the belief was true, and from that it would follow that she was not being deceived. But surely there must be a catch in that somewhere?

In the second deduction which I just outlined the catch seems to be in the assumption of (5). When Teresa worries about the Devil it is precisely about propositions such as (5) that she is worried. It is that the Devil may have deceived her into thinking that (5) is true. And so it seems perverse to suggest that Teresa could escape from the Devil simply by assuming (5) to be true. But, of course, (5) may be true after all. If it is true and if Teresa assumes it, then her deduction of (6) will be the deduction of a truth. If she believes (6) she will believe a truth. But it looks as though in that case she would believe it just by accident. And if she seeks a criterion it looks as though she wants something which will make her beliefs better than accidental.

But now, why should not the same argument be applied to the first of the two deductions which I outlined, the deduction of (4) from (1)? (1) is, after all, an assumption just as (5) was in the second case. Of course, (1) may be true – for all I know it is true. But (5) also may be true, and for all I know it is true. (1) and (5) do not differ in this respect. So if we (or Teresa herself) cannot make Teresa safe by assuming (5) how can she become safe by assuming (1)?

Now, maybe someone thinks that the difference is that (1), unlike (5), is safe for Teresa – it has that special kind of 'demon-proof' quality which I have called 'cartesian-safety'. But that would be a mistake. (1) is not cartesian-safe for Teresa or for anyone else. (1) is a statement to the effect that a certain proposition is cartesian-safe for Teresa, but (1) is not itself the proposition about which that claim is made. The proposition which is said to be cartesian-safe is one to the effect that Teresa has a certain property, H. But (1) does not say that Teresa has H, and it is perfectly compatible with her never having this property. And so the cartesian-safety of (1) cannot be the relevant difference between (1) and (5), because (1), just like (5), is not cartesian-safe at all.

It is important to note here that generally propositions of the form 'p is cartesian-safe for N' are not themselves cartesian-safe for N or for anyone else. And it is perhaps equally important to note that many propositions of this form are just downright false. Consider, for example, the following:

(7) *I was born in Bulgaria* is cartesian-safe for me.

This proposition is simply false, and it is false regardless of whether I or anyone else believes it (and also regardless of whether anyone believes the proposition to which it refers). It is just a mistake in analysis. But that, of course, need not prevent (7) from being believed. People make mistakes in logic and analysis every day, and often believe their mistakes. One need not concern oneself with the Devil at all in order to notice that.

This does bring us, however, to another important point, and one which may really involve a difference between (1) and (5). (5) seems to be a contingent proposition, a claim about a particular event in the life of Teresa. What is (1)? Well, it seems to be a piece of logic and analysis. One way of putting it is to say that it is a proposition about what possible worlds there are, and how they are ordered into sets and sub-sets. I am inclined to think that such propositions are not contingent, but necessary. If we take this view then we have discovered an important difference between (1) and (5). But is it a difference which will enable Teresa to outsmart the Devil? Unfortunately not.

It is to Descartes' credit that he recognized that one cannot escape the possibility of error and deception merely by retreating from the realm of the contingent into that of the necessary. 'As I sometimes think that others are in error respecting matters of which they believe themselves to possess a perfect knowledge, how do I know that I am not also deceived each time I add together two and three, or number the sides of a square . . . ?' [14] But surely the necessary truths are always true, and true in every possible world. How then can they be of use to a deceiving demon?

The answer is that they cannot. But a deceiving demon has no use for *contingent* truths either. As we have already noted, he wants to have no truck with truths at all. What he needs are falsehoods. But the realm of necessity contains the necessary falsehoods as well as the necessary truths. And the necessary falsehoods can be grist for the Devil's mill. When a demon sets himself to deceive us about some contingent matter he must get us to mistake some contingent falsehood for a truth of some sort or other. If he does not care about adding a logical error to the error of contingent fact, then he may be content to let us mistake a contingent falsehood for a contingent truth. In that case we will have the modality right and the truth-value wrong. But in a parallel way a demon might set himself to deceive us about some matter of necessity, pushing us to mistake a necessary falsehood for some sort of truth. If he does not care about adding a second mistake to the first he may well be content for us to take the necessary falsehood for a necessary truth. If so, then just as in the first case we will have the modality right and the truth value wrong.

Now, Descartes had presumably noticed that not all propositions in mathematical form, not all, say, which have the form $x + y = z$, are true, let alone being necessarily true. Some of them are false, perhaps necessarily false. And so he is worried that $2 + 3 = 5$ might be false, perhaps necessarily false, despite the fact that he has long taken it to be true, perhaps necessarily true.

We have, however, already noticed a similar fact about claims that some proposition is cartesian-safe. I think that such claims are necessarily true, *if they are true at all*. But some of them are false, and these are (as I think) necessarily false. (7), for example, is false, and on this view a necessary falsehood. And so we come back to Teresa. We have imagined her to be relying on a judgement about the cartesian-safety of some proposition. Of course, if she has got that right, then she is OK. The Devil has not deceived her. But might not a prudent Devil have first undertaken to deceive her about cartesian-safety, getting her to mistake unsafe propositions for safe ones, and then gone on to the business of deceptive visions and locutions? It would seem to be a reasonable strategy from his point of view. And so we seem again to conclude that if Teresa is right at all she is not right because of her criterion. She wants a criterion to determine the veridicality of some experience. But the judgements which she needs in order to make the criterion work seem to be just as much open to deception, and hence as much in need of a criterion, as is the original experience. Perhaps somewhere along this line the Devil has failed to deceive her, and so she winds up OK in the end. But we seem to have no reason to believe that the Devil's failure occurs at this particular point rather than that, and so no reason to think that Teresa's criteria function in any important way in foiling him.[15]

It may be worthwhile to introduce a word of caution here. I have argued a general point, that Teresa cannot make satisfactory use of a criterion for distinguishing veridical experiences from delusory ones, for detecting the deceptions of the Devil, and so on. And this is because a criterion will function only on the basis of a judgement. But whatever danger was to be averted by the use of the criterion will reappear as a danger that the judgement which the criterion utilizes is itself defective in the feared way. This will be the case, at least, for the criteria which Teresa mentions, and for any criterion whose application requires a judgement or belief. For example, it will apply to any criterion of veridicality which requires us to determine that the candidate experience has some property or relation, that it belongs in some particular class, and so on. But my argument does not entail that Teresa will not be able to distinguish veridical experiences from delusory ones, that she will not be able to detect the deceptions of the Devil, etc. For, as far as my argument goes, she may well be able to do such things without criteria at all.

III

The main body of my argument is completed in the preceding section. In this section I want to discuss briefly two avenues along which a person might attempt to evade the conclusion to which we seem to be drawn.

In the first place, it seems to me that Teresa cannot make herself safe from the Devil by giving up claims to certainty and replacing them with claims of probability. Teresa, for example, worries that the Devil may have given her a false and deceptive locution. But I have argued that the Devil might also deceive her in what appears to be an ordinary sense experience, in a judgement about her own spiritual state, and in judgements of logic and analysis. Suppose that Teresa admits this, but nevertheless asserts the following:

(8) The Devil is less likely to deceive me in matters of sense perception, logic, etc., than in visions and locutions.

And so she holds that, while her procedure is not infallible, if she checks her visions by reference to sense perception and logic she will have a better chance than if she uses no checks at all or if she should try to run the checks in the other direction. But this seems to leave Teresa in no better position *vis-à-vis* the Devil than she was before.

Of course, if (8) is true then Teresa's chances will be improved if she relies on sensation and logic, etc. But maybe (8) is not true. After all, not every statement of comparative probabilities is correct. Sometimes we are wrong about such things. Might not a prudent Devil have first deceived Teresa about (8)? And if he has done so, then if she relies on (8) she will in fact be decreasing her own chances and increasing those of her adversary. Furthermore, (8), just like the principles which we discussed earlier needs to be supplemented by particular judgements if it is to have any epistemic force. It must be supplemented by something like

(9) My belief that Christ was present, etc., is derived from a vision, while my belief that the bishop was present, etc., is derived from a sense perception.

But judgements which assign the origins of beliefs to visions, sense experiences, etc., are not bound to be true, as we see if we derive a new proposition from (9) simply by interchanging the references to the two beliefs. And so, may not the Devil first have deceived Teresa by getting her to accept (9)? If so, he need not worry even if she has got hold of a true estimate of probabilities in (8). For if (9) is false, then when it is combined with (8) it will redound to Teresa's damage and not to her benefit.

Perhaps someone objects that while (9) could be false nobody could make such a mistake in his own case. But this seems to be the claim that (9) is cartesian-safe for Teresa. Perhaps it is. I have no interest in denying it. But we have already seen that a judgement of cartesian-safety is of no benefit to Teresa.

Turning now to a different move, Teresa cannot escape from the Devil by becoming a conventionalist. And this is for somewhat the same reason that a geometer cannot avoid demonic deceptions in geometry by becoming a conventionalist there. For even if all of the axioms and postulates of Euclidian geometry were conventions there would still be a danger of being deceived in judging that a particular theorem, say the Pythagorean theorem, followed from them. And even if one took the notion of 'following from' to be purely conventional, and added to it the claim that all of the rules of inference and all of the logic to be used in developing this geometry are also conventional, there would still be a question of whether the Pythagorean theorem really does follow from these conventional (and even arbitrary) axioms in accordance with these conventional (and even arbitrary) definitions and rules. And we might be mistaken in answering that question.

Earlier I suggested that Teresa should worry about whether she might be deceived in believing such propositions as

(10) The bishop is present.

and

(11) *I have H* is cartesian-safe for me.

She might, following the present line, retreat into conventionalism by claiming that

(12) Propositions (10) and (11) are conventions.

Immediately our old question recurs. May not the Devil have deceived Teresa with respect to (12) itself? But let us again give Teresa the benefit of the doubt at this point. Let us assume that (12) is true. Then (11) is conventional. Let us also assume that if a proposition is a convention then one cannot be deceived in accepting it. (Is that really true? No matter.) Then Teresa is not deceived in accepting (11). And now, from (11) and the definition of cartesian-safety Teresa can deduce

(13) If I believe that I have H then I do have H.

If she adds to that

(14) I believe that I have H.

then she can deduce

(15) I have H.

And (15) is just the sort of proposition which we said earlier is the sort which Teresa needs to connect with one of her criteria. Has she now managed to salvage (15) by means of conventionalism? Unfortunately not.

Even if we raise no question about (14), which is required for the deductions, or even if we take it to be conventional also, we must still ask about the claim that (13) follows from (11), and that (15) follows from (13) and (14). Not every claim that one thing follows from another is true – there are plenty of mistakes of this sort. And so, despite the conventionalism of this approach, there seems to be room for the Devil and his nefarious activities. Of course, if he has not deceived Teresa about these deductions – if she is right about them – then she is OK. But, as we saw earlier, if he did not deceive her about the vision – if she was right about that – then she was OK from the very beginning. If in the end she has to rely on the assumption that the Devil has not deceived her in some one of her beliefs then it is hard to see why she should not make this move right away and be done with it.

IV

I come now to the concluding section of this paper. There are only three points which I want to make.

The first is a reiteration. The conclusion for which I have argued in the preceding sections is not that Teresa cannot know whether she is being deceived by the Devil. It is rather that she cannot have a criterion for determining whether he is deceiving her.

But I leave open the possibility that she might in some other way come to a knowledge of the truth.

Second, in the entire body of the argument, and on both sides of the argument, the references to the Devil are dispensable. I do not mean that Teresa was not serious about him. She was. And so may we be. But in the argument which I present, and in the objections and counter-arguments which I consider, he plays no essential role. Wherever there is a reference to the deceptions of the Devil we can simply replace them with references to our being mistaken. If we think it necessary to have some etiology for errors we can insert whatever we like – physiology, education, carelessness, or anything else. Teresa's problem, then, is a fundamental one in epistemology. She casts it, indeed, in a special form, and perhaps the problem does really arise for her in this special form. But even if *we* are not troubled by the Devil – even, for that matter, if there were no Devil – the fundamental form of Teresa's problem remains. We undertake to separate truth from error, and occasionally to distinguish the veridical from the non-veridical, by reference to what we already take to be true. But what if our mistake is really occurring at that point?

Third. Occasionally, it seems to me, Teresa suggests a different approach to this problem. Consider, for example, the following passage, which is part of her discussion of the vision of the feast day of St Peter:

> If I were blind, or in pitch darkness, and a person whom I had never seen, but only heard of, came and spoke to me and told me who he was, I should believe him, but I could not affirm that it was he as confidently as if I had seen him. But in this case I could certainly affirm it, for, though He remains unseen, so clear a knowledge is impressed upon the soul that to doubt it seems quite impossible. The Lord is pleased that this knowledge should be so deeply engraven upon the understanding that one can no more doubt it than one can doubt the evidence of one's eyes –

indeed, the latter is easier, for we sometimes suspect that we have imagined what we see, whereas here, though that suspicion may arise for a moment, there remains such complete certainty that the doubt has no force.[16]

In this passage, which has a few parallels in Teresa's works, I think we do not have any reference to a criterion of veridicality. We have no reference to properties of an experience which indicate that it is of divine, rather than demonic, origin. We have, instead, the report that 'to doubt it seems quite impossible' and 'the doubt has no force'. And in this experience, as she recounts it, a piece of knowledge 'is impressed upon the soul' and 'deeply engraven upon the understanding'. It is important that we not misunderstand this. Teresa is not saying here – so at least it seems to me – that this experience has certain characteristics (certainty, etc.) and that experiences with these characteristics are of divine origin. Against that sort of claim the arguments which we have been canvassing would apply with full force. Rather Teresa is here giving her testimony that, as this experience presented itself to her, its veridicality – the fact that it laid hold of a truth and delivered that truth to her understanding – was so plain and open upon the face of that experience itself that its purpose was accomplished. The truth was 'engraven upon the understanding', and doubt was banished. And it is this sort of experience, I think, and not the use of criteria, which is basic in Teresa's mystical knowledge.

Many of us will be strangers to mystical experience, at least of the richness, variety, and intensity which Teresa reports. That should not blind us, however, to the fact that we are not strangers to the sort of conviction which Teresa here reports. We, just as much as she, need to know a truth before we can use our criteria and our reasoning. And there is probably no one of us who has not sometimes found it in a way similar to the way Teresa reports. Sense experience often presents itself to us in this way (and Teresa herself calls attention to this parallel). But so also do experiences of other types. Some of you have probably had some such experience during the course of this paper. I suggested, for example, that the Devil may have deceived Teresa into thinking that proposition (15) follows validly from (13) and (14). But this deduction is a case of *modus ponens*, and I do not intend to suggest that *modus ponens* is not a valid form (though that would, of course, be another way of developing a similar argument). Rather I am suggesting that the Devil has deceived Teresa into thinking that these three proposi-

tions really do exemplify *modus ponens*. But if he has deceived her
in that way then we also must be deceived in the same way, whether
by the Devil or not. For we, too, are sure that this argument is an
instance of *modus ponens*. And so I sure that the suggestion
that Teresa might be deceived in *that* strikes some of you as laboured, pedantic, a philosopher's triviality. And so it seems to me,
too. I can find in myself no doubt that the derivation of (15) from
(13) and (14) is valid. I can say that Teresa might have been
deceived about it, but that represents in me no real possibility. But
also, it seems to me, I have no criterion for that (and I suspect that
you probably do not have one either). I *see*, somehow or other, that
these propositions match the form I know as *modus ponens*, and
that seeing seems to me to have no room in it for error. This is the
sort of thing which I may use in checking something else; it is not
now something which I think of checking.

Teresa's fundamental epistemological strategy, then, is one which
is common to us all. If she is mistaken in substance, then, either her
mistake is not traceable to this strategy, or else all of us, mystics
and non-mystics alike, stand on equally shaky ground.

And that brings us to the last question of this paper. If we are
attracted by the line of argument which I have presented, must we
too accept Teresa's experiences as veridical? No, I think not. Teresa
had her experiences, but she has not given them to us. She has
instead given to us a description of them, a report. But a description of a dinner is not itself a dinner, and a description of an
experience is not itself that experience. It may be that what happened to Teresa engraved something on her soul which her description will not engrave on our souls. I think that Teresa herself knew
this. As she concluded her discussion of another remarkable
incident in her life she said, 'If anyone thinks I am lying I beseech
God, in His goodness, to give him the same experience.'[17] When
Teresa prayed that prayer she may have done us her best service.

NOTES

1   'I saw your sister yesterday,' is a standard way of describing some-
    thing that happened to me yesterday, one of my experiences. I name it
    by reference to your sister.

    'You couldn't have,' you may retort. 'My sister is in New Zealand.'
    And if you persuade me that she is in New Zealand then I will agree
    too that I did not see her yesterday. Whatever may have been the
    psychology of my experience the true description of that experience

cannot be that of seeing your sister. I will take up for it some other form of words.

2   My interest in Teresa's treatment of her own mystical experience was first stimulated by a series of lectures given by Professor Nelson Pike.

3   St Teresa, *Life*, ch. 27 (p. 249). In this paper all quotations from this work are taken from *The Life of Teresa of Jesus*, translated and edited by E. Allison Peers (Garden City, N.Y., Image Books, 1960), and all page numbers refer to that edition.

4   Ibid., ch. 27 (p. 250).

5   Ibid., ch. 29 (pp. 269, 270). Cf. also ch. 28 (p. 260).

6   Ibid., ch. 7 (p. 100).

7   Ibid., ch. 25 (p. 239).

8   Ibid., ch. 25 (p. 233).

9   E.g., ibid., ch. 19 (p. 185).

10 Ibid., ch. 25 (p. 237).

11 Ibid.

12 Ibid., ch. 28 (p. 263).

13 René Descartes, *Meditations on First Philosophy*, second meditation.

14 Ibid., first meditation. The quotation is from *The Meditations and Selections from the Principles of René Descartes*, translated by John Veitch (La Salle, Illinois, Open Court Publishing Co., 1952), pp. 25, 26.

15 And, we might note in passing, a similar argument will show that Descartes was also mistaken in thinking that his judgements about the cartesian-safety of *I think* and *I exist* had established a secure base for operations against his own personal demon.

16 Teresa, ibid., ch. 27 (pp. 250, 251).

17 Ibid., ch. 29 (p. 275).

GEORGE I. MAVRODES, M.A. (Michigan), Ph.D. Professor Mavrodes has published *Belief in God: A Study in the Epistemology of Religion* (1970); *Problems and Perspective in the Philosophy of Religions*, ed., with Stuart C. Hackett (1967); and *The Rationality of Belief in God* (1970). He is also the author of many articles and reviews. He has taught at Carleton College and Princeton University, and at Kenyon College, Ohio, as Distinguished Visiting Professor of Philosophy. He is now Professor of Philosophy in the University of Michigan.

Index

Hindu 26–9, 45
Hindu mystic 47, 93–4, 97, 106, 121f.
Hinduism 26ff., 31, 32, 37, 43, 57f., 63, 171
Hintikka, J. 74
Hopkins, E. W. 73
Horner, I. B. 68, 71, 198
Horsburgh, H. J. N. 130
Horsch, Paul 83, 87, 98
Hsuan-tsang 199
Hulme, T. E. 206
Husserl, E. 63
Huxley, A. 2, 24, 49, 55, 67

Ibn Al Farid 94
Ibn 'Arabi 88, 99
Ibn atā Allāh 63, 74, 82, 88f., 92, 98f.
Ibn Tufayl 31
India 82ff., 86, 89, 94
Ineffability 17ff., 40, 46–50, 54–5, 56, 72, 102–7, 121, 138f., 141, 145, 148, 151–2, 178
Inge, Dean W. R. 2, 25, 70, 146
Intentional–Intentionality 63, 236–40, 244
Interpretation 12, 14, 22ff., 108–12, 117–19, 126, 152f., 171, 176f., 192f.
Isaiah 136
Isha Upanishad 106
Islam 45, 63, 171
Islamic 54
Islamic mysticism 27f., 31, 81f., 85–6, 88, 90–3, 95–6
Islamic tradition 53
Israel 215

Jainism 58
James, W. 2, 3, 25, 47ff., 55, 71–2, 114, 167
James' *Varieties of Religious Experience* 2, 25, 47, 71, 128, 167
Jayatilleka, K. N. 70f.
Jeffries, Richard 41, 50, 72
Jesus 26f.
Jewish mysticism 27f., 32–5, 38f., 45–50, 62–3, 65, 89, 114, 121, 176
Jhāna 16, 130
Joan of Arc 215, 228
Johansson, R. 68
John of the Cross, Saint 45, 105, 128, 216, 218, 232–4
John's *Ascent of Mount Carmel* 218, 233
Johnson, R. C. 130
Johnston, William 67
Jones, R. M. 2, 25, 148, 168
Joyce, James 208
Joyce's *Ulysses* 208

Judaism 40, 171, 180
Julian of Norwich 137ff.

Kabbalah 33, 52–3, 121
Kafka, F. 48, 72
Kalupahana, D. 68f., 73
Kamalasila 197f.
Kant, I. 59, 132–4, 200, 201
Kantian 59
Kaplaeu, P. 71
Karma 38
Karrat 73, 84
Katz, S. T. 21, 69, 73–4, 199
Kavvanah 34
Kavvanot 38
Keller, C. 4, 199
Kent, C. 8
Keter 52
Khānaqahs 44
Kharvass 44
Kitagawa, J. 71
Koans 43
Koch, H. 72
Krishna 16, 57

Lamotte, E. 71
Language, throughout
Laski, M. 130
Law, William 168
Leningrad Pedagogical Institute 116
Leonard, A. 67
Lerner, R. E. 129
Lessing, Gotthold 170
Lewis, H. D. 213
Lewis, I. M. 129
Locke, J. 211
Locution 214, 215, 216, 241–6, 251–2
Logos 201
Luria, I. 32, 70
Lurianic 27, 35, 43

Macdermot, V. 98
MacIntyre, A. 215, 220–8, 230–2
MacIntyre's(ed) *New Essays in Philosophical Theology* 215, 222
MacKinnon, D. M. 5
Madhyamika 17
Mahayana Buddhism 53, 94, 144, 166, 191f., 194, 198f.
Maitreya 161
Majjhima Nikāya 196
Mandukya Upanishads 48
Manet 30
Mānikkavācagar 93f.
Mansel, Dean 17
Mao by Ninian Smart 11
Mao Tse Tung 11